J. P. Mahaffy

A History of Classical Greek Literature

Vol. II. Part I.

J. P. Mahaffy

A History of Classical Greek Literature
Vol. II. Part I.

ISBN/EAN: 9783337179793

Printed in Europe, USA, Canada, Australia, Japan

Cover: Foto ©Thomas Meinert / pixelio.de

More available books at **www.hansebooks.com**

A HISTORY

OF

CLASSICAL GREEK LITERATURE

BY THE

REV. J. P. MAHAFFY, M.A.

KNIGHT OF THE ORDER OF THE REDEEMER
FELLOW AND PROF. OF ANCIENT HISTORY, TRIN. COLL. DUBLIN
HON. FELLOW OF QUEEN'S COLL. OXFORD
AUTHOR OF 'SOCIAL LIFE IN GREECE' 'PROLEGOMENA TO ANCIENT HISTORY'
'GREEK LIFE AND THOUGHT' 'RAMBLES AND STUDIES IN GREECE'
'THE GREEK WORLD UNDER ROMAN SWAY' ETC.

IN TWO VOLUMES

VOL. II. PART I.

THE PROSE WRITERS

FROM HERODOTUS TO PLATO

London

MACMILLAN AND CO.

AND NEW YORK

1895

ἐπεὶ δὲ τοῦ βίου μεταβολὴν ἅμα ταῖς τύχαις καὶ ταῖς φύσεσι
λαμβάνοντος, ἐξωθοῦσα τὸ περιττὸν ἡ χρεία, κρωβύλους τε
χρυσοῦς ἀφῄρει, καὶ ξυστίδας μαλακὰς ἀπημφίαζε, καὶ που καὶ
κόμην σοβαρωτέραν ἀπέκειρε, καὶ ὑπέλυσε κοθορνόν, οὐ φαύλως
ἐθιζομένων ἀντικαλλωπίζεσθαι πρὸς τὴν πολυτέλειαν εὐτελείᾳ,
καὶ τὸ ἀφελὲς καὶ λιτὸν ἐν κόσμῳ τίθεσθαι μᾶλλον, ἢ τὸ
σοβαρὸν καὶ περίεργον· οὕτω τοῦ λόγου συμμεταβάλλοντος
ἅμα καὶ συναποδυομένου, κατέβη μὲν ἀπὸ τῶν μέτρων, ὥσπερ
ὀχημάτων, ἡ ἱστορία, καὶ τῷ πεζῷ μάλιστα τοῦ μυθώδους
ἀπεκρίθη τὸ ἀληθές· φιλοσοφία δὲ τὸ σαφὲς καὶ διδασκαλικὸν
ἀσπασαμένη μᾶλλον ἢ τὸ ἐκπλῆττον, διὰ λόγων ἐποιεῖτο τὴν
ζήτησιν.—PLUTARCH, *De Pyth. Oraculis*, 24.

PREFACE

TO

THE THIRD EDITION.

THE publication of this new edition enables me to add a good many references to recent books, and to correct some errors which still remained. These corrections are far more numerous than would appear from the slight increase of the volume in size. As regards the bibliography of each author, it is hardly necessary, in the face of such works as Bursian's *Jahresbericht*, to attempt any complete catalogue of German books or tracts. But in the case of English commentaries, which are often ignored or neglected in the German and French periodicals, I thought it desirable to give the student a reference to at least the most recent English treatment of each author, where he will generally find the further information he requires.

I am not aware that in the department of prose literature there has been any remarkable addition to, or rectification of, our knowledge during the interval, unless Gomperz be right in attributing the Hippocratic tract περὶ τέχνης not only to the earliest moment of Ionic prose, but even to the pen of the famous Protagoras.[1] I have announced in its place a new discovery relating to the *Phædo* of Plato, and have added at the conclusion of the volume a scrap of an unknown historian recovered from an inscription.

As regards the peculiar views maintained in this book on the credibility of Thucydides' Sicilian archæology, on the estimate Xenophon has given us of himself, on the integrity of

---

[1] Cf. his curious edition and commentary just published in *Sitz.-Ber.* of the Vienna Academy, vol. cxx.

Demosthenes, on the comparative youth of Hypereides, I have found no reason to make me recede from the positions previously adopted. For in no case have these views been refuted by argument, though there have since appeared, and no doubt there will yet appear, many books adopting the traditional opinions on these points, without any attempt to re-think the problems independently. This is perhaps the most unsatisfactory feature in the study of a subject so long taught in schools and colleges. Those who profess it are generally unwilling to discover, or to admit, that what they have been long repeating to their classes is untenable or even doubtful. We must console ourselves with the maxim *magna est veritas, et prævalebit*, though we cannot but wish that this future victory were more definitely and proximately assured. The great difficulty seems to be a certain want of interest, a certain dislike to grapple with a new view, which affects the minds of those who have spent their years in teaching or learning what other people say, and setting or passing examinations in it. Let us only get over this obstacle ; let us have an honest discussion about a new and startling theory, and we shall have it either adopted or abandoned.

This, at least, has been the good fortune of Mr. Sayce, in his recent attack on Herodotus, that his views have received prompt attention ; and though I cannot but think he has been in the main refuted, he has enriched our knowledge of Herodotus by many criticisms which even his critics have adopted. The echo of this controversy has reached across the Channel, and not only has H. Diels exercised his acumen in showing that the alleged fragments of Hecatæus are not centos from Herodotus (as Cobet endeavoured to prove), but M. Alfred Croiset, in the just published second volume of a History of Greek Literature, has carefully rehearsed the whole charge, and given all the guide-posts through the controversy.[1]

[1] Cf. A. and M. Croiset, *Hist. de la Litt. grecque*, ii. 582, sq. He follows me in calling attention to Blakesley's earlier attack, and gives references

But here I do not think that we shall gain more than a new and more critical attitude towards a justly favourite Greek author. If, on the other hand, by accepting my arguments, the early Olympiads be discredited, or the birth of Hypereides brought down half a generation, we shall have facts to correct, and in the former case even to revise our whole conception of early Greek annals. In any case let us make our study of Greek, if we are to maintain it in the forefront of higher education, a living study; let us not talk of *injustice* to an ancient author if a critic speaks his candid opinion, and tells us that it is in conflict with the traditions on the subject.

The reader will find a brilliant argument of this kind in Mr. Rutherford's *Fourth book of Thucydides* (Macmillan, 1890), in which the condition of that text has undergone a searching revision, and an amount of corruption in the way of idle or futile additions is alleged which, if proved, would remodel many of our notions concerning Thucydidean Greek. But will the learned author receive the honest attention for his arguments which he deserves? Is it not more likely that those who have been exhibiting their cunning in analysing and explaining the Attic purity of the accretions which he condemns will fancy they feel the ground slipping from under their reputations, and will use every device, direct and indirect, to discredit his enquiry, and set it aside as a piece of idle ingenuity? The problem is too new to admit of solution, seeing that it awaits a fuller discussion, and for that reason I have merely referred to the book in my text.

For a different reason I have taken no notice of the bitter controversy between an Oxford and a Cambridge scholar concerning a certain commentary on Plato produced by the latter. Let us hope that this dispute will be as ephemeral as the interest it has excited. The only permanent feature about it is that

to Father Delattre in the *Muséon belge* for 1888. On the dispute about Hecatæus he gives a good summary (*op. cit.* ii. 547), and cites the article of H. Diels in *Hermes* for 1887, pp. 411, sq.

a

commonplace, which one greets with a smile as an old friend— I mean the assertion that the new commentator, whoever he may be, 'does not seem to have clearly comprehended Plato's theory of Ideas.'

Yet these disputes may have deplorable consequences; they may poison the mind of each side against all the work done by the other, and lead (especially on the side that feels defeated) to an unreasonable, lifelong, more than Corsican *vendetta*. Even our literary press becomes infected with these feuds; partisans who are afraid to strike openly do it by undue laudations, by undue depreciations, and so keep the quarrel alive by heaping up injustices which feed the flame; there are also those who come forward openly, without any interest in the question disputed, and seek to curry favour by seasoning their flattery of the one side with sneers at the other. No journal, however respectable, no editor, however conscientious, can secure himself against these vices in his staff, and so it happens that very indifferent work is often extravagantly lauded, while meritorious books have to wait for recognition till the reading public has slowly discovered what is really genuine and conscientious. However long delayed this recognition may be, there is one indirect consolation at hand: no command of the press, no amount of puffing has ever secured *permanent* popularity or respect for disingenuous or second-rate work. It is not so obvious or so certain, yet highly probable, that no really earnest and thorough work will ever be permanently ignored.

My new publishers have agreed with me that it is desirable to produce this volume in two parts, which can be procured separately. Thus the student of a particular portion of Greek Prose Literature can obtain what he requires without serious cost, and without being burdened with the minuteness of monographs upon the several authors.

J. P. MAHAFFY.

Trinity College, Dublin:
August 22, 1890.

CONTENTS

PART I.

HISTORY

OF

GREEK PROSE LITERATURE.

PART I.

———•◇•———

CHAPTER I.

INTRODUCTION—EARLY USE OF WRITING—THE INFLUENCES OF
RELIGION AND PHILOSOPHY AND THE DAWN OF HISTORY
IN THE SIXTH CENTURY B.C.

§ 295. *Introductory.*—The history of Greek prose literature,
as we possess it, begins almost at the close of the poetical
development of the nation, at least at the close of its original
development, for though many poets flourished later than our
earliest prose writers, no new species of poetry, except possibly
the bucolic, dates its origin from this time, and the later poets
were in few cases men of remarkable or enduring originality.
Hence it is that, in a logical survey of Greek literature, we may
allow ourselves to treat all the poetry before we approach the
consideration of prose writing. This, indeed, is now the
accepted order among the German writers on the subject.

I have in the former volume stated my belief that the
composition of any long or elaborate poem postulates the use
of writing, and I therefore proposed this condition as giving us
the earliest limit for the date of the Iliad as we have it ; but
many eminent critics have thought differently, and have argued
that poetry can be composed and preserved without any such
aid. Fortunately this divergence of opinion does not exist in

the case of prose literature. Everyone admits that prose is impossible without writing—nay, even without the well-established habit of fluent and sustained writing. A few words on the history of the alphabet in Greece may therefore suitably introduce our present subject.

§ 296. The materials for the investigation of early Greek writing are to be found in many various and scattered inscriptions, of which all those discovered up to a certain date are to be found in Boeckh's *Corpus Inscriptionum Græcarum*, but the later are scattered through various archæological journals. The stricter study of these documents must be prosecuted by means of photographs or facsimiles, as the shape and character of the letters are generally our only means of determining the age of the inscription. Investigations of this kind, when reduced to method, are called the science of *Epigraphik*, and, with the constantly increasing excavations and discoveries through the Hellenic East, have become the most important and fruitful branch of recent Greek studies. But in England the Universities have hardly awakened to this study, and the best English Hellenists, with a very few brilliant exceptions, are as helpless in the face of an old Greek inscription as if it were in a Semitic tongue. I can only refer the reader to a German summary of the main results—Kirchhoff's *Studien zur Geschichte des griechischen Alphabets* (3rd ed. 1877). In this very able book he will find it shown that our earliest inscription of determinable date—that of the Greek mercenaries on the leg of a colossal figure at Abu-Simbel—is by no means written in the most primitive form of the Greek alphabet. And yet this inscription cannot have been made later than 589 B.C., and possibly about 640 B.C.[1] The sepulchral inscriptions found at Melos

---

[1] ΒΑΣΙΛΕΟΣΕΛΘΟΝΤΟΣΕΣΕΛΕΦΑΝΤΙΝΑΝΨΑΜΑΤΙΧΟ
ΤΑΥΤΑΕΓΡΑΨΑΝΤΟΙΣΤΝΨΑΜΑΤΙΧΟΙΤΟΙΘΕΟΚΛΟΣ (sc. τῷ Θεοκλέος)
ΕΠΛΕΟΝΗΛΘΟΝΔΕΚΕΡΤΙΟΣΚΑΤΥΠΕΡΘΕΝΙΣ (sc. ἐς) ΟΠΟΤΑΜΟΣ
ΑΝΙΗΑΛΟΓΛΟΣΟΣΔΗΧΕΠΟΤΑΣΙΜΤΟΑΙΓΥΠΤΙΟΣΔΕ ΑΜΑΣΙΣ
ΕΓΡΑΦΕΔΕΜΕΑΡΧΟΝΑΜΟΙΒΙΧΟΚΑΙΠΕΛΕΦΟΣΟΥΔΑΜΟ (sc. son of nobody).

Cf. Lepsius, *Denk.* xii. 99, for a facsimile ; also Boeckh, *C.I.G.* 5126. Wiedemann, *Rhein. Mus.* xxxv. p. 364, and Abel, *Wiener Stud.* 1881, p. 110, refer it to Psammetichus II., though on different grounds. It should be added here, that the frequent proposal to read the ΟΥΔΑΜΟΥ of

and Thera, though perhaps not older in date, are far more archaic, and point to a condition of writing at least half a century older among the Ionians, who had modified their writing into the character found at Abu-Simbel. These and other facts show that the Phœnician alphabet of twenty-two letters must have been adopted by the Greeks, and quickly modified to suit the different character of their language before 700 B.C., and perhaps considerably earlier. But for our purposes we need not claim an earlier origin than 700, though perhaps the constant discoveries of old inscriptions at Olympia will soon afford us clearer and fuller evidence.

§ 297. These considerations are confirmed by another phenomenon which we find in Greece about the same period. The rise of lawgivers and of codes of law points distinctly to writing, for we can hardly conceive the ordinances of a statesman entrusted to vague tradition. The date and character of Zaleukos, Charondas, and Lycurgus are indeed subject to dispute, and the extant Spartan *rhetra* may be suspected to be later in form,[1] but no one can doubt that the Locrian and Spartan constitutions were early fixed in writing, certainly a considerable number of years earlier than those of Drako and Solon, which are fairly determined as shortly before and after the year 600 B.C. Quite in concert with this development of law we hear of the sayings of the Seven Wise Men, whose varying catalogue includes rather the politicians than the early philosophers, and whose wisdom was not only laid down in verse but in those short proverbs which easily fasten on the popular imagination. When Herodotus speaks of Æsop as a

the inscription, 'son of Udamos,' and to avoid the jocular rendering 'son of nobody' by the introduction of a Doric form, is directly in the teeth of the whole character of the writing. The 'son of Amœbicos' is not ὁ Ἀμοιβικο, but Αμοιβικο. The problem before us is not to invent a new text, but to translate what we have.

[1] It is cited and explained by Plutarch (*Lycurgus*, c. 6) : Διὸς Συλλανίου καὶ Ἀθανᾶς Συλλανίας ἱερὸν ἱδροσάμενον, φυλὰς φυλάξαντα καὶ ὠβὰς ὠβάξαντα τριάκοντα, γερουσίαν σὺν ἀρχαγέταις καταστήσαντα, ὥρας ἐξ ὥρας ἀπελλάζειν μεταξὺ Βαβύκας τε καὶ Κνακιῶνος, οὕτως εἰσφέρειν τε καὶ ἀφίστασθαι· δάμῳ δὲ τὰν κυρίαν ἦμεν καὶ κράτος· αἰ δὲ σκολιὰν ὁ δᾶμος ἕλοιτο, τοὺς πρεσβυγενέας καὶ ἀρχαγέτας ἀποστατῆρας ἦμεν. Cf. on this Rawlinson's *Herodotus*, iii. p. 346; or Grote's *Greece*, vol. ii. p. 465, sq., and notes.

λογοποιός of early date, he seems to point to some form of prose fable far older than his own time. It is remarkable that savage races in our own day have made beast-fables their first literary effort on the discovery of the use of writing.[1] But all these things have left us but faint and doubtful traces ; for the wisdom of the Seven Wise Men, and the fables of Æsop, have come down to us in a rehandled and modern form, and we know nothing of any early prose form in which these things were originally composed. But on the whole, we have ample evidence for the common use of writing throughout the seventh century, evidence which is, in my opinion, necessary to account for the development of Greek lyric poetry, the construction of codes of law, and the general literary culture of the age.

In fact, the wonder is, not that prose writing came so early, but so late in the history of Greek literature. But the national taste was so well satisfied by poetry that it required special influences, other than the mere familiarity with writing, to induce men to set down their thoughts in unmetrical form. To these we may now turn.

§ 298. We cannot embrace in this volume either the history of Greek religion or of Greek philosophy, both large and interesting subjects, and demanding special investigation. We are here concerned with them only so far as they produced a direct effect in moulding either the form or the tendencies of general literature. But as religion underwent great changes in the sixth century, and philosophy then originated, our sketch of Greek literature must embrace the remoter effects of both on the writers of that and succeeding generations.

We have already noted[2] in Pindar the allusions to a future world, and to its rewards and punishments, and that this doctrine was due to the Orphic mysteries, which were common through Greece in this century. The origin of these mysteries is uniformly referred to Picria in Thrace, from which they are said to have been brought to Lesbos, and then spread over Greece. They are closely identified, on the one hand, with the worship of Dionysus, which also originated in Thrace,

---

[1] Cf. my *Proleg. to Anc. Hist.*, pp. 118, 391.   [2] Vol. I. § 150.

but had assumed, by contact with Phrygia, an enthusiastic and orgiastic nature, so that the dithyrambs to the god, of old sung to the cithara, were adapted to flute and cymbal accompaniments ; on the other hand, the Orphic rites were bound up with the widely spread mysteries of Demeter and Persephone, celebrated at Eleusis. But still more remarkable, and more important than either of these indications, is the identification of Orpheus, as the priest of Apollo, with Dionysus, and the evidences that he and Apollo, with whom he is identified, once in hostility with Dionysus, became reconciled with that god, who, under the title of Zagreus, was made a sort of nightside to the sungod, and ultimately confused with him. This secret doctrine, the identification of Apollo and Dionysus, is said to have been that disclosed in Æschylus' trilogy about Lycurgus of Thrace, for which he was indicted as guilty of impiety. It is accordingly evident that the Delphic priests had recognised and adopted the Orphic rites as in harmony with their own creed, so that they must have been of real importance in Greece, and widely spread through the hearts of men.

§ 299. We may infer, however, from the scanty evidence of later writers that this religion of mysteries and rites, whether Orphic or Eleusinian or Dionysiac, was fundamentally distinct from the popular creed. It preached the identification of the most diverse gods, perhaps even the unity of all the gods. It approached the dogma of a world-soul, and of the divinity of the soul of man, if not of all the world, as a manifestation of God. It portrayed the wonder of a suffering deity, and of good overborne by the powers of darkness for a season. It held out the hope of immortality to those who embraced the faith, and made them a chosen people. It replaced, in fact, the old Homeric society of obvious human gods, with their vulgar amours and passions, by mystic principles and half-understood devotions. There seems little doubt that the established Delphic priesthood who adopted it borrowed from Egypt not only many elements of the new creed, such as the murder of the god and his resurrection from the dead, but more distinctly the policy of the Egyptian priests, who are known to have been monotheists or rather pantheists, yet who not only tolerated but taught a most complicated polytheism to the people. Thus the established religion went on : temples were built and statues consecrated, sacrifices offered and feasts celebrated to all the gods ; but the select, the initiated, the higher classes in religion found their comfort in far different beliefs, which could not be made public.

Yet they could not but make themselves felt. Inasmuch as perhaps all the literary men of the age knew these mysteries, we find among them, at least, two leading ideas engendered by their faith : the conception of law and order in both nature and the life of man, an order resulting from the control of one supreme principle, untouched by caprice or passion ; and the conception of mystery, of something unexplained in the world, of something revealed to privileged classes and hidden from the vulgar.

§ 300. While the belief in a future state takes but transient hold of the Greek mind, and even disappears in its vulgar form, these other larger notions seem to me to dominate most writers from Pindar onward, but above all to have affected the early philosophers, concerning whose views we must also say a few words. Most of them have unfortunately left us no fragments whatever ; but if they had, we should treat them as literature, not as philosophy.

The very same tendencies which suggested in religion the identification of various gods, and an increased appreciation of unity in worship, seem to have acted on the secular thinkers of Miletus, and set them to seeking unity in the substance or matter of the world. The doctrine of Thales that moisture was the common element of which all things were variously compounded, is directly analogous to the cult of Dionysus, the god of moisture, to whom all growth and fruitfulness are due, and who, in combination with Apollo, the god of light and heat, generates all the conditions of change in nature. The theories of the sixth century started in Ionia, and have this common point, the search after unity, as their leading feature. The followers of Thales found moisture too coarse a primeval substance, and substituted the more subtle air (Anaximenes) or imperceptible fire (Heracleitus). Others, such as Xenophanes and Pythagoras, advanced beyond the conception of mere matter, and sought their single principle either in number, with its eternal and certain laws, or in some higher abstract Unity, which embraced all apparent contradictions.

§ 301. The effect of these theories on literature was twofold: they taught that the matter of thought was worth recording apart from its literary form, and knowledge as such was to be pursued apart from elegance in diction ; secondly, they corroborated the religious teaching of the mysteries, that 'all things are not as they seem,' that public opinion and ordinary sense miss the truer and deeper meaning of experience, that there are secrets and difficulties in human knowledge, and many things hard to understand and still harder to explain. The first resulted in the origin of prose literature,[1] which according to consistent tradition was due to the wonder-working *Pherecydes* of Syros, son of Babys, who lived about the middle of the sixth century, and is called the teacher of Pythagoras. His semi-theological semi-philosophical book called Ἑπτάμυχος, on theogony and the revelation of the gods to the world, was the first attempt at a prose treatise.[2]

Neither Thales nor Pythagoras left anything written, and it is remarkable that Xenophanes, though he was a great adversary of the poets and of public opinion in general, and led the conflict between philosophy and poetry, nevertheless employed, not only the poetic form, but even the poetic habit of public recitation to disseminate his views. Perhaps there was as yet no reading public in the newer colonies of Italy and Sicily when he lived; but the fact remains certain, and also the similar practice of his follower Parmenides.

If, indeed, *Theagenes* of Rhegium, the first literary critic,

---

[1] The Greeks said prose *writing*, as they were fond of ascribing every step in culture to a definite inventor. But, as we have shown, and as the inscriptions above cited have since proved, mere prose writing must have long been in use for simple inscriptions, and for laws. But the use of prose for *literary* purposes was a distinct step, and much later than might have been expected.

[2] We have the opening sentence of it quoted by Diogenes : Ζεὺς μὲν καὶ Χρόνος ἐσαεὶ καὶ Χθὼν ἦν· Χθονίη δὲ οὔνομα ἐγένετο Γῆ, ἐπειδὴ αὐτῇ Ζεὺς γέρας διδοῖ. And again (Clem. Strom.) : Ζὰς ποιεῖ φᾶρος μέγα τε καὶ καλόν· καὶ ἐν αὐτῷ ποικίλλει γῆν καὶ ὠγηνὸν καὶ τὰ ὠγηνοῦ δώματα.

who wrote on Homer and introduced the principle of allegorical interpretation, really flourished about 525 B.C., the reason just assigned would not hold good ; but the date rests on the single authority of Tatian, and I hesitate to reckon a literary critic among the earliest pioneers of prose literature.

§ 302. On the contrary, HERACLEITUS of Ephesus [1] was perhaps the first great prose writer among the Greeks, and the source of a new current in the literature of his country. His treatise on Nature,[2] though not published by himself, was copied from the MS. he had deposited in the temple of Artemis at Ephesus, and was early known and read in Sicily, as appears from the fragments of his Sicilian contemporary Epicharmus, and from Attic references down to the days of Socrates. The whole philosophy of the man who had discovered that all organism grows, and that all growth implies motion, turned (like the Eleatic theory of Xenophanes) upon a contempt of ordinary opinions—nay, even a contempt of our ordinary senses, which are witnesses only to what is dead, as they perceive not the inner motion of every substance in the world. He therefore appealed to a select few, and made a severance among the members of society which had, perhaps, been unknown in Greek cities heretofore.

But what is more important as regards literature, he was the first Greek who ventured to write obscurely, and to profess to do so without a care. This is, to my mind, the important and novel side of Heracleitus in Greek literature : for from his day onward we had this style not uncommon even in the next generation, whereas in older literature it is unknown. In the following age we find it imitated by his followers, and even in Thucydides and in Sophocles, yet banished again by the good sense of the Athenian public. It does not reappear till the Alexandrian epoch, with which we are not concerned. When

---

[1] He was apparently of noble family, and certainly an exclusive aristocrat in sentiment. He flourished about 505-485 B.C., and seems to have been persecuted by the people. Diog. Laert. ix. 1, gives various stories concerning him and his views, with various readings.

[2] Alexandrians have left us on the MS. of Heracleitus in three books, which was the old number of these groups.

I speak of obscurity the word may, of course, be taken in different senses. First, there is the obscurity of allusions not clear to the reader ; and Pindar is full of this, but of this only, as he was one of the ordinary crowd in philosophy, and was not capable of any thoughts in themselves profound. Secondly, there is the obscurity of a crabbed or affected style. In Æschylus, on the contrary, we have not only the first kind of obscurity—the allusions to mysteries—but we have obscure thoughts, difficult to express and unintelligible to the most advanced Greeks ; for we have the evidence of Aristophanes, which I here believe, that Æschylus thought even the Athenians no judges of poetry, and would not accommodate his writing to their comprehension.

It has not, perhaps, been sufficiently remarked how important was the example of Heracleitus, and how easy it is to lead the fashion in obscure writing. We must remember that Heracleitus was really a quaint and original thinker, and a remarkable innovator, not only in thought, but in style ; for he wrote a rythmical, picturesque prose, at a time when prose was in its infancy. His fragments are far more poetical in the higher sense than the verses of Xenophanes, and for this very reason he may have scorned the shackles of metre, and set down unchanged the utterances of his teeming mind. This accounts for the remark of the rhetor Demetrius,[1] who says that the frequent asyndeta were the greatest cause of his obscurity. Each thought was thrown out by itself, and the reader must find its logical connection with the rest for himself.[2]

In addition to Zeller's exhaustive chapter on Heracleitus,[3] I may recommend the various brilliant essays of J. Bernays, reaching from 1848 to 1869 ; some separately published, others

[1] § 192.

[2] Specimens of Heracleitus' style are the following : ἔμπεδον οὐδέν, ἀλλά κως ἐς κυκεῶνα πάντα συνειλέονται. ἐστὶ τωυτὸ τέρψις ἀτερψίη, γνῶσις ἀγνωσίη, μέγα μικρόν, ἄνω κάτω περιχωρέοντα καὶ ἀμειβόμενα ἐν τῇ τοῦ αἰῶνος παιδιῇ. αἰών παῖς ἐστι παίζων πεσσεύων συνδιαφερόμενος. τὰ δὲ πάντα οἰακίζει κεραυνός. οὐ ξυνίασι ὅκως διαφερόμενον ἑωυτῷ ὁμολογέει · παλίντροπος ἁρμονίη ὥσπερ τόξου καὶ λύρης.

[3] *Phil. d. Griech.* i. 566–677.

in the seventh and ninth vols. of the *Rhein. Mus.* We have also, from Mr. I. Bywater of Oxford, a new critical and more complete edition (1877) of the fragments, 130 in number, with Diogenes' *Life*, and the spurious *Letters*, done with that conscientious care which distinguishes all his work.

§ 303. The example of the theologians and philosophers was however, active in another direction ; for it stimulated writers on the genealogies of gods and of men to set them down in prose. The earliest of these are enveloped in mist ; it is even doubtful whether *Cadmus* of Miletus, the reputed father of history, ever existed, or whether his account of the settlement of Ionia was not a late forgery. *Acusilaus*, of the Bœotian Argos, near Aulis, the son of Cabas, who devoted himself to mythical genealogies chiefly adapted from Hesiod, is a real personage, of whose work some thirty notices are preserved in the scholiasts ; but we know nothing more about him. Equally obscure is *Dionysius* of Miletus, the reputed author of a Persian history ; and the prose works attributed to Eumelus of Corinth were certainly later paraphrases from poetical treatises. *Pherecydes* of Leros (the second of the name) certainly did some service in genealogies, which even at his time (B.C. 460) were the only phase of history esteemed and understood. A society consisting of clans always lays the greatest stress on genealogies ; as, for example, the ancient Irish, whose histories are little more than enumerations of names.[1] Xanthus, Charon, and Scylax are only of interest in connection with Herodotus (below, p. 26).

§ 304. But the second or critical element of history was added presently by a greater man, HECATÆUS of Miletus, who seems to me to have the best right to be called the Father of History among the Greeks. For he was the forerunner of Herodotus in his mode of life and his conception of setting down his experience. He attained such eminence as to be consulted pub-

---

[1] Those who ridicule these Irish genealogies are ignorant that they were practically title-deeds, for any man proving himself an O'Neill or a Maguire had a right to graze cattle in the O'Neill and Maguire country, and to till it. Hence these genealogies were early kept, and no doubt early disputed, and this gives them an exceptional value. I perceive the same anxiety to show hereditary rights in all the usurpers of power throughout early Greek history.

licly by the Ionians at the time of their revolt (incited by
Aristagoras) from the Persians.   He knew the Persian empire
from personal examination, and advised strongly against any
revolt.   When he could not persuade them, he advised them to
secure the supremacy of the sea, a common capital, and a cen-
tralisation of forces ; which could only be done, he considered,
by applying the treasures given by Crœsus to Apollo's temple
at Branchidæ to supply the sinews of war.   These views show
him to have been a man of large political insight.   He also
advised Aristagoras, at the end of the revolt, to fortify the
island of Leros,[1] and there await the tide of events ; but
for the third time, his advice was unheeded.   These facts all
rest upon the authority of Herodotus, who mentions him elsewhere, and systematically, as λογοποιὸς ἀνηρ, or ὁ λογοποιός.
In one place he tells us that Hecatæus boasted to the priests of
Egyptian Thebes that he could trace his origin through fifteen
generations back to a god, which they denied, saying that
at least 345 generations could be proved by them to have
lived on the earth since the reign of the gods.   Herodotus also
mentions without criticism his theory of the unjust expulsion of
the Pelasgi from Attica, and he often alludes to his predecessor slightingly, without expressly mentioning his name.

From these facts, along with the notices of Suidas, it appears that the historian was born about Ol. 57-8, and died after
the conclusion of the Persian war, about Ol. 76.   His high
position in society is proved not only by the story just mentioned, but by his wide and careful travels, which imply good
means and connections.   Whether he learned from Pythagoras
we cannot tell.   His travels apparently embraced Egypt, Persia,
Pontus, Thrace, as well as the Greek world, and were probably
made before the Ionian revolt in 500 B.C., when his wide experience was publicly recognised, and after 516 B.C., when the
town of Boryza in Thrace became Persian, which he states it
to be in a geographical fragment.   Thus the settled and orderly

---

[1] There is an inscription published in Ross's collection (ii. p. 28), in
which some Hecatæus is honoured as a founder and benefactor by the
Lerians.   Whether this person be the historian, or a relative, I am unable
to tell.   The fact is mentioned by Mure (iv. 143).

condition of the Persian empire, when Darius was established on the throne, seems to have enabled Hecatæus to acquire his geographical materials. It has been inferred from a story preserved in a fragment of Diodorus that he was sent as an ambassador to Artaphernes after the conquest of Ionia, and that he obtained good terms for his countrymen. He is mentioned as a man of exceptional learning (along with Hesiod, Pythagoras, and Xenophanes) by his younger contemporary Heracleitus, and classed by Hermogenes with the great historians of Greece.

§ 305. Of his works we can recognise two : a geographical description of the known world, and an historical work, sometimes called *Genealogies*. He seems to have had one predecessor in each—Scylax of Caryanda, who explored the Indus for Darius Hystaspes, and wrote a *Periplus* which was soon lost, and Acusilaus of Argos. He completed and improved the map first constructed by Anaximander, and it was, doubtless, this copy which Aristagoras brought with him to exhibit at Sparta. He narrated curious natural phenomena, just as Herodotus, but naturally believed more than Herodotus did, and is accordingly criticised by him for credulity. But he was, nevertheless, the first Greek historian who did apply rational criticism [1] to test

---

[1] The following are the chief specimens :—

Müller, frag. 346 : Ἐποίησαν δὲ Ἑλλήνων τινὲς ὡς Ἡρακλῆς ἀναγάγοι ταύτῃ τοῦ "Αιδου τὸν κύνα, οὔτε ὑπὸ γῆν ὁδοῦ διὰ τοῦ σπηλαίου φερούσης, οὔτε ἕτοιμον ὂν πεισθῆναι θεῶν ὑπόγαιων εἶναί τινα οἴκησιν, ἐς ἣν ἀθροίζεσθαι τὰς ψυχάς· ἀλλὰ Ἑκαταῖος μὲν ὁ Μιλήσιος λόγον εὗρεν εἰκότα, 'ὄφιν φήσας ἐπὶ Ταινάρῳ τραφῆναι δεινόν, κληθῆναι δὲ "Αιδου κύνα, ὅτι ἔδει τὸν δηχθέντα τεθνάναι παραυτίκα ὑπὸ τοῦ ἰοῦ· καὶ τοῦτον ἔφη τὸν ὄφιν ὑπὸ Ἡρακλέους ἀχθῆναι παρ' Εὐρυσθέα.'

Frag. 349 : 'Γηρυόνην δέ, ἐφ' ὅντινα ὁ Ἀργεῖος Ἡρακλῆς ἐστάλη πρὸς Εὐρυσθέως, τὰς βοῦς ἀπελάσαι τὰς Γηρυόνου καὶ ἀγαγεῖν ἐς Μυκήνας, οὐδέν τι προσήκειν τῇ γῇ τῶν Ἰβήρων,' Ἑκαταῖος ὁ λογοποιὸς λέγει, 'οὐδὲ ἐπὶ νῆσόν τινα Ἐρύθειαν ἔξω τῆς μεγάλης θαλάσσης σταλῆναι Ἡρακλέα· ἀλλὰ τῆς ἠπείρου τῆς περὶ Ἀμβρακίαν τε καὶ Ἀμφιλόχους βασιλέα γενέσθαι Γηρυόνην καὶ ἐκ τῆς ἠπείρου ταύτης ἀπελάσαι Ἡρακλέα τὰς βοῦς, οὐδὲ τοῦτον φαῦλον ἆθλον τιθέμενον.'

Frag. 357 : Ἡ πολλὴ δόξα κατέχει μὴ ἐλθεῖν τὸν Αἴγυπτον εἰς Ἄργος, καθάπερ ἄλλοι τε φασὶ καὶ Ἑκαταῖος γράφων οὕτως· 'ὁ δὲ Αἴγυπτος αὐτὸς μὲν οὐκ ἦλθεν εἰς Ἄργος· λέγεται δε τις ἐν Ἄργει πράν, ὅπου δικάζουσιν Ἀργεῖοι.'

popular beliefs , and his originality in this point, the result, no doubt, of the contemporary philosophy at Miletus, must not be overlooked.   From his geographical work some 330 citations have been collected by Carl Müller, most of them names of towns in Stephanus of Byzantium, and a few in Strabo.[1]   From his *Genealogies* (of which the genuineness was disputed by Callimachus, but defended by Eratosthenes and Strabo) a smaller number of more interesting passages still survive, bringing up the total number (together with the *fragmenta incerta*) to almost 400. The very opening sentence of the *Genealogies* is characteristic.[2] On his style we have three very interesting notices : Strabo says[3] that the school of Cadmus, Pherecydes, and Hecatæus, though abandoning metre, were in other respects poetical writers.   Hermogenes[4] has a general description of his style, which is somewhat as follows : ' Hecatæus of Miletus, from whom Herodotus profited most, is a pure and clear writer, and in some respects possesses no ordinary charm.   Using

Mure says (iv. 71) that while his foreign geography was full of good observations of an historical kind, his genealogies and his Greek notices were confined to the mythical period   The passages just cited show that he applied criticism here also, and that Mure's distinction is probably unfounded.

[1] C. Müller thinks it unlikely that the genuine work survived till Stephanus' time, and holds that he used an interpolated and modified copy. Thus Capua was called Vulturnum in Hecatæus' day, and yet is cited from his work (fr. 30) with its new name.   A map of his views is published in most good ancient atlases, and also in the appendix to Mure's fourth volume.   The gap in his description of the coast from Naples to Genoa is well noted by the latter, and points to some distinct prohibition on the part of the Romans and Tyrrhenians, which kept Greek vessels from landing on their coasts.   Probably Greek ships were compelled to sail from Naples by way of Sardinia to Mentone, the first town mentioned on the coast above Naples, at least in the fragments we have in Stephanus.   But the like omission of Athens, Argos, and other renowned Greek towns, shows that there was some other cause of gaps either in Hecatæus' book, or in Stephanus' quotations from it.

[2] Frag. 332 (from the rhetor Demetrius) : Οῖον ὡς 'Εκαταῖός φησιν ἐν τῇ ἀρχῇ τῆς ἱστορίας· ''Εκαταῖος Μιλήσιος ὧδε μυθεῖται.'   Cf. also § 12 : 'Εκαταῖος Μιλήσιος ὧδε μυθεῖται· τάδε γράφω, ὥς μοι ἀληθέα δοκέει εἷναι· οἱ γὰρ 'Ελλήνων λόγοι πολλοί τε καὶ γελοῖοι, ὡς ἐμοὶ φαίνονται, εἰσίν.

[3] i. p. 34.   [4] *De gen. dic.* ii. 12

the Ionic dialect pure, and not mixed with epic and other elements, as Herodotus did, he is in diction less poetical.[1] Neither is he so finished a writer. His charm is, therefore, not comparable to that of Herodotus in treating similar subjec's ; for the matter of a book is not its only element as regards delighting the reader, but the diction, in all its details, is of great importance. Thus Hecatæus, not having given equal thought and care to his diction, was completely surpassed by his successor.' The modern reader will of course observe that the last remark is wrongly put. No doubt, Hecatæus, with ten times the labour, could not have attained the elegance in style of Herodotus, who did not write till Greek prose had been studied and practised for nearly a century longer ; but the facts on which Hermogenes based his remark are doubtless strictly true. Lastly, in *Longinus de Sublim.*, chap. xxvii., the author says : ' Sometimes when a historian is speaking of a person, he suddenly leaves his own attitude and passes into that of the person he is describing. This figure should be used when a sudden crisis brooks no delay in the writer, and, as it were, compels him to pass at once from person to person. So it is in Hecatæus. ' Ceyx being grieved at this, immediately requested the Heracleidæ, his descendants, to leave the country. For I am not able to help you ; in order then that ye may not be yourselves destroyed, and, moreover, injure me, go [2] to some other community.'

§ 306. I have dwelt at considerable length on Hecatæus, who represents most distinctly the positive tendencies of the sixth century as opposed to its speculative and mystical aspirations. With him all was matter of fact, observation, and plain

---

[1] This is quite in a different sense from Strabo's remark.

[2] Frag. 353 : Ἔτι γε μὴν ἔσθ' ὅτε περὶ προσώπου διηγούμενος ὁ συγγραφεύς, ἐξαίφνης παρενεχθεὶς εἰς τὸ αὐτὸ πρόσωπον ἀντιμεθίσταται.—Διὸ καὶ ἡ πρόχρησις τοῦ σχήματος τότε ἡνίκα ὀξὺς ὁ καιρὸς ὢν διαμέλλειν τῷ γράφοντι μὴ διδᾷ, ἀλλ' εὐθὺς ἐπαναγκάζῃ μεταλαίνειν ἐκ προσώπων εἰς πρόσωπα· ὡς καὶ παρὰ τῷ Ἑκαταίῳ· ' Κῆυξ δὲ ταῦτα δεινὰ ποιούμενος, αὐτίκα ἐκέλευε τοὺς Ἡρακλείδας ἐπιγόνους ἐκχωρεῖν· Οὐ γὰρ ὑμῖν δυνατός εἰμι ἀρήγειν· ὡς μὴ ἂν αὐτοί τε ἀπόλησθε κἀμὲ τρώσητε, ἐς ἄλλον τινὰ δῆμον ἀποίχεσθαι.'

Note the infin. ἀποίχεσθαι. Did he return here to the narrative form? More recently Cobet (*Mnemos.* xi. 1) has argued that the works

recording of observations. Thus the positive tendencies, which culminated in the splendid histories and geographies of later days, owed their origin to this early school of practical enquirers. But I will not prosecute this side of Greek literature further here, and shall consider the successors of Hecatæus in relation with their most illustrious and perfect type, Herodotus. We are justified in doing so, not merely because the Persian wars form so great a crisis in Greek history that no sort of literature, save the choral lyric poetry, passed through it unchanged, but also because Miletus—the great intellectual hothouse of Greece, the centre of her art, her philosophy, and her history—was completely destroyed by the Persians at the opening of the fifth century, and so the splendid continuity of Greek thought received a disastrous check. Up to this date, the title Milesian meets us in every field of thought; from henceforth it disappears for centuries from our studies. Simple stories of rude shepherd life, and the loves of rustic swains, were known long after as Milesian tales—a faint and wretched afterglow of the most lurid and stormy sunset in the history of Greek intellect. Prose literature received a blow from which it never recovered; for while the tendency of Ionic prose had been (as it ought to be) to assume the narrative, or the philosophical form, the destruction of its proper home threw the balance into Attica, where the rhetorical element became so predominant as to control all descriptions of prose writing. Hence, as Mure observes,[1] Greek prose has permanently suffered, and we have only one great specimen of what narrative prose might have been but for the dominating influence of Athens. Herodotus, with all his genius, was unable to stem the tide of Attic influence; yet his great work shows us clearly what might have been expected but for the subjugation of Ionia and, above all, the destruction of Miletus.

The dramatic elements in the religious mysteries of the sixth century, especially in the worship of Dionysus, have been treated in a separate chapter.[2]

attributed to Hecatæus at Alexandria, and quoted (as above) by Hellenistic critics, were all forgeries, made up chiefly out of Herodotus, who thus seemed to have copied him. I fear the great critic was failing when he wrote this article.   [1] iv. 127.   [2] Vol. I. chap. xiv.

CHAPTER II

HERODOTUS AND THE CONTEMPORARY IONIC PROSE WRITERS.

§ 307. THOUGH Miletus, the great centre and mainspring of Ionic culture, was untimely destroyed, the influence it had already exerted over eastern Hellas could not disappear in an instant. A series of men attempted to utilise prose for historical purposes, and communicated the old Milesian spirit to Herodotus, who, although he lived to see the Peloponnesian war and to witness the teaching of the sophists and the rise of rhetoric at Athens, was, nevertheless, so strictly a writer of Ionic genius, so completely a coequal in spirit and in culture of Epicharmus and Pindar, and Æschylus, that in a rational survey of Greek literature he must be placed among his predecessors as one born out of due season. But the culture of Athens had, perhaps, not yet swallowed up all the rest of Greek literary genius, and the style of Hellanicus, a younger contemporary, or, at least, not older than Herodotus, makes us suspect that Herodotus was not so unique as he is generally considered.

We have the late, but respectable, authority of Dionysius of Halicarnassus, that he was born 'a little before the Persian wars,' which would make him older than the account of Pamphila, who gives B.C. 484 as his birth year. As it seems likely, from the absence of later allusions, that he died before 420 B.C., he may have been born before the battle of Marathon. It is generally agreed that Halicarnassus was his native town, though from his long residence at Thurii he is called the Thurian by Aristotle, when quoting the opening words of his history in the *Rhetoric*.[1] He is also called the Thurian

[1] iii. 9.

logopoïos in a passage cited from an epistle of Julian by
Suidas. But Strabo mentions both titles, and explains them
in the obvious way just mentioned. Suidas says his parents'
names were Lyxes and Dryo, or Rhœo, through one of whom
Panyasis was his uncle. An extant epitaph or epigram con-
firms his father's name, and the obscurity of both, though
Suidas calls them illustrious, seems some warrant for the trustworthiness of the tradition.

I see no reason for doubting the relationship with Panyasis,
which is rendered internally probable by the peculiar and exceptional education which Herodotus must have received. His
intimacy with Homer's poems has been shown from a comparative table of phrases [1] to be such as we should not expect from
ordinary circumstances, but can easily explain by his intercourse
with Panyasis, the learned reviver of epic poetry. In the same
way he quotes the cyclic poets, Hesiod, the gnomic and lyric
poets, and the earlier tragedians, Æschylus and Phrynichus.
It seems by accident, rather than from ignorance, that he omits
Callinus, Tyrtæus, the elder Simonides, Stesichorus, Epime-
nides, and Epicharmus, from references which otherwise embrace all the older literature. The two Sicilian poets may
possibly not have been known to him till he went to Thurii,
but he writes like a man with all the greater authors at hand,
as they may have been in the house of Panyasis and, of course,
at Athens, which he visited in mature age. Suidas, indeed,
says that he was exiled to Samos by Lygdamis, grandson of the
Artemisia whom he delights to honour in his history ; that he
returned and obtained his country's liberty by expelling Lygdamis, but finding himself disliked, left for Thurii, where he
settled and died. But all these facts, if true, could hardly have
escaped corroboration by his own allusions, or, at least, by
early witnesses.[2] We hear nothing of Herodotus having married
or left any descendants.

§ 308. We can therefore assert nothing, save that a good deal

[1] Mure (vol. ii., Appendix Q) gives an imperfect list.

[2] All these legends are rejected by A. Bauer, in his researches, as invented when Herodotus began to revive in popularity after long oblivion.
But this ground for scepticism is refuted by H. Weil in the *Revue Critique*
for Jan. 1, 1880.

of his earlier life was spent in travelling, and apparently travelling for the purpose of his history.[1] This he must have brought with him to Athens in sufficient completion to make him famous, if Sophocles, as Plutarch and Suidas tell us, composed an ode to him in the year 440 B.C. It is probable, therefore, that before this time he had visited Upper Egypt, Susiana, Babylonia (as far as Ardericca and Ecbatana), Colchis and Scythia, Thrace, Dodona, Zakynthos, and Cyrene, with most of the countries within this great circuit. The spread of mercantile enterprise from Miletus and Phocæa, and the security afforded by the Persian conquests and good administration of Asia and Egypt, made such voyages not only possible, but perhaps not unusual. Even in the days of Solon it was part of a perfect education to visit, at least, the Lydian court and the wonders of Lower Egypt.

Herodotus' eastern travels seem to have been made before his retirement to Thurii, but we cannot fix the years and order of them, except that he saw the battle-field of Papremis after the year 460 B.C.,[2] probably while the Athenian armies were in possession of part of the country. He is said by the pseudo-Plutarch to have recited his history when he came to Athens, and (by Suidas) afterwards at Olympia ; but the latter tale is plainly an invention suggested by the later fashion of exhibiting there, and the earlier is not much more probable, unless a mere reading among distinguished friends were intended. But if this were so, the alleged public vote of ten talents would of course be inconceivable.[3] Yet I see that most recent German critics accept both the public recitation and the state reward.[4]

It is probable that he resided at Athens for some years until he joined, with many other celebrated men, the colony

---

[1] Travelling for literary purposes was so rare in those early times, that I do not share the confidence of K. O. Müller and others, who assert positively that Herodotus had no other object. Commercial reasons may have existed, though it is not easy to imagine such various voyages conducive to any systematic business. As Stein observes, his personal wanderings seem to have extended precisely to the limits of the Persian dominion ; beyond them he only speaks from hearsay.

[2] iii. 12.   [3] Cf. *Euseb. Chron. ad Ol.*, 85 (Ed. Schöne).

[4] Stein, *Introd.* to his Edition, i. p. xxii, note.

which founded Thurii, near the old site of Sybaris, in 443 B.C.[1] There can be little doubt that at Athens he learned to know many of the splendid intellects then collected there, besides Sophocles, who seems indebted to him (cf. § 185) for several passages : that in the *Antigone*, brought out in 440, where the greater loss of a brother than a husband is curiously discussed ; the attack on the habits of Egyptians in the *Œdipus Col.* 337, sq., as well as the rehearsal of human misery in the chorus (1211, sq.), if this be not modelled on Theognis, 424, sq.[2]

It also appears from the strongly democratic temper of the later part of his history, in spite of his aristocratical antecedents and parentage, that he came under the influence of Pericles and his policy. Yet if we assume this, and even that he re-visited Athens after the Propylæa was built (430 B.C.), we are astonished at the small effect which Attic thought and Attic style made upon his history. The compressed logical speaking of Antiphon, the stately emphasis of Pericles, the subtlety of Euripides, and the whole sophistical school, seem the offspring of another age and another atmosphere. In this society we may conceive him, intellectually at least, a sort of Oliver Gold-smith, often ridiculed by his friends for simplicity, and no doubt underrated, but, withal, far exceeding his clever critics in direct-ness, in grace, and in pathos, and so gaining a place in the literature of his country which his contemporaries never antici-pated. But perhaps this is too fanciful, and I would rather

---

[1] As K. O. Müller observes, there is no evidence that he left Athens in 443 ; it is even possible, according to the same authority, that he did not leave till after the opening of the Peloponnesian war. But this would throw the composition of his history far too late, if we suppose with Müller that it was not written till his retirement to Italy.

[2] Cf. further, frag. 380, on the discovery of games to stave off the pangs of hunger ; and frag. 967, on the melting snow causing the inundation of the Nile. The passage above mentioned in the *Antigone* is considered spurious by some critics, but is defended on very reasonable grounds by Kirchhoff, *Ent. des herodot. Gesch.*, pp. 8–9. Though, as he says, we can conceive no later time at which such an interpolation would be popular, it is more likely that Sophocles obtained the story privately from Herodotus than that he copied it from a just published history. Cf. Stein's *Introd.*, p. xxv.

infer from this curious want of influence that the main body of
his work was finished when he came there, and that he spent
his leisure in completing and perfecting it. There are, it is
true, a good many references to current events after 431 B.C.,[1]
and these notices are woven into the tenor of the narrative;
but, nevertheless, these later allusions which touch the opening
of the Peloponnesian war, and some events which may not
have occurred till 425 B.C., are easily severed from the main
narrative, and are probably additions made to a corrected
copy, in which he even refers to the incredulity with which
one of his statements had been received. He alludes[2] to a
separate work on Assyria, of which hardly any trace seems to
have survived, so that many have thought he only referred to
a longer episode which he intended to introduce in his book.

§ 309. His life, which some critics have prolonged beyond
all probability into the next century, was ended either at Thurii,
where he was even said to have been buried in the market-
place, or at Athens. The restless and troubled state of Thurii,
together with the late allusions to Athens, make the latter alternative probable enough. A third account transfers his tomb to
Pella in Macedonia, which is incredible. The complete absence
of allusions to the Sicilian expedition, coupled with his habit
of 'writing up' his book to recent times in its allusions, is
strong evidence for his death before that event. It has been
debated whether the work was finished, and, as usual, critics
have held opposite views on the subject : some alleging that
the capture of Sestos is a natural and proper end ; others that
he must have intended to proceed to other events in connection with it. I can only state my opinion that though the
author meant to add some details, as is proved by an unful-
filled promise,[3] the main subject was completed with the

---

[1] v. 77 ; vi. 91, 98 ; vii. 137, 233 ; ix. 73 and elsewhere.

[2] i. 106 and 184. Prof. Rawlinson cites a passage in Aristotle's *Natural
History*, and some notices of Parthian manners in John of Malala, which
may possibly be taken from it ; but according to the best MSS., which
Kirchhoff supports by the expression πεποίηκε, used by Aristotle, the passage comes from the poet Hesiod.

[3] i. 184.

repulse of the Persians from Europe, and the work substantially and properly concluded.

Similarly it has been debated whether he wrote his work in middle or in advanced life ; and, as Mure has observed, its tone and style, in the absence of outward evidence, are certain to produce the impression of an aged man telling his long experiences to a younger generation. This feeling is enhanced by the strong contrast to his Attic contemporaries which has already been mentioned. Most of the debates about his life are of this vague and uncertain character, and are after all but waste of time. I will only observe that his most elaborate biographer, Dahlmann, seems to me more unfortunate and illogical than the rest in his conjectures, none of which I have here adopted.

§ 310. But of late years A. Kirchhoff has taken up the question with his usual acuteness, and has discussed in a special pamphlet[1] the evidences in the work itself, which are, as he rightly says, our only real evidence. He thinks the earlier part of the work shows traces of familiarity with Athens, from the comparison of the circuit of Ecbatana with that of Athens,[2] from the comparing of a distance with that from the agora at Athens to Olympia,[3] from his knowledge of Æschylus' poetry, and from his reducing Persian measures to Attic.[4] Hence he infers that the historian arrived at Athens from his travels about 446 B.C., and finished up to iii. 119 (the story of Intaphernes' wife) at Athens early in 442 B.C., so that Sophocles came to know it. He thinks that the criticism of his dialogue among the Persian conspirators,[5] to which he afterwards pointedly refers,[6] may have been one of the causes for his suspending his work and going, in the interests of Pericles, whom he admired greatly, to Thurii. From there he visited Sicily and Magna Græcia, and thus resumes his history with special knowledge of Crotoniate legends. From v. 77, in which the Propylæa at Athens, which were not finished till

---

[1] *Die Entstehungszeit des herodotischen Geschichtswerkes*, 2nd ed., Berlin, 1878, ably criticised by Mr. E. Abbott (*Transact. Oxf. Philol. Soc.* for 1880, p. 31).

[2] i. 98.   [3] ii. 7.   [4] *Op. cit.*, p. 12.

[5] iii. 80.   [6] vi. 43.

431 B.C. are mentioned, and from other hints in the later books, the historian seems to have returned to Athens about that time, and proceeded with his work up to 428 B.C., which contains the latest references to contemporary events. Kirchhoff holds that the work was then interrupted by the death of Herodotus, as it should have included the victory at the Eurymedon.[1]

But the whole of this acute argument is based on the hypothesis that our text stands exactly as it was originally composed, and that allusions were not afterwards inserted. The argument from silence used to limit the last year of Herodotus' writing to 428 B.C. is also very precarious. It is also certain that a successful recitation, followed by public rewards at Athens, which Kirchhoff accepts, cannot possibly have been a reading of the first three books, but rather of the last three, in which Athens is really glorified. This consideration upsets either the tradition or Kirchhoff's theory.

There are two busts of Herodotus in the Naples Museum, neither of which is of good workmanship, and which are, moreover, not duplicates or referable to the same original. One is a double Herme, with Thucydides at its back ; the other is a smaller and plainer bust, but with a peculiar ugly and friendly face, not unlike the bust of Socrates, and with much of the gentle and gossiping expression which we might expect in the historian. I should be disposed to consider this as our best authority, but for the recent confirmation of the Thucydides on the double Herme (cf. below, § 363).

§ 311. Turning from the historian to his work, it must be at once premised that no abstract of each book will here be attempted, because such an account gives a false idea of the work, which, while following a general plan, abounds in so many digressions, small and great, in so many stray remarks of interest in literature and archæology, i~ so many anecdotes of national or individual peculiarities, that any reader can take it up anywhere, and find it both instructive and amusing. Even a careful and lengthy digest of the general argument, such as is given by Mure,[2] conveys no idea of the general effect, which can be far better appreciated by a perusal of any twenty chapters.

The plan is distinctly stated at the opening. It is to narrate the great conflict of Greeks and barbarians ; so that the glorious deeds of both may not perish, and that their true causes may be known. Herodotus thus chooses no petty quarrel between neighbouring Greek cities, no dispute of transitory moment, but the great shock of East and West, of liberty and despotism, which has lasted in many Protean phases up to the present day. The first result of this large conception, which rises above the narrow nationalism of his successors, is that his history gives us more information about the state of ancient nations and their culture than all the other Greek historians put together.

§ 312. His preface is on the mythical conflicts between the Greeks and the Asiatics ; but after a very brief sketch in five chapters he boldly lays aside the mythical point of view, without caring to decide upon the question of aggression there disputed, and states his intention of starting from the first Eastern aggressor upon the Greeks for whom he can vouch from his own knowledge, not forgetting to tell of cities, both great and small, as he proceeds, seeing that the fortunes of men change, and their glory waxes and wanes with the lapse of time. He enters at once upon Crœsus of Lydia, and proceeds to give an account of the kingdom since its foundation by Gyges to its destruction by Cyrus, turning aside constantly to explain its gradual encroachment upon and conquest of the Ionian cities. The antiquities of Ionia, and its connection with Attica and Achaia, are probably drawn from his uncle Panyasis' poem, and are highly interesting as regards the federal constitution, the dialects, and the culture of the early Ionians.[1] But there are also interwoven digressions of dramatic interest—the legends of the visit of Solon to Crœsus, and the affecting story of Atys ; others of historical importance, such as the reign of Peisistratus, the rise of Sparta through Lycurgus, and her early struggles with

---

[1] i. cc. 142–51. Niebuhr thought the grand catalogue of the Persian forces was borrowed from Chœrilus (cf. § 109). But this poet was younger than Herodotus, though contemporary.

Tegea. The conquest of Lydia by Cyrus leads him to go back to the rise of the Median empire, and its merging into that of the Persians by the revolt of Cyrus. The customs and religion of the Persians are described, and then their conquest of Ionia, Caria, and Lycia, with constant notes on these latter nations and their customs. The next war of Cyrus leads the historian to Babylon, which is carefully described and its later history sketched.[1] The first book ends with the death of Cyrus in battle with the northern barbarians.

§ 313. Herodotus passes through these and a vast number of other subjects with the most perfect ease and mastery. The reader is never disappointed at the delay of a result, or annoyed at the irrelevance of a digression. When Crœsus comes in contact with Cyrus, he reverts to the older history of Cyrus' empire; when Cyrus attacks Babylon, he reverts in the same way to the older history of Babylon and of Assyria; but finding this episode too cumbrous, he relegates it to a separate 'Assyrian history.' The second, third, and fourth books are a detailed account of the progress of the Persian empire under Cambyses, the false Smerdis, and Darius; but the campaigns against Egypt, Arabia, Scythia, and Libya afford a proper place for a full and interesting discussion of the geographical features, natural peculiarities, or society of these countries. These digressions, which occupy the whole of the second book (on Egypt) and almost all the fourth (Scythia and Libya), are so complete in themselves as to suggest the theory that Herodotus, when he first travelled, intended to put his careful and systematic observations together into a geographical work— on the model of Scylax, but something far greater, which would describe the less known countries of the East and South, not only in their natural, but in their political history. This plan must have been abandoned before he went to Thurii, or he would certainly have composed a similar digression on the less known parts of Italy, and probably on the Carthaginians. But as the work proceeds, and the interest in the coming catastrophe grows warmer, the episodes and halting places are sparingly admitted, and the great struggle advances with epic grandeur

[1] cc. 178 ss.

to its close. The narrative finds its natural conclusion in the
capture of Sestos, the last point which the Persians held in
Europe, and their repulse into that Asia which they always
claimed as their own. There is, therefore, no reason to doubt
whether the author lived to finish his task. The very last chapter
is, indeed, a sort of appendix, like several in the work, which
a modern author would have thrown into the form of a foot-
note ; but as this device was then unknown, all these collateral
points find their place in the text.[1] Yet even in these parts
of the work we should deeply regret the omission of the short
notes on the character and privileges of Spartan royalty, on
the Athenian acquisition of Lemnos, and on older Attic history ; nay, even the scandalous anecdotes about the courts of
Periander and of Xerxes are agreeable diversions, though by
most critics censured as beneath the dignity of history. On
the affairs of Samos[2] he is so explicit in several places that he
was supposed to have retired there when in exile from Halicarnassus, and learnt the Ionic dialect ; but the affairs of
Samos, especially under Polycrates, the greatest of Greek
despots, if we except those of Sicily, are sufficiently important in themselves to warrant the share assigned to them,
and the inscriptions found on the site of Halicarnassus by Sir
Charles Newton are in the Ionic dialect.

A fuller inventory of this great and complex work is accessible in many good editions and translations mentioned
below ; nor is it the duty of a historian of literature to discuss the many historical problems raised by a comparison
of the statements of Herodotus with those of other ancient
authorities, or with the evidence of inscriptions newly discovered in our own times. We must here confine ourselves to
the literary character of his book, and his qualities as an
author and an artist.

---

[1] It is, moreover, noticeable that very few of the historical works left
us by the Greeks have formal conclusions—a fashion which seems some-
how contrary to literary taste in those days, and of which the absence is
perhaps connected with the practice which many authors followed of tack-
ing on their narratives to that of a predecessor by taking up the thread
where he had dropped it. [2] iii. 120, sq., &c.

§ 314. The extant fragments of Xanthus show that Herodotus used his *History of Lydia* less than might have been expected, there being no extant coincidence between them, although Ephorus states that Xanthus afforded a starting point
to our author.   The case is only different in degree with Charon
of Lampsacus, whose fragments (on the annals (ὧροι) of Lampsacus) show a good many points of identity in subject with
Herodotus, though there are equally points of difference ; and it
has been argued from Herodotus' missing the point of a joke on
the old name of Lampsacus (Pityusa), made by Crœsus,[1] that
he cannot have read Charon's annals of the town, in which this
older name is prominently mentioned.   Charon's annals of the
Spartan kings are not definitely referred to in vi. 55.   The
works of Hippys of Rhegium, and of Antiochus of Syracuse, were
chiefly devoted to the affairs of Magna Græcia, which Herodotus does not touch at length ; and this is, I think, a strong
argument against the composition of his work at Thurii in his
later years.   Had the whole scheme and plan of it not been
matured before he settled in Italy, it is more than probable
that he would have gathered materials for more interesting
episodes, and told us something of the early fortunes of the
Hellenes in the West.   The memoirs of Ion and Stesimbrotus,
and the history of Hellanicus, must have been later than the
date to which his history is here assigned, and do not therefore
require notice in this place.   As to geographical literature,
Herodotus cites [2] the *Arimaspea*, a geographical poem of
Aristeas, as an authority on Scythia ; and Scylax of Caryanda's
Periplus on Arabia and India.   He also criticises the maps
then current, and I have already noted (pp. 11, 14) references
to the work of Hecatæus.   It is, indeed, notable, at the dawn
of an epoch of research, how often men despise their immediate
and ablest predecessors, while they treat with respect the earlier
and weaker attempts of the same kind.   Herodotus appears to
feel in Hecatæus a rival, while the rest were hardly in the same
plane of literature.

§ 315. The books now enumerated, together with the poetical
library above described, were all the literary sources accessible

---

[1] vi. 37.   (Müller, *FHG.* i. p. 33, frag. 6.)   [2] iv. 14.

to Herodotus, if we except the personal intercourse with all the high culture and knowledge to be found at Periclean Athens. Commanding these materials, Herodotus had set to work from an early period of his life to enlarge and complete them by a long series of travels and careful observations ; endeavouring, where it was possible, to see both geographical curiosities and monumental records with his own eyes, or else giving us the evidence of those who had seen them, often with careful scrutiny and cautious reserve, when they were beyond his personal ken. Thus, in the Greek world he consulted those ancient registers or lists of kings, priests. or victors, which were preserved in various temples.   Charon had already published the list of Spartan kings ; Hellanicus added the priestesses of Juno at Argos and the Carnean victors, probably after Herodotus' researches were concluded.   These lists were of the last importance to early chronology, and were collateral with the system afterwards adopted in Greece—that of reckoning by Olympiads.   There were also a vast number of inscribed pillars in important cities, and of rich offerings dedicated to ancient shrines, on which the donors had told their circumstances, and so left records of their life and acts.   The treasury at Delphi, for instance, was full of such offerings, one of which, the tripod dedicated by Pausanias to the Greeks after the battle of Platæa, was lately found in the hippodrome at Constantinople.[1] By means of these documents, as well as by sifting the traditions of the nearer times orally, the historian attained considerable accuracy and clearness about the earlier portions of Greek history, properly so called.   The trivial points at which Thucydides sneers show how free of serious errors Herodotus must have been in this part of his work, and we may safely say that, with all his love of the marvellous and his taste for gossip, he has told us more, and told it better, than his critical followers contrive to tell us with far greater compression and the omission of endless points of interest.

§ 316. When he goes beyond the Hellenic world, his want of linguistic knowledge causes a great difference in his power of attaining 'truth.   He takes care, indeed, to express doubt con-

---

[1] Cf. Rawlinson's *Herod.*. vol. iv., Note A (p. 483).

cerning the many wonders told him of the ends of the earth
—northern Scythia and southern Arabia—which he repeatedly
tells us he could not learn from an eye-witness ; but concerning these nothing trustworthy was perhaps then attainable.
But in the case of the old cultures of Asia, and in Egypt,
where ample records positively teemed on rocks, and pillars,
and public buildings, his ignorance of the languages threw him
into the hands of cicerones—inferior priests, mercenary soldiers,
and other incompetent and untrustworthy persons—who often
did not know the truth, and, perhaps, sought deliberately to
mislead the curious Greek enquirer.   Hence, while his pictures
of the life and manners of these nations are of inestimable
value, his attempts to sketch their past history have often been
corrected, or even reversed, by the recent deciphering of inscriptions which he could have seen and transcribed.   Even
here he is *generally* right ; it is hard for an honest enquirer not
to discover a great deal of truth ; but he is not reliable, and
it is one of the great boasts of modern research to have been
able to extract the truth where the venerable Greek enquirer
was fain to be content with a cross-examination of doubtful
witnesses and a comparison of their negligences and igno-
rances.

It has often been urged in addition, that even under his
untoward circumstances, Herodotus might have done better
had he been endowed with the critical faculty of Thucydides,
and had he not started with a theory of Divine interference,
and an innate love of the marvellous and the quaint.   This
so-called childishness of Herodotus has been unduly mag-
nified by the fact that we do not possess his forerunners, but
only his most sceptical successor, wherewith to compare him.
This is evidently unjust ; for while he appears credulous from
this point of view, he was probably far in advance of the
Greeks of his day, if we except the Periclean circle.   He is
constantly sceptical, and even disposed to censure others as
too easy of belief ; but as is natural with all nascent scepticism,
this feeling breaks out only here and there, and is illogically co-
ordinated with credulity on kindred points, which the author
has not thought of disputing.   A most interesting catalogue

might be made of such survivals of credulity in the works of
the sceptics of all ages.

§ 317. But no German editor has approached the question
of Herodotus' credibility with such boldness and originality
as Mr. Blakesley in the very remarkable introduction to his
edition. Of course others have pointed, as he does, to the
influence of *Sophistic* on the historian, to his wandering life,
like Protagoras or Gorgias, to his alleged reading out of his
performances, to the conventional turns of his moral advices,
and the repetition of the same ethical commonplaces in the
mouths of divers and dissimilar characters. He is the first to
lay proper stress on the close identification of Herodotus,
by Thucydides and other ancient critics, with the *logopoioi*
who composed not to instruct but *to please.*[1]   He believes that
this class of men, as soon as they attained any facility in prose
composition, selected such events, and attributed such motives,
as they thought would be striking and popular without any
misgivings as to the accuracy of their statements ; for the
historic sense is a late and gradual acquisition which Thucydides acquired only by his extraordinary genius and circumstances in those early days. If this be so, the credibility of
Herodotus as to particular facts will stand on a very different
basis from that of modern historians. It has been hitherto
assumed that wherever he speaks as an eye-witness his faith-
fulness is beyond dispute ; but if he be a mere story-teller,
which is our nearest English to a λογοποιός, nothing is so
universal an attribute of such people in all times as to narrate
secondhand facts as if they were personal experiences. It is
done without the least bad faith, for the teller may firmly
believe his authority, and merely wish to complete his picture
without critical statements as to his authorities. Mr. Blakesley
is clearly of opinion that Herodotus did this, and that he
copied personal narratives from other people and set them
down as his own. He gives as an example the alleged
copying[2] from Hecatæus of facts about the crocodile, the

---

[1] He compares the speeches of Solon and Crœsus (i. 23 and iii. 36)
with the notions ascribed to Hippias in Plato's *Hipp. Maj.*, p. 236.

[2] ii. 68–73. Prof. Sayce, in his *Herodotus*, has pushed this criticism
to its utmost limit.

hippopotamus, and an account of the phœnix. This Herodotus does without acknowledgment, and with such deviations from the truth as seem to preclude a personal investigation. If these considerations be well founded, a vast deal of learned talk about the travels of Herodotus and his valuable evidence as an eye-witness will be blown to the winds. But of course it would not place him in the rank of a modern novelist, or even in that of De Foe, which Mr. Blakesley suggests. The real parallel he gives is that of Marco Polo, whose work at first circulated in MS., like that of Herodotus, and underwent curious alterations, not only at the hands of interpolators, but at the author's own, before it was printed. There is the same mixture in both of credulity and scepticism, of veracity in spirit, and yet ready acceptance of the doubtful or the false, of effort to be historical in an age when strict history was hardly yet defined.

§ 318. This speculation belongs to the estimate of his genius, which it may properly introduce, and is naturally suggested by the contrast of the Father of History with his greatest and most immediate successor, Thucydides ; nor is it reasonable to waive the question by merely insisting upon the contrast of their natural characters, and the different social and political atmosphere in which they were educated. Had Herodotus been a cold and sceptical critic, a despiser of all the domestic and personal features in great men or in dominant nationalities, a Periclean Athenian whose exclusiveness raised the pettiest Greek quarrel above the largest revolutions among barbarians, he might, no doubt, have sifted such materials with greater acumen, but he certainly would have had neither the desire to possess them nor the temper and the patience to collect them. The genial simplicity and wide sympathy of Herodotus not only supplied him with the stimulus to seek, but his informants with the inclination to impart, what they knew, and thus vastly counterbalanced any inferiority of judgment by the larger field of knowledge which he embraced.[1] His just estimate of the

[1] The only authority I can quote for this view, which I have implied long ago in my *Prolegomena to Ancient History*, is that of the Comte de

older civilisations of the Lydians, the Medes, the Persians, and
the Egyptians, has made his great work a picture, not of Greece,
but of the old world at one of its most interesting periods. To
the student of ancient history in any large and comprehensive
sense, it must be pronounced a work of infinitely greater
value and more permanent interest than the struggle for
ascendancy between the two leading states of Greece, which
had no general effects upon the changes of the world. While,
therefore, the conceptions of history in Herodotus and Thucy·
dides were mainly the consequence of the temper of the men
and of their surroundings, it must be declared that, *for an
historian*, the atmosphere in which the latter lived, while giving
him critical acumen and freeing him from theological prejudices, narrowed his view and distorted his estimate of the
relative importance of events. We may indeed feel very grate-
ful that Herodotus was not attracted in early life by this brilliant exclusiveness, and that he remained an Ionic instead of
becoming an Attic historian.

§ 319. There is a like contrast between the style of the earlier
and the later historians. Herodotus was thought the master of
the λέξις εἰρομένη, or style of simple co-ordination of clauses,
while Attic rhetoric brought them into complex connections,
so as form ingeniously constructed periods.[1] There are, indeed,
speeches introduced by Herodotus, such as the discussion on
the best form of government by the fellow-conspirators of
Darius,[2] where he shows ample acquaintance with the rhetoric
of the day, and where the periods are formed with some skill

Gobineau, in his exquisitely written but fantastic *Histoire des Perses* (i. 247,
sq.). He goes further than I do, and makes a curious *apologia* for the
Oriental chroniclers in connection with the receptive and uncritical temper
of Herodotus.

[1] Dionysius Hal. gives, as an example, Herodotus' words : Κροῖσος ἦν
Λυδὸς μὲν γένος, παῖς δὲ Ἀλυάττεω, τύραννος δὲ ἐθνέων τῶν ἐντὸς Ἅλυος
ποταμοῦ ; which, if periodically constructed, would be : Κ. ἦν υἱὸς μὲν Ἀ.,
γένος δὲ Λ., τύραννος δὲ τῶν ἐντὸς Ἅλυος ποταμοῦ ἐθνῶν. He even adds
a forced and unnatural construction. This loose and easy style was sometimes affected by Attic rhetors, as, for example, by the tyrant Critias, and
may be seen in fragment 25 of his *Lacedæmonian Polity*.

[2] iii. 80, sq.

and intricacy. This intermediate sort of writing was the *historic period* as opposed to the stricter *rhetorical* or *logical period.* These speeches, which are a common feature of all the classical historians, are by no means so signal a blemish to his work as are the rhetorical harangues in later literature ; for his speeches are well contrasted with those in Thucydides as *dramatic,* and coming in so naturally as to produce a lifelike picture of scenes and characters.[1]   I add a passage from one which strikes us as very peculiar, from its Thucydidean tone, and which proves

---

[1] The most elaborate instance just referred to is most severely censured by all the critics, who think it absurd that the great Persian nobles should discuss aristocracy and democracy after the manner of Greek sophists. Nevertheless Herodotus insists, in spite of the disbelief of his contemporaries, that this discussion really took place.   It seems to me a very bold thing to deny flatly the truth of an assertion which Herodotus— a man of undoubted honesty and intelligence—makes in the face of hostile criticism ; and, even had I no stronger reason, I should hesitate to disbelieve him.   But Gobineau has clearly shown the elements of truth in the story, and how the historian puts in a Greek form the really vital problem of the Persian empire.   It is usual to regard it as an Oriental despotism, which was occasionally the case, when the central power came into strong hands ; but this is really a false view.   The Iranian nobles were a feudal aristocracy, divided into classes, within which each member was really free, though bound by immemorial customs to render certain dues of respect and service to the chief.   The independence of all these clans and families really constituted a democracy, not of course a city democracy, with an agora and public debates, but a country democracy, with liberty and equality of rights, and this was somewhat the form of constitution into which Persia relapsed under the Arsacidæ, when the tyranny of the central king of kings was found too oppressive.   Cambyses, succeeding to the wealth of Cyrus, and to the possession of his conquests, which of course did not belong to the hereditary nobles of Iran, began to make them feel this tyranny.   Hence the discussion of the conspirators : were they to continue this imposing but dangerous monarchy ?   Could the seven lords in council control the other feudatories, and maintain the empire ? or should they revert to the natural condition of old Iranian society, and let all the clans live under their immemorial customs ?   It is also to be noted that they do not resolve on a monarchy, without limiting it beforehand by reserving to themselves certain hereditary privileges, thus showing their appreciation of the danger. I must again refer for an excellent statement of this matter to Gobineau, *Histoire des Perses,* i. 583, sq.

how fully Herodotus sympathised with the enterprise of imperial Athens, as expounded in Thucydides' speeches.[1]

But the general character of his writing, with its gossiping resumptions (ἐπαναλήψεις) and its natural anacolutha (which old grammarians noted and admired), is that of a peculiarly easy and artless flow, more like a charming conversation than a set composition ; and this is characterised by a constant passage from narrative to dialogue, which comes in so naturally as to be often unperceived. There is reason to believe (above, p. 14) that Hecatæus followed the same practice, which may have been a typical feature of Ionic historical prose. But it is not likely that many writers could have attained this art to such perfection as Herodotus. He employs it constantly to paint characters, which he never describes in a formal paragraph, but brings, as it were, living and speaking upon his stage. It has, nevertheless, been justly remarked that he is more successful in portraying types than individuals, national characteristics than personal features. His Persians, and Lydians, and Spartans are very distinct ; but his Crœsus becomes a Solon in captivity, and his Eastern grandees all use the same formulæ of contempt for unknown Hellenes of the West. This monotony was doubtless fostered by the gentle fatalism which prevails throughout early Greek literature, and which finds its perfect expression in the dialogues of Artabanus and Xerxes.[2] But this same feeling

[1] vii. 50 : Ἀμείβεται Ξέρξης τοισίδε· ''Ἀρτάβανε, οἰκότως μὲν σύ γε τουτέων ἕκαστα διαιρέεαι· ἀτὰρ μήτε πάντα φοβέο, μήτε πᾶν ὁμοίως ἐπιλέγεο. Εἰ γὰρ δὴ βούλοιο ἐπὶ τῷ αἰεὶ ἐπεσφερομένῳ πρήγματι τὸ πᾶν ὁμοίως ἐπιλέγεσθαι, ποιήσειας ἂν οὐδαμᾶ οὐδέν· κρέσσον δὲ πάντα θαρσέοντα ἥμισυ τῶν δεινῶν πάσχειν μᾶλλον, ἢ πᾶν χρῆμα προδειμαίνοντα μηδαμᾶ μηδὲν παθεῖν· εἰ δὲ ἐρίζων πρὸς πᾶν τὸ λεγόμενον μὴ τὸ βέβαιον ἀποδέξεις, σφάλλεσθαι ὀφείλεις ἐν αὐτοῖσι ὁμοίως καὶ ὁ ὑπεναντία τούτοισι λέξας. τοῦτο μέν νυν ἐπ' ἴσης ἔχει· εἰδέναι δὲ ἄνθρωπον ἐόντα κῶς χρὴ τὸ βέβαιον ; δοκέω μὲν οὐδαμῶς. τοῖσι τοίνυν βουλομένοισι ποιέειν ὡς τὸ ἐπίπαν φιλέει γίνεσθαι τὰ κέρδεα, τοῖσι δὲ ἐπιλεγομένοισί τε πάντα καὶ ὀκνεῦσι οὐ μάλα ἐθέλει. Ὁρᾷς τὰ Περσέων πρήγματα ἐς τὸ δυνάμιος προκεχώρηκε· εἰ τοίνυν ἐκεῖνοι οἱ πρὸ ἐμεῦ γενόμενοι βασιλέες γνώμῃσι ἐχρέοντο ὁμοίῃσι καὶ σύ, ἢ μὴ χρεόμενοι γνώμῃσι τοιαύτῃσι ἄλλους συμβούλους εἶχον τοιούτους, οὐκ ἄν κοτε εἶδες αὐτὰ ἐς τοῦτο προελθόντα· νῦν δὲ κινδύνους ἀναρριπτέοντες ἐς τοῦτό σφεα προηγάγοντο. μεγάλα γὰρ πρήγματα μεγάλοισι κινδύνοισι ἐθέλει καταιρέεσθαι.

[2] vii. 10, sq. ; and thus in 46, sq. : Μαθὼν δέ μιν Ἀρταβανος ὁ πάτρως,

of the transitory nothingness of life—Euripides' τὸ μηδὲν εἰς οὐδὲν ῥέπει—may have aided his candid nature in the very just and impartial view he takes of the virtues and vices of men. He has often been accused, but never convicted, of bias or unfairness. He is most explicit in telling the good points of those who suffer his severest censure. Perhaps the most disagreeable personage in his history is the deity 'who permits no one to feel proud but himself' [1]—a sort of singular, but impersonal Providence, in whom a leading attribute is jealousy, a curious and early reflection of the most ingrained national vice of the Greeks from Homer to the present day. The enigmatical warnings of this Providence, through dreams and oracles, occupy, no doubt, too prominent a place among his causes for great events, but, nevertheless, convey to us the feeling of the Greek public, even of later days, far more faithfully than the uncompromising positivism of Thucydides. If, also, he assigns trivial origins to great consequences, such as the selfishness of Demokedes involving his whole race in misfortune, we must remember in palliation that the caprices of

---

ὃς τὸ πρῶτον γνώμην ἀπεδέξατο ἐλευθέρως οὐ συμβουλεύων Ξέρξῃ στρατεύεσθαι ἐπὶ τὴν Ἑλλάδα, οὗτος ἀνὴρ φρασθεὶς Ξέρξεα δακρύσαντα εἴρετο τάδε· Ὦ βασιλεῦ, ὡς πολλὸν ἀλλήλων κεχωρισμένα ἐργάσαο νῦν τε καὶ ὀλίγῳ πρότερον; μακαρίσας γὰρ σεωυτὸν δακρύεις. Ὁ δὲ εἶπε· Ἐσῆλθε γάρ με λογισάμενον κατοικτεῖραι ὡς βραχὺς εἴη ὁ πᾶς ἀνθρώπινος βίος, εἰ τουτέων γε ἐόντων τοσούτων οὐδεὶς ἐς ἑκατοστὸν ἔτος περιέσται. Ὁ δὲ ἀμείβετο λέγων· Ἕτερα τούτου παρὰ τὴν ζόην πεπόνθαμεν οἰκτρότερα. ἐν γὰρ οὕτω βραχέϊ βίῳ οὐδεὶς οὕτω ἄνθρωπος ἐὼν εὐδαίμων πέφυκε, οὔτε τουτέων, οὔτε τῶν ἄλλων, τῷ οὐ παραστήσεται πολλάκις, καὶ οὐκὶ ἅπαξ, τεθνάναι βούλεσθαι μᾶλλον ἢ ζώειν. αἵ τε γὰρ συμφοραὶ προσπίπτουσαι, καὶ αἱ νοῦσοι συνταράσσουσαι καὶ βραχὺν ἐόντα μακρὸν δοκέειν εἶναι ποιεῦσι τὸν βίον. οὕτω ὁ μὲν θάνατος μοχθηρῆς ἐούσης τῆς ζόης καταφυγὴ αἱρετωτάτη τῷ ἀνθρώπῳ γέγονε· ὁ δὲ θεὸς γλυκὺν γεύσας τὸν αἰῶνα φθονερὸς ἐν αὐτῷ εὑρίσκεται ἐών. The author of the *Epitaphios*, ascribed to Lysias, has used this passage with great effect, and without any servile imitation, in his admirable p[er]oration, §§ 77, 78.

[1] vii. 10. It is, however, but just to add that he thinks the gods (θεοὶ) have their name from setting in order (κόσμῳ θέντες), and that he recognises in many places a wise and benevolent Providence. Thus, iii. 108, καὶ κως τοῦ θείου ἡ προνοίη, ὥσπερ καὶ οἰκός ἐστι, ἐοῦσα σοφή, makes harmless and edible animals prolific, whereas the reverse is the case with birds of prey.

despots, however contemptible in themselves, may be as vast in results as the rational policy of deliberative assemblies.

The same tendency makes him attentive to female character, and to the indirect influence of women on public affairs. His sketches of Queen Artemisia and the Spartan Gorgo, of Amestris and of Labda, are very spirited, and full of feeling; but here again, like a tragic poet, he rather paints types than peculiar individuals. If he is anywhere peculiarly felicitous in individual features, it is in such scenes as Cleisthenes' feast for the suitors of Agariste, or the attempt on Kypselus in his infancy. Here it is that a certain humour, which almost passes for mere simplicity, makes him paint small and comic detail, and so fill in with definite and peculiar colour the outline of the fixed types which generally occupy his pages. We naturally associate this humour with its opposite, the pathetic, as both are the offspring of a quick and delicate sympathy. Nor are we disappointed in Herodotus, whose profound pathos is not surpassed by any tragic poet. The legend of Atys, the story of the Periander's family troubles, and the dramatic forebodings of the great catastrophe in the dreams and confessions of Xerxes and Artabanus, are prominent among many instances of this rare and splendid quality in Herodotus' narrative.

§ 320. Turning to the dialect of Herodotus, we find ourselves in presence of a problem which has been raised by the minute criticism of the present day, and which seems not likely to receive a satisfactory solution. We can perceive from the author's careful observations [1] on the four subdivisions of the Ionic dialect of Asia Minor that he had studied the question, and that his language was not unconsciously determined by the circumstances of his education, but was the carefully chosen and purified instrument in which he determined, for æsthetic reasons, to clothe his thoughts. This agrees with the repeated observations of Greek grammarians, that his dialect was mixed or various, as opposed to the pure Ionic of Hecatæus and Hippocrates; it is therefore idle to assert that his history represents the Samian or any other local speech. But beyond this the observations of such critics as Hermogenes and Dionysius are un-

---

[1] i. 142.

fortunately confined to general statements that he is the chief master of Ionic—as Thucydides of old Attic—prose. They do not determine in any detail what combinations or variations were admitted by Herodotus. This silence was probably owing to the absence of any special studies among the Alexandrian critics,[1] who left so much material on Homer and on the Attic writers. As a natural consequence the readings of our texts seem regulated by no fixed principles, and not only are various dialects admitted, but the same word appears, even in our best MSS., in divers forms. While there are thus difficulties about the original form of individual words which will probably never be solved, we can indicate two certain sources of variety.

The first is the rise of epic language, with which Herodotus was always acknowledged to have been thoroughly imbued. This strong tincture, not only of epic phrases, but of thoughts, seems to result from his early intercourse with Panyasis, a learned student of epic diction, who may possibly have educated his nephew, and endeavoured to induce him to follow in his own footsteps. If this be so, seeing that Panyasis must have studied epic diction critically, we should have ample reasons for this complexion in the dialect of Herodotus. It is, however, carefully to be remembered that all the later researches into Homeric language tend to the theory of an old Attic recension, and to the consequently old Attic character of the diction as we have it. There can be little doubt that this old Attic and the Ionic dialects of Asia Minor were closely allied, so that many apparently epic forms may be mere archaic words in the language of Herodotus' parents. The theory that our Homer was recast in the days of Herodotus, and so brought into accord with his language, is part of Mr. Paley's doctrine of the late composition of our Iliad and Odyssey which has been above rejected (§ 48).

The second source of variety in Herodotus seems to be the adoption of Attic forms, and of some Doric forms, almost all of which are, however, in use with Attic writers. It is even

---

[1] Abicht, i. p. 9, says the Alexandrians were much occupied with him, and that to them we owe the division into nine books. If so, why have we no body of scholia extant?

doubtful whether the dialect of Halicarnassus was Doric in
Herodotus' day ; its exclusion from the Hexapolis, which he
mentions, and the discovery of two early Ionic inscriptions
by Sir C. Newton during his researches, make it unlikely that
it was. And as regards the Attic forms, we are uncertain
both how far old Attic and Ionic forms may have coincided,
and how far our present MSS. may have been tampered with
by Atticising transcribers. The difficult problem of determining
the dialect of the book has, nevertheless, been attempted by a
series of scholars, beginning with Struve in 1828, who worked
out the evidence of the MSS. on a few very frequent forms,
such as the declension of Βασιλεύς ; Dindorf followed in his
preface to the Didot edition (1844). and even gave an alpha-
betical catalogue of proper Ionic forms ; then comes Bredow
(1846), and the later German editors of the text. They start,
in my opinion justly, from the principle that Herodotus did not
vary in his writing of the *same* word, and that therefore the
balance of MS. evidence in favour of one form should make
us correct the less authenticated variants of the same word.
There are cases where the evidence is so evenly balanced that
no decision seems possible, and there are still editors, such as
Mr. Wood, who will not accept the principle, and think that
Herodotus carried his epic imitations so far as to use various
forms for euphony's sake. This question is therefore likely to
remain open, and it is a matter of great satisfaction that it inter-
feres hardly at all with the understanding of the text. The age
immediately succeeding Herodotus drifted away so rapidly from
his tone of thought and style that he soon lost his popularity.
Thucydides and Ktesias still think him worth criticism, but the
rest snub him as a mere story-teller, and in the days of Theo-
pompus (a century later) he was so forgotten that that rhetorical
historian published an abstract of his work in two books.[1]

§ 321. As already observed, there is no evidence that the text
of Herodotus occupied the Alexandrian critics like those of
Homer or Aristophanes. But the Roman rhetoricians, especially
Dionysius of Halicarnassus, fully appreciated his perfection in
style, though they, of course, set it down to a conscious theory,

---

[1] But Aristotle, in his *Rhetoric*, speaks of him as a typical historian.

and not to the natural conditions of early prose. Dion Chrysostom seems quite saturated with him ; he cites or transcribes no author, except Homer, so often. In the age of Hadrian the father of History again revived in general estimation, and became the object of much comment and admiration. Thus we may thank the taste of a degraded and artificial age for having saved us this splendid monument of early genius. Porphyry mentions *Miscellanies on the Emendation of Herodotus*, by the grammarian Philemon, who notices even in his day the many corruptions of the existing texts. I suppose all Greek literature affords nothing else so like a smart and adverse modern review as the tract on the *Spitefulness of Herodotus*, which has reached us under Plutarch's name. The author takes all the history to pieces, especially the Hellenic history, and endeavours to show at every turn a spirit of malevolence and injustice, which is so strong as to result in self-contradictions and inconsistencies of various kinds. Some of the points made, especially as regards the Corinthians, seem very good, and perhaps the attack has not been sufficiently considered ; but the smartness of the writing is singular for a Greek criticism.[1] At the same time the writer insists upon the extraordinary charm exercised by Herodotus' style, and thus bears witness to his popularity in that day. Accordingly, he was constantly imitated in late Roman and Byzantine days.[2] But no body of scholia seems to have reached us in any of the extant MSS. Of these some thirty are known, the oldest and best of which is the Codex Mediceus of the tenth century. There are also good texts of the eleventh and twelfth centuries at Rome. But ever since Gaisford's edition the peculiar codex S (Sancroftianus), which he first made known, was considered of higher authority, and was made the basis of all the recensions down to Stein's earlier text ; while Abicht has in our day argued successfully

---

[1] Here is a specimen (c. 33) : Θηβαίους δὲ καὶ μηδίζοντας λέγων ἐν Θερμοπύλαις στιχθῆναι, καὶ στιχθέντας αὐτοὺς ἐν Πλαταιαῖς μηδίζειν προθύμως, δοκεῖ μοι, καθάπερ Ἱπποκλείδης ὁ τοῖς σκέλεσι χειρονομῶν ἐπὶ τῆς τραπέζης, εἰπεῖν ἄν, ἐξορχούμενος τὴν ἀλήθειαν, οὐ φροντὶς Ἡροδότῳ. He refers to the story of the marriage of Agariste (vi. 129).

[2] Cf. the curious references in Nicolai, *L.G.* i. p. 271.

against this course, and has again asserted the Mediceus as the proper groundwork for a critical text.   This is admitted in Stein's larger critical edition, and the third edition of his commentary.

Herodotus was first printed in the Latin version of Laur. Valla at Venice, in 1474.   The princeps of the Greek text is that of Aldus (1502), but it is based on a Paris MS. not of the highest authority.   Gronovius (1715) first collated the Laurentian codex, but Wesseling (1763) commenced the really critical labours on the text by a larger collation of many MSS.   Early in the present century there are two laborious and learned editions by Schweighäuser and by Gaisford, followed by that of Bähr (second ed. 1856).   Blakesley's (*Bib. Class.* 1854) does not give any of the newer lights, but shows great acuteness in the appendices on various historical questions.   The best critical books of the newer school are the annotated editions of Abicht and Stein, with German notes.   The former has also written important monographs on the text ; [1] the latter has published a large critical edition (Berlin, 1869), in which he has discussed and classified the MSS., and given the fragments of lexicography and the few scholia attached to our extant copies.   He promises (in a third volume) a full *lexicon Herodoteum.*   Both have given at the close of the preface to their editions an excellent conspectus of the peculiar forms used by Herodotus. Schweighäuser's *Lexicon Herodoteum* is a painstaking book, but was published before the later labours in the text.   Moreover, all the exegesis before 1850 is rendered obsolete by the reading of the cuneiform inscriptions, which have thrown immense light on the Persian and Assyrian histories.   The same may be said as regards the results of Egyptology, which are brought to bear on the second book in Stein's edition by the learning of Brugsch Besides the early version of Valla, there is an excellent French translation by Zaccher, and a fine English edition by Prof. George Rawlinson, which is illustrated with the learning and research of Sir Henry Rawlinson and Sir G. Wilkinson : this edition is the only English one up to modern requirements in exegesis, seeing that Mr. Sayce's edition of books i-iii. is mainly

---

[1] Especially in the *Philologus*, xxi. p. 79, sq.

on the history of the East. There is now a new translation by Mr. G. C. Macaulay (Macmillan, 1890). Stein's edition, which has been made the basis of a critical recension by Cobet in the *Mnemosyne* for 1883, is severely criticised by Gomperz in the *Trans. of the Vienna Academy* for 1883.

§ 322 The most important rival of Herodotus as a writer of Ionic prose history was HELLANICUS of Mitylene, who was older in years, according to Pamphila, and prior, according to Dionysius; but who mentioned circumstances concerning the battle of Arginusæ (408 B.C.),[1] and must therefore be regarded as a later writer than Herodotus. Nevertheless, he seems not to have been so perfect an artist, and to have fallen short as regards the conception of welding all his various researches into one great whole. Some thirty titles of his works are mentioned in various citations, and though some of these may be amalgamated, there can be no doubt that he was author of many distinct books, of which some were even in poetical form. Carl. Müller discovers in their subjects something of a plan like that of Herodotus, first handling Persian and other barbaric nations, and then approaching Greece. The Greek legendary history of Argolis, Thessalia, Arcadia, and Attica, would come under the titles Phoroneus, Deucalion, Atlas, and Cecrops, whose genealogies were handled after the manner, we may suppose, in which the 'Annals of the Four Masters' treated early Irish history; but the Attic history was carried down to the historian's own days. The later events of other Greek states may have been noted in connection with the lists of the priestesses of Argos and the Carnean victors. This scheme is ingenious, and in itself probable, though it can hardly be proved from the scanty and indirect citations which remain. But this much seems plain, that Hellanicus, like Herodotus,

---

[1] This appears from schol. Aristoph. *Ran.* 706. τοὺς συνναυμαχήσαντας δούλους Ἑλλανικός φησιν ἐλευθερωθῆναι, καὶ ἐγγραφέντας ὡς Πλαταιεῖς συμπολιτεύεσθαι αὐτοῖς (fr. 80, Müller). The schol. on Soph. *Philoct.* 201, makes him use the work of Herodotus, and therefore distinctly younger as a writer. He is also cited by Plutarch, and in the *Life* of Andocides as having shown that orator's descent from Hermes. This again points to the latest decade of the century, before which time Andocides could hardly have been prominent. Nevertheless, in the tract on the *Spitefulness of Herodotus* (c. 36) he is apparently referred to as older than that writer.

pursued at the same time historical and geographical researches. His history did not however escape, like that of Herodotus, the vice of dwelling upon the mythical period, from which little but genealogies could be related. But these mythical accounts of the old poets were not merely transcribed into prose ; they were apparently compared with and corrected by the local traditions. It may have been originally to extend and improve this local knowledge that geography was studied, and no doubt commercial reasons added their force. Thus geography and mythical history became combined in the same hands, and in the case of Herodotus the avoidance of myths, and descent to real history, made the combination natural and artistic. Though we know that Hellanicus wrote in the Ionic dialect, the 179 allusions collected by Müller do not contain any materials for a criticism of his style or for any judgment of his literary merits.

Hermogenes and Dionysius both rank him below Herodotus, and no doubt justly. Whether he wrote a few years before Herodotus or after him, the fact that a distinguished literary rival in the same field made so widely different a figure tends to increase our respect for our father of history, and our conviction that his work was not the natural outcome of a general progress in prose literature, but the discovery of an original and unique genius. As to mere research, Hellanicus may possibly, as Mure asserts,[1] have been superior, seeing that he had some notion of the Latin language, and mentions Spina, Cortona, and Rome, which belonged to a part of Italy almost unknown to the Greeks of his day. But these, and his other notices of Italy and Sicily, may have been borrowed from Hippys of Rhegium, or Antiochus of Syracuse, who is cited (fr. 7) by Dionysius of Halicarnassus as mentioning Rome. All these lost authors do not properly belong to a history of extant classical literature ; their statements, quoted at second hand, and in altered phrase, are important to the historian who is sifting the age and character of the authorities for some alleged fact, but they have no claim whatever to be called literature. I refer all those who desire a full list of these

[1] iv. 237.

writers, and the conjectures of the learned about them, to Mure's fourth volume, or to Carl Müller's first volume of his inestimable *Fragmenta Historicorum Graecorum.*

§ 323. But I will not pass on without saying a few words about two other contemporaries who were among the Ionic prose writers (though also otherwise celebrated), because they seem to have struck out a new vein in literature, and one which did not find favour for a long time after they made their essays. I refer to the personal memoirs of STESIMBROTUS of Thasos, and ION of Chios. The latter has already occurred (§ 228) in the list of the lesser known tragic poets, and he might have achieved in this direction an undying fame but for the excessive splendour of his rivals. He may have been a good poet ; 'nevertheless he did not attain unto the first three.' As an historian we find him cited as the author of two works—the *Settlement of Chios,* in which he gave the antiquities and early history of his native island, and a book variously called his ὑπομνήματα or ἐπιδημίαι, his memoirs or foreign travels, that is to say, his travels to Athens and other famous towns. He seems to have made notes of the eminent men he met, and their social qualities, and these he put together into piquant chapters, which are occasionally cited by Athenæus and Plutarch. The long fragment on Sophocles (fr. 1) is very curious, and so are the notes on Kimon and Pericles ; but the utter silence of all early writers concerning this work, and some chronological difficulties about the campaign of Sophocles, have made Ritter suspect that the whole treatise is a later forgery. If we consider the undeveloped state of Greek prose before the year 421 B.C., when Ion is alluded to as already dead, it is indeed somewhat strange that familiar memoirs should have been written, and still more strange that such a branch of prose should have found no school of cultivators ; for Stesimbrotus (born Ol. 72), who was a contemporary sophist, and wrote about Homer and about the mysteries, is quoted by Plutarch in a very similar way for gossiping anecdotes, but is never cited in the better days of Greek literature. He wrote a book about Themistocles, and Thucydides (son of Melesias), and Pericles, from which a good deal is

quoted about Kimon, and Pericles and Themistocles. But
these memoirs seem, even from our scanty fragments, of a
very different complexion from the pleasant social sketches of
Ion. Plutarch ranks Stesimbrotus with the comic poets in his
savage attacks on Pericles, nor did he give even of Kimon so
agreeable a picture as Ion's. According to Adolf Schmidt
(*Perikl. Zeit.* vol. ii.) this is unjust. and not only is he a main authority of Plutarch, but even of Thucydides, as regards Themistocles' life. We cannot say whether Stesimbrotus, who doubtless
spoke Ionic at Thasos, but who lived from about 470 at Athens,
wrote in that dialect ; however, the distinctly Ionic character of
Ion's fragments leads us to suppose that this familiar sort of prose
was not composed in severe Attic purity, but in the easy dress
of Herodotus' co-ordinate constructions and semi-poetical dialect. But the days of Ionic prose were numbered : not even
the splendour and variety of Herodotus' great history could
stay the influence of Attic taste, of Attic rhetoric, of Attic preci-
sion, which invaded Greek literature at this time and overcame
all other tendencies. Thus it may possibly be the form in
which they wrote which condemned these two anecdotists
to oblivion for centuries. Rhetorical prose became the only
prose tolerated ; even narratives were regarded as species of
eloquence, and so the familiar homeliness and artless charms of
the chroniclers gave way to political oratory and political history. It is indeed not unlikely that Stesimbrotus formed a
sort of connecting link, and that under the pretence of writing
memoirs he composed a bitter political pamphlet against the
liberal policy of the day. His trade as a sophist, and the
strong protests of Plutarch against his unfairness, make us suspect that we are drifting away fast from the candid spirit and
the large views of Herodotus.

§ 324. For even Herodotus had his early and formidable
detractor, who set himself deliberately to contradict the historian's accounts of Persia and Assyria, and to show their general
untrustworthiness. As this man, KTESIAS, the private physician
of Artaxerxes at the battle of Cunaxa, wrote in Ionic prose,
and in the style of earlier historians, it will be well to include
him in the present chapter, though his work cannot have

appeared till after the year 400 B.C.   But both his opposition
to Herodotus and his general attitude, which owing to many
years' residence in Persia was not affected by the revolution of
taste at Athens, bring him together logically with the earlier
prose of Asia Minor.

We know that he was the son of Ktesiochus of Knidos, and
Galen describes him as a relative of Hippocrates the physician ;
so that he may have been an eminent practitioner attracted by
high pay to the court of Ochus, where he remained fourteen
years (415–1 B.C.), as well as the first three of Artaxerxes' reign.
He described himself as a person of great importance at that
court, and as an envoy, not only to the Greeks after the
battle of Cunaxa, but to Evagoras, prince of Cyprus, and
afterwards to Sparta.   His two principal works, the *Persica*,
which included Assyrian and Median histories leading on to
the Persian, and his *Indica*, or description of the wonders of
India, were composed after his return home.   A *Periplus* and
a tract on *Mountains and Rivers* are also quoted.   We do
not possess a single direct quotation from these works, our
knowledge of him being derived from copious paraphrases in
Photius, who gives the facts in his own language.   Hence we
can only take on trust the statement of ancient grammarians
that he wrote in good Ionic, and with elegance, but without the
simplicity of Herodotus, for he was always seeking for sudden
and striking effects and pathetic contrasts.[1]   But he set himself
deliberately to overthrow the authority of Herodotus on Eastern history by asserting that he himself had access to the
royal records, the βασιλικαὶ διφθέραι, in the archives of Artaxerxes ; and he remodels all the Median history, changes the
names of the personages allied with and opposed to Darius,
and in every point makes it his duty to show Herodotus a
liar.   Though successful for a time, and perhaps to some
extent causing Herodotus to be neglected, he did not satisfy
critics like Aristotle, or even Plutarch, who in the *Life of*

---

[1] His fragments 23 S contain what appears to be the earliest prose
narrative of a romantic love-story, that of the Median Stryangeus and the
queen of the Sakae, Zarinaea.   Cf. Rohde, *der griech. Roman*, p. 39.

Artaxerxes throws doubts on his authority. But the pseudo-Plutarch follows him in his tract *On the Spitefulness of Herodotus,* so does Diodorus.[1]

His fragments were first edited and his credibility upheld by Stephanus in 1566, and this is the attitude of the two learned editions of Dindorf (Didot's *Herodotus*) and Bähr, both of which were published just before the newly deciphered cuneiform inscriptions were brought to bear upon the question. The learned arguments and the judicial attitude of these critics, who insist upon the better sources of information of Ktesias, and the impossibility of his being quite incredible where he insists upon a distinct version, have been rendered amusing by the reading of the inscriptions, which prove that Herodotus was nearly always right, and that the colossal errors of Ktesias must have arisen from a deliberate attempt to deceive.[2] From this point of view the work is a literary curiosity, and it is to be hoped that some learned German will think it worth his while to re-edit the fragments, with all the monumental evidence appended, in order that we may know what residuum of truth is left in them, and whether it is worth while discussing their authority where they contradict Herodotus only, and are not themselves contradicted by monumental evidence. For my own part, I do not believe it is possible to lie consistently, and think there must be some elements of real history in every such fabrication.

§ 325. It is, however, very remarkable that while the Ionic dialect found little favour in history or in any kind of poetry during this epoch, and the resuscitation of its old epic form was not more successful than its very perfect narrative style in the hands of Herodotus, still in the department of pure science this dialect was dominant, and maintained itself far into the next century. The earlier Ionic philosophers and their

[1] The latter tells us (xiv. 16) that Ktesias brought down his Persian history to the year of the Sicilian Dionysius' declaration of war against the Carthaginians (398 B.C.) For adverse judgments cf. Clinton's *Fasti, sub an.* 398 B.C. There is now a good ed. of the remains of Ktesias (except the *Indica*) by Mr. Gilmore (Macmillan, 1889).

[2] Cf. Rawlinson's *Herodotus* (i. 77). Mr. Sayce has since endeavoured in his *Herod.* (books i–iii., Macmillan, 1884), to reverse this decision, but not, I think, with success, in spite of his great special learning and acuteness.

Eleatic offshoot had used epic hexameters to convey their speculations. From the time of the profound Heracleitus, Ionic prose, and probably the dialect of Miletus, came into use ; and we find in the latter half of the fifth century, not only the Samian Melissus,[1] and the Clazomenian Anaxagoras, but the Thracian Democritus, the Cretan Apollonius, and the cosmopolitan Protagoras[2] writing in this accepted philosophic tongue. It is remarkable, too, how the many actual quotations from these men show that terseness and vigour were perfectly attained in the language which strikes us as so diffuse and easy in Herodotus. Perhaps the most splendid specimen of this incisive and almost more than Thucydidean force and brevity is found in the genuine works of Hippocrates, who, though he may have taken that historian for his model, writes in pure Ionic, and approaches the style of Heracleitus far more than he does that of the Attic politician. The many treatises by later hands, which are transmitted to us under the name of Hippocrates, are composed in the same dialect, which had evidently become the established language of the school or medical guild of Kos. Such guilds are very tenacious of language, and Latin is not more universal in the medical pre-scriptions of the present day than Doric became at Athens in the next century, when Doric schools of medicine were highly esteemed.

The scientific development of the Greek mind at this epoch does not belong to our subject, but I have called attention to the prevalence of Ionic prose among the most serious

---

[1] Though it seems that the Elean Zeno, the comrade of Melissus in philosophy, agreed with him in adopting prose (instead of the epic verse of his master Parmenides) as his method of conveying his subtle dialectic, there is still no evidence that he wrote in Ionic prose. The citations from his book are in Attic, but may possibly have been all paraphrased by Aristotle, Simplicius, and Diogenes. The silence concerning his dialect is, however, good negative evidence that he wrote in old Attic. Blass (*Att. Ber.* i. 52) speaks of Gorgias as the first Attic orator, on some-what similar evidence. But if the Sicilian rhetor, who only visited Athens in old age, was able to compose in Attic, Zeno, who came there in middle age, may have also done so, though he was not a professional orator.

[2] Zeller, *Phil. der Griechen*, i. p. 1020, note.

thinkers, as well as among the most frivolous anecdotists, to show how easily we may make rash judgments about Greek dialects, and talk of the softness and weakness of the Ionic speech as an evidence of luxury and mental relaxation, whereas all the really earnest science of the day—I here waive the claims of the sophists—was expressed in this very dialect, and with a strength and compression which savours rather of harshness and obscurity than of simple and artless transparency.

§ 326. The life of HIPPOCRATES is shrouded in a strange mist, considering the extraordinary celebrity of the man. In the late biographies which remain to us the following facts seem worthy of record. A certain Soranus of Kos, otherwise unknown, is said to have made special researches among the records of the Asclepiad guild, in which Hippocrates was set down as the seventeenth in descent from the god Asclepios, and born on the 26th of the month Agrianus, in the year 460 B.C. The inhabitants were still offering him the honours of a hero. He seems to have travelled about a good deal, particularly in the countries around the northern Ægean, and to have died at an advanced age at Larissa in Thessaly, leaving two sons, Thessalus and Drakon. Many of his descendants and followers in the school of Kos were called after him—Suidas enumerates seven in all—so that this additional uncertainty of authorship attaches to his alleged writings. The many statues of him agreed in representing him with his head covered, a peculiarity which excited many baseless and some absurd conjectures. Abstracting carefully from the numerous Hippocrates mentioned in contemporary Attic literature, there are two undoubted references to the great physician of Kos in Plato,[1] and one in Aristophanes,[2] which confirm the epoch assigned to him in the biographies. He is said to have been instructed by Herodicus of Selymbria, and Gorgias of Leontini, a legend arising merely from the confusing of this Herodicus with another physician who happened to be the brother of Gorgias. There is no vestige of either Herodicus' practice or Gorgias' rhetoric in the extant treatises ; but Hippocrates assuredly, like Pericles,

---

[1] *Protagoras,* 311, A ; *Phædrus,* 270, C.　　　[2] *Thesmoph.* 274.

trained himself for a large knowledge of his special pursuit by a familiarity with the metaphysic of the day. His alleged study of the great plague at Athens is not corroborated by a comparison with Thucydides' account. The works pronounced genuine by Littré in the large collection of Hippocratic writings which still survive are these : the treatises on *Ancient Medicine*, on *Prognosis* (which includes our diagnosis in the largest sense), the *Aphorisms*, the tract on *Climate* (air, water, and situation), the *Epidemics* (i. and iii.), the *Treatment of Acute Diseases*, the tracts on joints, fractures, and surgical instruments applied to them, on head wounds, and the *Oath* and *Law* of the guild.

It need hardly be added that several of these are disputed by more sceptical critics ; but some of them, for example, the tracts on *Climate* and the *Epidemics*, are certainly genuine, and show that Hippocrates was not only a great physician and philosopher, but a literary genius of the highest order. It is, of course, quite mistaken to say that he originated Greek medicine ; a large body of recorded facts, and of contesting theories, were before him ; a great deal of practical knowledge had been accumulated, and had guided the treatment of disease among his predecessors. In the Asclepeia or temple hospitals established at Athens, Epidauros, Knidos, Kos, Cyrene, and elsewhere, a great many cases were recorded in an empirical way. On the other hand, the physical philosophers, such as Empedocles, Democritus, and Anaxagoras, were constantly putting forth theories on the nature of man and the composition of the body. What was perhaps more important than either was the close study of physical conditions by the trainers in the palæstras. These men made hygiene and diet a matter of first-rate importance, and both they and the philosophers banished superstition from the study of health, and introduced that purely human and rational method of discussion which is so prominent in Hippocrates, and which gives his reasoning so strong a likeness to that of his contemporary Thucydides.[1] From all these sources we can see materials

---

[1] Here is a specimen :

(*De aëre, aquis, locis.* cap. 29.) Οἱ μὲν οὖν ἐπιχώριοι τὴν αἰτίην προστιθέασι θεῷ, καὶ σέβονται τούτους τοὶς ἀνθρώποις καὶ προσκυνέουσι, δεδοικότες

drawn together to form a large and comprehensive system of medicine. Discarding all assumptions of abstract elements, or of various phenomena being deduced from one substance, Hippocrates seems to have insisted upon taking man as he appears in experience, and from an accurate induction of particular cases to establish the laws of health and disease. The gymnasts had taught him to lay stress on hygiene, and he insists that an accurate analysis of health is vital for teaching us the true symptoms of disease. But while thus starting from particulars, and building his inferences on them, he learned from the philosophers that large view which, as it were, neglects local symptoms, and seeks to classify each case under general conditions of disease, bringing out the common features in each, and comparing them with the general conditions of normal health. Hence he paid special attention to climate and situation, and his most interesting tract is that on the effects of air, water, and situation, in which he compares Asiatic and European races, and suggests to Plato and Aristotle the celebrated political division of mankind so often quoted from the *Politics.* The minute noting of cases in his *Epidemics* shows

περὶ γε ἑωυτῶν ἕκαστοι. Ἐμοὶ δὲ καὶ αὐτῷ δοκεῖ ταῦτα τὰ πάθεα θεῖα εἶναι καὶ τἄλλα πάντα, καὶ οὐδὲν ἕτερον ἑτέρου θειότερον, οὐδὲ ἀνθρωπινώτερον. ἀλλὰ πάντα ὁμοῖα καὶ πάντα θεῖα· ἕκαστον δὲ ἔχει φύσιν τῶν τοιούτων καὶ οὐδὲν ἄνευ φύσιος γίγνεται. Καὶ τοῦτο τὸ πάθος ὥς μοι δοκέει γίγνεσθαι φράσω. Ὑπὸ τῆς ἱππασίης αὐτοὺς κέδματα λαμβάνει, ἅτε ἀεὶ κρεμαμένων ἀπὸ τῶν ἵππων τοῖς ποσί· ἔπειτα ἀποχωλοῦνται καὶ ἑλκοῦνται τὰ ἰσχία οἳ ἂν σφόδρα νοσήσωσι. Τοῦτο δὲ πάσχουσι Σκυθέων οἱ πλούσιοι, οὐχ οἱ κάκιστοι, ἀλλ' οἱ εὐγενέστατοι καὶ ἰσχὺν πλείστην κεκτημένοι, διὰ τὴν ἱππασίην· οἱ δὲ πένητες ἧσσον, οὐ γὰρ ἱππάζονται. Καίτοι ἔχρην, ἐπεὶ θειότερον τοῦτο τὸ νόσευμα τῶν λοιπῶν ἐστι, οὐ τοῖς γενναιοτάτοις τῶν Σκυθέων καὶ τοῖς πλουσιωτάτοις προσπίπτειν μούνοις, ἀλλὰ τοῖς ἅπασι ὁμοίως καὶ μᾶλλον τοῖσι ὀλίγα κεκτημένοισι· εἰ δὴ τιμώμενοι χαίρουσι οἱ θεοὶ καὶ θαυμαζόμενοι ὑπ' ἀνθρώπων καὶ ἀντὶ τούτων χάριτας ἀποδιδοῦσι. Εἰκὸς γὰρ τοὺς μὲν πλουσίους θύειν πολλὰ τοῖς θεοῖς, καὶ ἀνατιθέναι ἀναθήματα, ὄντων χρημάτων, καὶ τιμᾶν· τοὺς δὲ πένητας ἧσσον, διὰ τὸ μὴ ἔχειν, ἔπειτα καὶ ἐπιμεμφομένους, ὅτι οὐ διδόασι χρήματα αὐτοῖσι· ὥστε τῶν τοιούτων ἁμαρτιῶν τὰς ζημίας τοὺς ὀλίγα κεκτημένους φέρειν μᾶλλον ἢ τοὺς πλουσίους. Ἀλλὰ γάρ, ὥσπερ καὶ πρότερον ἔλεξα, θεῖα μὲν καὶ ταῦτά ἐστι ὁμοίως τοῖς ἄλλοις· γίγνεται δὲ κατὰ φύσιν ἕκαστα· καὶ ἡ τοιαύτη νοῦσος ἀπὸ τοιαύτης προφάσιος τοῖς Σκύθαις γίγνεται οἵην εἴρηκα. Ἔχει δὲ καὶ κατὰ τοὺς λοιποὺς ἀνθρώπους ὁμοίως.

the other side of his mind; and there are points of diagnosis ('prognosis,' as he called it) on which modern physicians have nothing to add to his observation.

Turning from details to the general features of the man, so far as we can discern them in the acknowledged treatises, we are struck with the honest, earnest, scientific spirit of all his researches. He is in direct antagonism with the spirit of charlatanism, and of seeking after sudden effects and surprises, which must have been a very general feature among medical men when they had but lately separated themselves from priests and soothsayers—in fact, from the 'medicine men' who impose upon early and superstitious societies. The celebrated opening sentence of the *Aphorisms* is a memorable manifesto against this spirit,[1] and in a hundred places he warns against ostentation, recommends simplicity and patience, and confesses with true and deep modesty his errors and his failures. Here, again, we are reminded of Thucydides' description of his own work, no ἀγώνισμα ἐς τὸ παραχρῆμα, but a κτῆμα ἐς ἀεί. In fact, as Littré has observed, the polemic of Hippocrates against the charlatans is as serious and sustained as that of Socrates against the sophists.

§ 327. The style of Hippocrates is nervous, exceedingly compressed, and, at times, obscure from its brevity; but, on the other hand, profoundly suggestive, picturesque, and full of power and pathos. He uses poetical words and images freely, but always to increase the fulness of his meaning, never for mere ornament. He is far terser in thought than Thucydides, though he resembles him in shortness of expression; indeed, as I have before said, he more resembles Heracleitus than any other Greek prose writer.

The questions about his dialect are quite similar to those which beset the text of Herodotus. Though dwelling in the Doric settlement of Kos, he used the Ionic dialect. It appears, however, not only from our texts, but from the remarks of ancient critics, that his language was closer to old Attic than that of Herodotus, and we do not know whether it

---

[1] ὁ βίος βραχύς, ἡ δὲ τέχνη μακρή, ὁ δὲ καιρὸς ὀξύς, ἡ δὲ πεῖρα σφαλερή, ἡ δὲ κρίσις χαλεπή.

was merely another of the four dialects distinguished by him, or whether it was an artificial language with Atticisms introduced.   Our MSS. are hopelessly vacillating in their various transcriptions of the same words ; and here, as with Herodotus, the ignorance of scribes, who substituted a familiar for a provincial form, has destroyed the evidence which we might have had concerning the literary dialects of Asia Minor.

The whole history of the text of this author is, indeed, full of doubt and difficulty.   The researches of Littré have disentangled the following facts.   Ktesias of Knidos, though said to be a relation of Hippocrates, belonged to a rival school, and is reported by Galen to have criticised some points of practice recommended by Hippocrates.   As these physicians were contemporary, Ktesias cannot have referred to any later or spurious writings.   But such soon came into existence.   The sons and the son-in-law of Hippocrates, as well as other members of the school, edited, enlarged, and circulated his writings.   Some of the tracts are evidently mere rough notes thrown into shape ; and thus a body of Hippocratic writings, not unlike the collection of Aristotelian writings, began to be formed, in which the genuine and spurious were almost inextricably combined.   Aristotle, who shows many traces of intimacy with Hippocrates, quotes one of the existing tracts (*On the Nature of Man*) under the name of Polybus, his son-in-law.   We hear in the succeeding generations of Diokles of Karystus, Apollonius and Dexippus of Kos, as commentators upon his doctrine.   With Herophilus, who founded a celebrated school at Alexandria, the real criticism of the text seems to have begun ; for the lists of Hippocratic writings varied, and the learned men, called ' sifters ' (χωρίζοντες), drew up a short list of what they held genuine.   No author was more commented on, both as to style and as to matter, than Hippocrates.   While the school of Herophilus carried on fierce polemics on his principles, and on the genuineness of certain tracts, the verbal critics, like Aristarchus, discussed his dialect and style.   I must refer the reader to Littré's fifth chapter for a full list of all these critics down to Galen, who is our best authority upon Hippocrates, but whose medical criticisms only have survived; a trea-

tise on the genuineness of the several tracts, and another on the
historical allusions in them, are unfortunately lost. We may
pass in silence the few later names which follow upon Galen,
the last of the great ancient physicians. Three *Lives* are to be
found : in Suidas (very full), in Tzetzes, and one ascribed to
Soranus (not Soranus of Kos).

§ 328. *Bibliographical.* A great number of MSS. of Hippocratic writings remain, but we are still in want of any complete catalogue of them. Those in Paris have been collated
with exemplary care and diligence by M. Littré, who discovered that one of them (No. 2253), of the tenth century,
contains a text far superior to all the others, and is derived
from a purer archetype. He also shows that none of our
MSS. represents the texts of Artemidorus, Rufus, and Sabinus,
prepared in Hadrian's time, and criticised for their innovations
by Galen, who comments, even in his day, on the variations
in the MSS. Concerning the Viennese, Marcian, or Vatican
copies I can find out nothing certain. The text first appeared
in a Latin translation of Fabius Calvus, the friend of Raphael,
in 1525 (Aldus); the Greek text in 1526 (*ibid.*). Then come
the great Basle and Dutch editions of Cornarius and Foës.
The only modern editions of note are Littré's (4 vols. Paris,
1839), based on the Paris MSS., and Ermerins' Dutch edition
(1859–64), which only adds a collation of two trivial Leiden
MSS., and many notes of Cobet on a Marcian codex. The
Histories of Medicine, such as Sprengel's and Daremberg's,
must be consulted for closer information.

At last we have, in the *Revue des études grecques* for 1889
(vol. ii. pp. 342, sq.), a learned enquiry into the extant MSS.
on medical subjects by M. Costomiris, himself both a Greek
and a physician. He gives a catalogue of the treasures of the
Paris libraries, and adds that there are many tracts of Galen
and others still unprinted !

CHAPTER III.

THE DEVELOPMENT OF PHILOSOPHY AND THE RISE OF TECH-
NICAL EDUCATION IN THE FIFTH CENTURY—THE SOPHISTS
AND SOCRATES.

§ 329. WE now proceed to consider the speculations and
the teaching of Greek philosophy—a large and special study—
so far as they had a direct influence upon letters. There was
a time when Greek philosophy assumed the garb of epic
poetry, and though very novel in subject, did not modify the
form which it adopted, or create a new kind or species in
literature. I have mentioned Xenophanes, Parmenides, and
Empedocles as the most remarkable representatives of this
epoch in Greek thought. There came also a time when prose
had long been the received organ for earnest thinking, when
philosophy, with equal indifference about the form, used that
received organ without adding any other feature to literature
than seriousness of tone and the introduction of some technical terms. Such, for example, was the prose of Chrysip-
pus and of Aristotle. But at the crisis in the Greek mind
which we have reached with the middle of the fifth century—a
period of seething restlessness in politics and in speculation, of
scepticism in religion, of vagueness in the yet unformed theory
of morals—philosophy must necessarily become an important
thread in the variegated tissue which the historian seeks to un-
ravel. The rise of a new character in Greek literature produced
by these causes must of course have been gradual, and marked
off by no gap of time from what preceded, and we might
expect to find even contemporaries variously affected by it—
some adhering to the old, and some to the new ideas. But by

a peculiar good fortune we still have two remarkable pairs of writers, contemporaneous in most of their life, who illustrate the wide gap in style and in sentiment which may be produced by a very small difference in age. Sophocles and Euripides were not twenty years apart in age, Herodotus and Thucydides not more, and yet the mellowness of the old, and the crudeness of the new ; the acquiescence of the old, and the scepticism of the new ; the clearness of the old, the depth of the new, are shown in them as if there were a century intervening. It is for this reason that, having concluded our survey of Herodotus and Sophocles, the last and most perfect bloom of Ionic and of old Attic culture, we ought not logically to pass to their rivals and younger contemporaries, Thucydides and Euripides, without pausing to survey the remarkable intellectual forces which had come into play throughout Greece, and which found in them their earliest and greatest exponents. But for the severance of prose and poetry in this work I should accordingly have assigned to the Sophists a place which might seem peculiar in literary history.[1]

There are periods in the life of men when a few years make little difference in intellectual matters. If a new theory or a new way of thinking is broached to men of forty and men of sixty, the former are nearly as unlikely to embrace it as the latter. The case is widely different if we compare men of twenty with men of mature and settled convictions. For the time of opening manhood and growing intellect is the time when the mind is for a very few years peculiarly open as well as retentive, when passion intensifies study and inflames enthusiasm, and thus the prominent teachers of our earliest manhood, whether preachers, or poets, or politicians, have an influence upon us which seems absurd to our elders, who keep quoting the leaders of their own youth as the ideals for *our* imagination. Thus a very few years make a wide gap in our intellectual sympathies, and this is probably the most natural account of the gap between Sophocles and Euripides. Sophocles heard the same philosophers or sophists whom Euripides heard, but

---

[1] Viz. between Caps. XVI and XVII. of Vol. I.

they were not fashionable at Athens till his education was completed, and his career and artistic style determined.[1]   Thus
they would have but little effect upon him in comparison with
their effect on the rising Euripides, who may have met Zeno
and Anaxagoras before his genius had found its expression, or
at least before he had adopted his philosophic creed.

§ 330. If we enquire what influences were at work when
the dominion of Athens in literature, as well as in politics,
was secured, and every leading thinker, whatever might be his
home, came to Athens as the natural field for preaching his
system, we shall find several distinct schools — Grote enumerates twelve—whose main object was physical speculation
carried on to some extent by observation, but mostly by deduction from certain metaphysical hypotheses.   Among the latest
of these was the teaching of Empedocles of the four heterogeneous elements, and their mixture by Love and Hate ;
there was the atomic theory of Leucippus and Democritus, of
the homogeneity and indivisibility of all the particles of matter
which are mechanically combined in the void.   But there were
also two theories which probably had far deeper influence on
such men as Euripides—the one on account of its striking and
fruitful dogma; the other on account of the new method
whereby its tenets were maintained.

Anaxagoras, while agreeing with the Eleatics on the impossibility of creation or annihilation, and with various of his
other predecessors on the qualities of the elements of matter,
could not explain the composition and harmony of the world
without assuming as the prime cause of motion Νοῦς, or spirit.
This postulate of a heterogeneous, non-material cause to account for the harmony and order, as well as the composition

---

[1] The dates of all the leading earlier Sophists are not accurately determinable, but I think the weight of evidence is in favour of the assertion in
the text, which has, moreover, general reasons in its favour.   This is the
general result of the careful and elaborate discussions of the dates in the
notes to the last edition of Zeller on the Sophists (*Phil. der Griechen*, vol. i.
sect. iii.).   Of course I do not put Diagoras of Melos in Ol. 78, as Suidas
does, but about Ol. 98.   On this point cf. Meier's article *Diagoras* in
Ersch und Gruber's Encyclop.

of material nature, though only assumed in the most timid way, and for the purpose of introducing physical explanations, was nevertheless an innovation of capital importance, and opened the way to a philosophic adoption of the unity [1] of God, and the general idea of a divine Providence which we have already met in its popular form in the history of Herodotus. It moreover caused the gradual abandonment of that habit of personifying natural objects which was the universal feature of the untutored Greek mind ; and though the contemporaries of Anaxagoras held it gross impiety to call the sun a mass of white-hot metal, these views must infallibly prevail as soon as the unity of God was seriously adopted, and his action required to explain the course of the world.

We have secondly, among the metaphysicians of the day the Eleatic doctrine in the hands of *Zeno*, who did not add to the theory of the unity of Being, and the unreality of variety and change, but merely strengthened it by a polemical method of reasoning which had a vast effect on the style as well as the thought of his day. He sustained his somewhat unintelligible and abstract dogma by attacking the opinions of his opponents, and showing that what they assumed as obvious—such notions as variety and change—involved greater absurdities and contradictions than the doctrine which he professed. This *negative dialectic*, this habit of pulling to pieces the doctrine of the adversary by question and answer, was carried out to its full completeness by Socrates, who made it the most powerful instrument of philosophic teaching ever known in the history of human intellect. It must be carefully kept in mind that Zeno did not use this dialectical method for the purpose of teaching scepticism ; he was no sophist or technical rhetorician, but nevertheless his method was naturally adopted by them, and they used it as a model.

§ 331. This leads us to consider the influence upon literature of the Sophists, the practical teachers of education in the fifth century, who sprang up to meet a sudden and pressing want, and who professed each in his own way, and without any

---

[1] The reader will remember that this does not necessarily imply His Personality.

concerted plan or system, to instruct for money, and to train the youth of any city in the political and literary acquirements necessary for attaining and holding a prominent place in society. Only one of these celebrated men, Gorgias of Leontini, takes an actual place in the history of Greek literature, and that from his rhetorical side, in which he was the direct forerunner of Attic eloquence. This rhetorical side of the Sophists, and their grammatical and linguistic studies, will properly be treated when we come to another department of Greek prose literature. I am here only concerned with their indirect effect on literature, and especially upon history and tragic poetry, by means of their metaphysical and ethical speculations. These are, indeed, not easy to sever from their rhetoric ; for as with them form seemed always more important than matter, and an immediate result than a permanent gain, they were perpetually turning philosophy into rhetoric, and proclaiming rhetoric as philosophy.[1]

Grote was the first to dispel the cloud of misconception which had been diffused about the Sophists by ancient calumny and modern dulness, nor is there any part of his monumental history of Greece more enduring in value than the famous sixty-seventh and sixty-eighth chapters on this subject. While all the works of the Sophists have perished, there have remained to us the ablest and the most systematic attacks ever made upon them, and from opposite sides. Aristophanes, representing the old Conservative party, which hated all enlightenment and progress, attacks them in his *Clouds,* where he makes Socrates, as the most familiar at Athens, their representative, though attributing to him many tenets which he is well known to have opposed. Still Socrates, though he did oppose the Sophists and ridiculed them, and did not travel about or take pay, was, broadly speaking, one of them. He was a professional educator, he kept shaking old prejudices and received opinions, he practised dialectic, he trained men to think and speak accurately, and so he might fairly be made by the comic

---

[1] Thus Philostratus, at the opening of his *Lives of the Sophists,* says τὴν ἀρχαίαν σοφιστικὴν ῥητορικὴν ἡγεῖσθαι χρὴ φιλοσοφοῦσαν, and this theory was carried out strictly down to the time of Isocrates and proclaimed by him.

poet a vehicle for his furious onslaught on all the weaker and immoral features in the Sophistic education, though it was Socrates
who had really reformed and rendered it the noblest outcome
of the age.   On the other hand, Plato, representing the ultra-
Radical party, which advocated not the reform but the reconstruction of society, attacked them for the opposite fault—for
not being thorough enough, for preaching mere hand-to-mouth
expedients, and having no systematic principles at the basis of
their slipshod philosophy.   For this purpose he represents in
his Dialogues such men as Callicles and Polus and Euthydemus
as impudent assertors of a selfish morality or as mere intellectual mountebanks, who are overthrown and humbled by the
elenchus of Socrates.   But even Plato, the professed enemy of
the Sophists, does not venture to traduce the great leaders
who had inaugurated the movement, and made it popular and
lucrative.   Protagoras, Gorgias, and Prodicus are even in
Plato's Dialogues treated as important and respectable thinkers,
who though not a match in argument for Socrates, yet advocate
reasonable and moral theories, and advocate them with ability.
But all these circumstances, which Grote has brought out into
clear daylight, were jumbled together by the former editors of
Plato, and by most of the historians of philosophy, into a
stupid tirade against all the Sophists whom Plato chose to
oppose.   Critics ascribed to them the lowest and most impossible motives, and attributed to their influence a complete
degradation of Greek society, which, as a fact, is historically
false, and even if true could never have been produced by a
few wandering teachers of open immorality.   The dramatic lam-
poons of the old comedy, and the hardly less dramatic pictures
in Plato's Dialogues, are used indiscriminately as absolute proofs
against the Sophists, and yet as quite untrustworthy or merely
ironical when they record anything in their favour.   There is no
more prominent proof of the prejudiced estimating of evidence
common among distinguished classical scholars than the
German literature on this subject, and it is an equally curious
evidence of either preoccupation, or perhaps of the slow
effect which an argument in a foreign tongue produces, that
though most of them cite Grote's arguments, they fail to see

their force, and set down his logic to his democratic party spirit.[1]

§ 332. These Sophists, who sprang up to meet the want of their age, and were morally neither better nor worse than the public they addressed, attempted to give practical instruction to such as desired it in philosophy, in morality, and in politics. They did not form a sect or school, but nevertheless resembled one another in certain important features, which they had indeed —be it noted—in common with the older and more profound philosophers, such as Xenophanes, and more particularly Empedocles. They travelled about from city to city, because in those days of city states it was not convenient to send youths to a special university town, where they must have lived as aliens; and therefore, as they could not go to their university teaching, it must come to them. For the sophistic teaching corresponds very closely to what we should call university teaching, and in later days a 'pupil of Isocrates' is spoken of as we should say 'an Oxford man.' In the next place they were said to make very great fortunes by their profession, which Isocrates opposes by the bad argument that Gorgias, the richest of them, left but a small property. For though they were men of good morals and temperate habits, we perceive in them all a certain ostentation and expensive style of dress and living, which they evidently thought necessary to their importance, and which doubtless absorbed their profits.

These external points, along with their encyclopædic pretensions and practical system of teaching, make it just to call them by a definite class-name. Honoured and fêted by the richer youth, suspected and mostly despised by the older and more staid people, a brilliant and yet a second-rate profession, they afford an exact parallel to the artists of the present day—I mean especially singers and actors, who travel about the world in great luxury, and are received with much ambition and pride by younger people of the highest class, but who, nevertheless, spend great fortunes and acquire brilliant reputations without rising to that position in society which the

[1] To this Oncken, and Zeller in the latest edition of his *History of Greek Philosophy*, are honourable exceptions.

better classes assert for themselves [1] An Athenian gentleman whose son turned sophist, however celebrated, would have felt as an English squire whose son turned operatic singer. The worship of these merely material artists—actors and dancers —appeared in Greece also, at a later and degenerate time ; in the classical epoch even such a social position could only be attained by artists in intellectual perfections.

§ 333. But, as might be expected from their somewhat superficial character, which resulted naturally from the number of subjects which they professed, the Sophists found scepticism very convenient where positive theories were abstruse and disputed, or when moral objections were brought against purely intellectual education. *Protagoras* of Abdera, the earliest and perhaps the greatest of them, asserted in the opening of his book : ' Respecting the gods, I neither know whether they exist nor what are their attributes ; the uncertainty of the subject, the shortness of human life, and many other causes, debar me from this knowledge.' This statement, which is not verified by any allusion in Plato's portrait of the man, is said to have so offended the orthodox public of Athens that they exiled Protagoras, and had his book publicly burnt. More certain is his theory that ' man was the measure of all things ;' in other words, that all knowledge was relative, and depending upon the faculty of knowing—a statement of vast importance, and the basis of all idealism and of most scepticism from that day to our own. Profound as these dogmas appear in themselves, they were peculiarly convenient for a teacher who desired to draw his pupils from theological and moral speculation into the more positive and practical pursuit of rhetoric and of politics. If individual man is the measure of all he can know, and of all he ought to do, the moral consequences are doubtless very serious, and they became obtrusive enough in the sequel ; but the earlier Sophists did not teach these developments.

---

[1] I should be stating an absurdity were I to say, or imply, that there are not thorough gentlemen, in every sense, pursuing these artistic callings ; but it is notorious that this is not the rule, and that it is possible to be a renowned artist without more than a special cultivation of a particular dexterity.

Similarly, *Gorgias*, as a philosopher, wrote a book denying any possibility of a scientific knowledge of nature, apparently in the absolute sense. It was called *On the non-existent or on Nature* (περὶ τοῦ μὴ ὄντος ἢ περὶ φύσεως),[1] and argued, (1) that nothing exists, (2) that if it does it cannot be known, (3) or even if known cannot be communicated. These propositions were sustained by a negative dialectic similar to that of Zeno, offering the adversary an alternative and then disproving both members. In morals these two sophists seem to have taught nothing peculiar, though the logical result of their psychological scepticism could not be doubtful. *Prodicus* of Keos, on the contrary, to whom the apologue of the *Choice of Heracles between Virtue and Vice* is ascribed, was apparently a teacher of the orthodox sort, and merely graced with the ornament of rhetorical diction the principles of popular morality. I will not here follow the history or the catalogue of the Sophists further. But in the absence of any philosophical treatises written by the Sophists, or of any closer information than mere titles on their method, we may say a word here upon the fragments of one of the more obscure of their number, which are nevertheless preserved in no inconsiderable number.

§ 334. *Antiphon*, the sophist, also called τερατοσκόπος and ὀνειροκρίτης, often confused with the contemporary rhetor, is introduced by Xenophon disputing with Socrates ;[2] but he is not there represented as preaching any opinions save a contempt for asceticism and a vindication of human pleasure, as well as being the advocate of paid teaching. Hermogenes criticises his style only, and thus we are reduced to his fragments to tell us the nature of his teaching. He wrote a work in two books about *Truth*, which, as in Protagoras' treatise, meant Being or Reality, and in this work seems to have embraced most of the physical enquiries of the day. Its tendency was sceptical, for he denied Providence, and there were scientific

---

[1] Perhaps this title was intentionally parodied from the title of Protagoras' work, which seems to have been inscribed περὶ ἀληθείας ἢ περὶ τοῦ ὄντος. I do not think this remarkable resemblance is noted by the historians.

[2] *Mem.* i. 6.

(as opposed to theological) explanations of astronomical phenomena.   To this physical treatise he added a moral or
ethical discourse, as is plain from the elegant extracts quoted
from him, without special reference, by Stobæus, which illustrate worldly wisdom and human fortunes in graceful and
poetical diction, and with anecdotes possibly in the style of
Prodicus.   But the tone is not so much that of a preacher as
of a mere painter of human life.   I would call special attention
to frag. 131,[1] which is closely analogous to the speech of
Medea in Euripides,[2] with additional points of considerable
merit, on the balance of happiness and misery in marriage.[3]
There was a third book, called *Poiiticus*, which was probably
a handbook for a young citizen who desired to prepare himself
for public life.   These fragments are sufficiently full to show
us both the encyclopædic turn of the man and his super-
ficiality, so that his aim was rather to clothe knowledge in an
attractive form than to stimulate to deep enquiry.   Hence we
can still see the justice of his nickname λογομάγειρος, which
Suidas has preserved.   If he recommended pleasure, and to
snatch the happy moment as it came, his pictures of human
sorrow and labour may have been meant to enforce this view,
as well as the denial of Providence with which he is credited.
But still the moral fragments are elegant in expression, and
refined in the feeling which they show, so that we may be sure
this forerunner of Aristippus did not choose to pass for anything
else than a moral and respectable teacher.   His fragments
can best be studied in Blass's edition of the orator Antiphon,
and in the discussion[4] in which he has considered their contrasts with his namesake's speeches.

§ 335. It seems established that the successors of these men
gradually degenerated into polymaths and then into mountebanks in education, and that they soon sank in importance.

---

[1] Ed. Blass (Teubner).   [2] *Medea*, vv. 200, sq.

[3] It ends with the words φέρε δὴ καὶ παῖδες γενέσθωσαν· φροντίδων ἤδη
πάντα πλέα καὶ ἐξοίχεται τὸ νεοτήσιον σκίρτημα ἐκ τῆς γνώμης καὶ τὸ
πρόσωπον οὐκέτι τὸ αὐτό.   Blass thinks these extracts belong to his book
περὶ ὁμονοίας, from which the express quotations only prove that it was an
exhortation to harmony among citizens.

[4] *Attische Beredsamkeit*, i. 99.

Before Plato composed his later Dialogues they had become too insignificant to merit refutation, and in the following generation[1] they completely disappear as a class.   This is of course to be attributed not only to the opposition of Socrates at Athens, but to the subdivision of the profession of education. Its most popular and prominent branch—that of Rhetoric—was taken up by special men like the orator Antiphon, and developed into a strictly defined science.   The Philosophy which they had touched without sounding its depths was taken up by the Socratic schools, and made the rule and practice of a life. The Politics which they had taught were probably found too general, nor were these wandering men, without fixed home, or familiarity with the intricacies of special constitutions, likely to give practical lessons to Greek citizens in the art of state craft.   Thus they disappear almost as rapidly as they rose—a sudden   phase   of   spiritual   awakening   in   Greece,   like   the Encyclopædists of the French.[2]

These were the intellectual disturbers of society, who began to tell on poetry when Euripides approached the problems of the drama.   It is indeed absurd to say that moral and metaphysical difficulties had not been agitated by earlier poets. The conflict between the duties of avenging a murdered father and of filial affection to the murderess, is one which might make the most thoughtful doubt and hesitate.   The conflict between obedience to the law and obedience to the holiest affection, in the *Antigone,* is an *antinomy* far deeper and more interesting than those of Zeno.   But the tragic poets did not press for a general solution, they did not insist upon a full statement and argument on both sides ; they taught, after their manner, philosophy, but not dialectic.   Euripides   could   no

---

[1] Isocrates indeed in his speech περὶ ἀντιδόσεως (especially §§ 198, sq.), not delivered till 353 B.C., says a great deal about popular objections to himself, and to the Sophists, as a class to which he was supposed to belong.   But probably he was merely repeating the arguments of his youth, which were important enough when he opened his school, about 408 B.C., but were quite obsolete in his later years.   Isocrates shows the peculiar tenacity of a narrow intellect in repeating a once acquired idea.

[2] Cf. Zeller, *Phil. der Griechen*, i. pp. 1027, sq

longer avoid these explicit controversies. The physical theories
of Anaxagoras, and his theological difficulties, were current
among thinkers at Athens, and demanded a more popular
exponent than a dry prose treatise. If man be indeed the
measure of all things, the passions and the miseries of man
take their place in philosophy, and require exposition and
analysis as well as his higher principles. Above all, the weak
and the ignorant, the woman and the slave, have their rights in
the democracy where all men have been already equalised, and
their wisdom, their fortitude, and their temperance are not less
suitable to excite our terror and our pity than the sufferings of
heroic men. Such were the altered conditions of tragedy in
the hands of Euripides.

§ 336. But I must add a word, lest it should be imagined
that the great poets and prose writers, whom I have described as rising just before the movement, had remained
absolutely untouched by it. Both Sophocles and Herodotus
were too clear-sighted and too sympathetic to permit of their
standing altogether aloof from the current of thought in their
maturer years. Hence we find in Sophocles *Eristic*, as in the
dispute of Teucer and the Atridæ (*Ajax*), we find in Herodotus
scepticism, we find in both a rhetorical skill which, though concealed by the garb of poetry or of conversation, shows that
neither was insensible to the charms of the new artistic study
of diction. The appearance of a break with the old beliefs in
Herodotus, and the insistance upon personal evidence, have
caused him to be named, though unjustly, the sophist of Greek
history. There is in Sophocles an approximation even to the
compression and obscurity of Thucydides, which indicates (I
suppose) the reaction of Antiphon and his school against the
obvious and stilted periods of Gorgias. But nevertheless,
when all due allowances have been made, the broad fact
remains, that Sophocles and Herodotus belong to a different
generation and a different school of thought from Euripides
and Thucydides. Hence it is not only justifiable, but even
necessary, to separate them in treatment, though they stand
almost side by side in chronology.

§ 337. If this history were a history of Greek philosophy, we should class SOCRATES not with the Sophists, but as the head of a new movement, and the father of Ethical philosophy, and of critical method in the succeeding century. But from a literary point of view, it must not be forgotten that he was a man of the Periclean age, and the contemporary of those who made the fifth century the most splendid in Greek literature. Nevertheless we cannot trace his effect upon the books of his own day, except in the attacks of the Old Comedy, and the many traditions which make him a friend and admirer of Euripides. It is only after his death that all Hellas begins to ring with his name. We may therefore connect him either with the influence which brought him forth, or with those which were derived from him. I prefer the former, though less usual course, as being best suited to show his position in Greek literature.

It must be remembered that Socrates never wrote anything, and that his literary prominence is solely due to the extraordinary stimulus he gave to others. For he not only suggested all the philosophy of the succeeding centuries, but he really created a new form of Attic prose—the philosophical dialogue, which in the hands of Plato outshines every other form of Greek writing in the fourth century, except perhaps the speeches of Demosthenes. Let us first consider what he owed to his predecessors, and then what were his special points of originality as compared with them.

§ 338. It is hardly true to say that he was the first to bring down philosophy from heaven—from abstruse physical speculations—to earth—to ethical questions concerning the rules of human life. More than one of the greater sophists, such as Prodicus, had concerned themselves with morality, and professed the teaching of virtue. It is not less inaccurate to say that he invented negative dialectic, or the method of arguing with an adversary by raising difficulties, and proving absurd consequences, for this had been the special field in which Zeno had already attained remarkable results. But Zeno had only applied his dialectic to purely speculative metaphysic, and the Sophists had only regarded moral lessons as a small part of the cycle of practical education. The novelty in Socrates was the application of the scientific method of dialectic to practical questions, and his severance of these, of ethical enquiries, from the physical and theological speculations of older philosophers. This was accordingly another step in the severance of the branches of education, which was perhaps commenced by Antiphon's exclusive adherence to rhetoric.   Now this latter was the very branch which Socrates wholly avoided, and which he protested against in the pursuit of clear ethical notions.   He insisted upon perpetual question and answer, upon keeping up the pupil's attention by making him join as an equal or fellow enquirer in the search, and he sought, from an induction of the particular uses of any term, to arrive at some general definition which should comprise them, and thus convey a clear and consistent idea to those who used that term.   Thus he not only laid the foundations of the science of ethics, but he stimulated his followers to an accurate use of abstract terms, and to set down their enquiries in the form of question and answer; in other words, philosophical accuracy, and the conversational form, were his positive contributions to literature.

His main importance arose from his wholesome antagonism to the taste for rhetoric, for flowing periods, and plausible statements, which infected and had almost completely leavened Attic literature at the close of this period.   His whole life was a protest against rhetoric as an engine of education or of self-culture.   Talking well about a subject was a mere disguising of ignorance to oneself and others.   The real thing was to sift each point, and discuss each statement.   So deeply did Socrates feel this necessity of clearing up one's own mental condition, that he held all virtue to be knowledge, and that vice arose not from passion, but from ignorance, or perhaps rather from confusion of thought.   This part of his teaching was indeed as it were an inheritance from the Sophists whom he combated all his life, for they too professed to make good citizens by teaching, and if virtue can be taught, it must be a kind of knowledge.   But the whole spirit of Socrates' teaching was nevertheless directly opposed to the rival educators, with whom he was often classed.   They were brilliant and superficial; he was homely and thorough; they rested in scepticism, he advanced through it to deeper and sounder faith ; they were wandering and irresponsible, he was fixed at Athens, and showed forth by his life the doctrines he preached.

§ 339. But I will not digress into Socrates' philosophy or into his life. These things are fully discussed not only in the philosophical, but in the political history of Greece. It may be sufficient here to state that he was the son of the sculptor Sophroniscus and Phænarete (a midwife), and that having followed his father's trade for a short while—an alleged specimen of his work was preserved in the Acropolis, where Pausanias saw it—he turned to ethical speculation. But he started with self-examination, and, rejecting all superficial solutions, he soon came to test his researches by examining those around him, and seeking from them answers to the moral questions which puzzled him. He performed the public duties which fell to his lot with constancy and bravery, and bore with great equanimity the extreme poverty—μυρία πενία—which was the result of his devotion to the training of others. But as all the foremost young men of Athens—Alcibiades, Critias, Charmides—attended him, he was attacked by the orthodox and democratic party after the Restoration, with the charge of corrupting the youth and teaching the worship of strange gods. His defence, which we must not identify with the famous *Apology of Socrates* by his pupil Plato, justified his conduct, and assumed so bold and patronising a tone to the jury, that he was condemned by a small majority, and executed 399 B.C. The real causes and the significance of this sentence have much occupied modern critics, but do not belong to our present subject. Thus Athens lost a striking and familiar figure, which had for half a century frequented the market-place; but his spirit lived on in the schools which sprang from his teaching.

§ 340. The many extant busts agree with the indications in Plato's *Symposium* concerning the very ugly type of his face— round eyes, snub nose, and thick protruding lips. But if the type was that of a Silenus, there was much kindliness and geniality about him, along with great bodily vigour and endurance. We have two detailed portraits of his life and conversation in the

Dialogues of Plato, and in the Dialogues of Xenophon, who also wrote *memoirs* of his master. These latter are by modern scholars thought to give a less idealised portrait of the man, but in many traits they agree with the more elaborate and grander picture found in the Dialogues of Plato. There is a peculiar group of these Dialogues specially devoted to drawing a true picture of Socrates in his last days—the *Euthyphron,* a discussion on his views concerning piety at the moment when he was charged with impiety by Meletus ; the *Apology,* which professes to give his defence in court; and the *Crito,* in which he refuses the chance of escaping, and lays down the strict duty of obedience to the law as the great civic virtue. This last dialogue shows us clearly enough the Xenophontic side of the man, who together with intellectual scepticism inculcated plain orthodox morality in practice. The *Phædo,* which completes the dramatic picture, and paints the last hours of his prison life, seems a later composition, and attributes to him metaphysical theories, which were rather Platonic than Socratic. But the scenery is no doubt fairly accurate. This group then gives us Socrates in his death. The best Platonic picture of him in his life is to be found in the introductions to the *Lysis* and *Charmides,* and in the latter portion of the *Symposium,* where the drunken Alcibiades gives that wonderful, audacious, and unparalleled account of him in his most secret moments.

It is suspected that Plato has introduced many of his own theories under the ægis of Socrates' name. This very probable conclusion is, however, apparently opposed to the testimony of Aristotle, who constantly in his extant writings quotes the opinions of Socrates, and quotes them from his words in the Dialogues of Plato. But he probably assumes it as known that the Platonic Socrates is an idealised portrait. Nor does he ever quote the Socrates drawn by Xenophon or any other of the numerous authors of Socratic dialogues.[1] There is a third sketch of the man in the fragments of Aristoxenus, who states on the authority of his own father that he was a man of strong passions and irascible temper, taking money for teaching, and altogether of a lower type than

[1] In the chapters on Plato and Xenophon I will return to this question.

the fuller accounts compel us to believe. This shows us at least that he had many opponents and detractors, who looked upon him as anything but a great moral and social reformer.

§ 341. It is indeed not difficult to see injurious tendencies suggested by his teaching, which might alarm more earnest thinkers than the old conservatives, who feared that he was shaking all the foundations of traditional morality and religion. There is no doubt that by his discouraging the pursuit of practical politics, of oratory, and of physical science, until men had cleared up all their first principles by ample discussion, he encouraged a strong and very mischievous tendency among all social people—that of wasting their time in conver· sation, the λέσχης τερπνὸν κακόν of Euripides. It is no doubt very well to say that these dialectical talks were all-important. Even in the Dialogues of Plato, which are of course vastly better than the actual discussions, there is much prolixity, and much waste of time and ingenuity. Accordingly the charge that Socrates taught young men to idle in talking over what they ought to do—ἀδολεσχεῖν as the Greeks called it—is not unfounded. Again, the doctrine that each man's first and most absolute duty was to purify his own soul from moral ignorance, and attain to that knowledge which was virtue—this doctrine asserted the infinite value of each man's own good as contrasted with the good of others and of the State. Hence Socrates preached what the Germans call that *absolute subjectivity* which was ultimately the destruction of the whole ancient idea of the State. Though himself an exemplary citizen, it may be asserted that none of his known pupils ever turned out even a moderately good one. Young aristocrats like Alcibiades, Critias, and Charmides set up their 'absolute subjectivity' as above the laws, and endeavoured to use other men as slaves or playthings. Men of pleasure like Aristippus used the virtuous and vicious alike for their own convenience, and escaped by voluntary exile from the intolerable duties of promoting the welfare and good government of their fellows. Last of all the Cynics, such as Antisthenes and Diogenes, broke with society altogether, lived as strangers under the protection of laws which they despised, and offended and shocked their fellow-citizens by the

grossest rudeness and the most shameless indecencies. **No**
doubt these men were parodies of Socrates. They omitted all
the refinement, all the grace, all the wonderful attractiveness,
which his threadbare cloak and naked feet could not impair.
They exaggerated his somewhat prosy homeliness about
cobblers and tinkers and tailors as the proper illustrations in
moral enquiry. They travestied his noble contempt of a false
and unjust public opinion into an insolent disregard of all the
traditional decencies of social life. Still they *were* parodies.
They followed up his rejection of the ordinary culture of
sophistic education with a rejection of all culture, and thus for
the first time that closest of all alliances in Greek social life
was dissolved. Unfortunately, perhaps indeed fortunately, the
books of all the Socratic philosophers, except those of Xenophon and Plato, have perished. The myriad tracts enumerated
by Diogenes Laertius in his Lives of Euclid of Megara, of
Stilpo, of Antisthenes, of Diogenes, of Aristippus, and of the
other *viri Socratici* are gone, and have hardly left a trace
behind. But though we thus have escaped commenting upon
their style and method, it was necessary to say a word in passing
on the extraordinary revolution produced by Socrates in Greek
thought. Had these men lived a century earlier, they would
assuredly have been Sophists. In the fourth century they were
all developed in antagonism to the general features of the
Sophists.

§ 342. But we must now take up another thread in the complex woof, and show how great men of a totally different stamp
stood out at Athens, together with the poets, the historians, and
the Sophists. We have seen in the last chapters how, from the
writing of treaties and drawing up of registers, the first
attempts had been suggested of setting down first mythical
histories, and then annals in unfettered or prose diction—
a very important and late step in a society whose poetry
had long reached a splendid literary form, and had been
employed for politics and for philosophy as well as for more
emotional and romantic subjects. These bald and dry attempts were gradually refined into the narrative form by
Hecatæus, and perfected by the introduction of dramatic

elements—of humour and pathos in the matter, and mixture
of dialogue with narrative in the form, by the great and
consummate genius of Herodotus. But with him this branch
of Greek literature reached its highest point. The later
attempts to write Ionic historical prose, such as that of Ktesias,
strove merely to enhance the effects attained by Herodotus,
and made no lasting impression upon their age. Indeed, it is
very remarkable how little even his splendid work is cited
among contemporaries, and how intent the men of his day were
upon a different style and a different ideal in prose writing.
Not even the great body of Greek speculation which was
written in Ionic prose, and which contained the deepest
thoughts of their deepest thinkers—Heracleitus, Democritus,
Anaxagoras—could stay the current which set in a new direction.

Perhaps an account of the Sophists should not close without
a word about Hippias of Elis, whom the Platonic dialogues
called after him describe as an ostentatious, but clever and ver-
satile man, accomplished in many arts, but specially in rhetoric.
His writings are completely lost, and there remain from him
but a couple of antiquarian notes, such as that in the *Argument*
of the *Œdipus Rex* on the history of the word *tyrant*. Among
his other researches, he undertook to publish for the Eleans a
complete list of the Olympic victors, and this list, surviving
in Eusebius' *Chronicon*, has ever since been quoted as the
earliest and most authentic register of events kept in Greece.
But Plutarch (*Numa*, cap. 1) says expressly it was a late work
(that is, resting on no ancient or earlier researches), and that
Hippias *started from no trustworthy foundation*. If so, the
learned world has been mistaking a sophistical *tour de force* for
an authentic record of facts. I have discussed the question in
the *Journal of Hellenic Studies*, ii. 164, sq., where my results
have not been shaken by any of the recent discoveries at
Olympia. The early Olympiads were plainly manufactured, and
Pausanias, who searched for archaic work, could find no dedi-
cation older than the so-called 29th Olympiad. But he speaks
of rewritten and spurious epigrams.

CHAPTER IV.

THE BEGINNINGS OF ORATORY AND THE RISE OF ATTIC PROSE COMPOSITION—GORGIAS, ANTIPHON.

§ 343. THE new direction was itself determined by two great causes—the spread of education among the masses, and the increase of democratic constitutions throughout the Greek world. For the consequent importance of conversation and discussion raised eloquence above all other branches of literature, and no sooner was critical attention directed to its power and charm, than they were found to be reducible to a theory which could be taught to a degree impossible in the case of poetry. This was the teachable or artificial element in oratory, by which the speaker, in addition to the natural gifts of genius and of outward grace, adds the technical skill derived from the science of rhetoric, the τέχνη, as the first inventors called it.

In the simpler sense eloquence had always been at home among the Greeks. The Homeric poems assume it as a great gift in their heroes, and one not generally possessed by them. Odysseus, and Nestor, and Phœnix are the orators of the heroic age, and the specimens of their persuasive speaking in the poems show how keenly the rhapsodists and their audiences appreciated this high quality. In Hesiod it is an inspiration of kings by the muse. The deficiency of the Spartan Menelaus almost seems suggested by Doric, not by Achæan Sparta. But in early historical days, it is remarkable how little we hear of eloquence. None of the early tyrants is reported to have owed his power to this quality, not even Peisistratus, who was a literary and perhaps an eloquent man. In the pages of Herodotus we can only find the Athenian Hippocleides, who outshines the other suitors of Agariste in social eloquence at the

feast, and Themistocles—the first notable historic instance, which
the evidence of Thucydides corroborates.   Though Herodotus
does not remark upon it, his dramatic narrative leaves us in no
doubt as to the secret of Themistocles' influence.   It is, however,
certain that his speaking was not more based on technical knowledge than that of the orators in the Iliad, and that, like the
many other speakers in Herodotus, he trusted to a persuasive
manner, and to weighty facts to produce the effect he desired.
The period after the Persian wars was that which we have
already discussed in connection with tragedy, and the development of philosophy and sophistic.   The democratic right of
free speech, and the love of talking and disputing, so dear to
Greeks of all ages, comes out everywhere.   Tragedy is the
poetry of argument and of eloquence, rival systems of philosophy
are the arena of polemic and exposition ; sophistic is little
more than the setting up of this formal readiness as the highest
and most perfect accomplishment of life.   But far more important than all these luxuries of education were the practical
uses of eloquence, not only in public deliberation, but in pleading before democratic assemblies or courts of justice.   Hence
the necessities of the age must produce teachers of eloquence
in all these branches.

§ 344. The earliest practical development was due to the
Sicilians, who seem to have been always remarkable among
the Greeks for their *Attic* qualities, their quickness of intellect,
and love of clever speaking.   There are signs of this talent even
in the scanty fragments of Epicharmus and Sophron ; nor did it
become extinct down to the days of Cicero, who specially
notes it in many places through his Verrine speeches and
his rhetorical writings.   But the introduction of democracy
at Syracuse in 466 B.C., and at Agrigentum a few years later,
gave a great impetus to the study of oratory ; and so it comes
that while Aristotle, speaking loosely, mentions Empedocles
of Agrigentum as the master of Gorgias and the father
of rhetoric, Syracuse certainly produced in Korax the first
founder of the art of preparing court speeches, with a view
to persuading the judges by artful attack and defence.   It
is said that the expulsion of the tyrants produced so many

claims for property wrongfully seized and transferred by them, that Korax wrote his *techne*, and probably prepared speeches for pay, to meet this public outburst of litigation. But the special point about him and his successor Tisias, was their avoidance of the trade of sophist, and their strict adherence to the practical profession of *rhetor*. We are told in the *Lives of the Orators*, ascribed to Plutarch, that Tisias gave lessons to Lysias at Thurii, and to Isocrates at Athens. Pausanias even says that he came with Gorgias on his celebrated embassy (427 B.C.) to Athens. All these anecdotes are of little authority. There is no good evidence that Korax, who taught early, and Tisias, who taught late, in the fifth century, wandered about like Gorgias. It is also certain that they composed their speeches for Syracusans in Doric dialect, and were therefore inconvenient models for Attic orators. A *techne*, or rhetorical treatise, by Tisias was extant in antiquity, in which he developed the importance of the εἰκός, or putting probable points, which Plato adopts and developes in his *Phædrus*.

It is evident that these Rhetors, just like the Sophists, cared nothing for truth and falsehood, but altogether for persuasion. This was generally called ' making the worse argument appear the better,' and is attacked by both Plato and Aristophanes, as if the whole profession of advocates were not necessarily founded upon the principle of leaving the truth to be ascertained by the judge, and of confining themselves to the strengthening of the side on which they have been retained. This charge against the Sophists, which all the German scholars repeat with great devoutness, might be brought with equal justice, and equal irrelevancy, against the great profession of the law in the present day. It is Machiavelli's adherence to this scientific neglect of moral considerations in a general policy, instead of a particular cause, which has excited against him the same kind of charge with greater force.

As has been just observed, we have no evidence of the influence of Korax and Tisias on Attic judicial oratory, and yet it is almost certain that Antiphon must have studied them. For he was essentially their successor, and not the successor of the Sophists, strictly so called, who taught at Athens during the fifth

century. Protagoras was indeed supposed by some to have made
advances in rhetoric, but it was not in forensic, but in dialectical
speaking.   He discussed the accurate sense and use of words.
and noted grammatical anomalies ; he expounded poets, and
discussed politics—in fact, he did everything but lay down strict
rules for judicial argument.   Nevertheless, his general studies
must have greatly influenced style ; and if Pericles thought
it worth while spending a day in discussing with him the real
cause of an accident, he can have been no mean or unsuggestive
thinker.   But neither he, nor Prodicus, nor Hippias of Elis,
though the one set forth the praise of virtue with elegant
diction, and the other brought together an encyclopædia of
knowledge in his lectures, can be called special masters in the
art of Attic prose.   It is indeed possible that they all, like
Protagoras, continued to use the Ionic dialect.

§ 345. But while these men were promoting in a formal
way accuracy of diction and elegance of form, *political* oratory
of a more solid kind, such as had been employed by Themistocles, was receiving a great impulse at the hands of Pericles.
There can be no doubt as to the extraordinary effect of his
public speaking.   Even the comic poets who upbraid his
policy, and assail his motives, cannot deny it.   They speak
of him as the Olympian, whose eloquence was very thunder
and lightning ; they speak of him as charming the audience
with magic power, and alone of the speakers of that day
leaving a sting behind.[1]   Yet we know that he left nothing
written save a few decrees, that he never thought of publish-
ing his speeches, and that the wonderful effects produced
were not by a violent or impassioned manner, but by the
weight of his character, the dignity and calmness of his de-
meanour, and the solid and convincing nature of his arguments.   The few sayings remembered of him are remarkable
for pithiness, and for a deep poetic feeling, and we know that,
in addition to his political speeches, he made some of those
semi-political harangues at public funerals, which were of the
nature of an epideictic display, and which excited an ungovern-
able enthusiasm in the Athenian women then present, whose

---

[1] Cf. Vol. I. § 256, note.

seclusion debarred them from hearing elsewhere the great orator. But we may be certain that, though we have no remains of the speeches which he delivered, the compositions put into his mouth by Thucydides have no resemblance to them except in the policy they advocate. The rhetorical antitheses and verbal subtleties of Thucydides were quite foreign to the genius of Pericles, who clearly owed his power to his profound thoughts, which were doubtless clothed in poetical and figurative, but clear diction. This purely political oratory, which despised the trammels of rhetorical form, was probably the oratory aimed at by such democratic speakers as Cleon and Lysicles and Hyperbolus, though we know that the first of them added vulgar and extravagant action—a thing quite contrary to Greek taste. In after days there may have been a few proud and careless aristocrats who trusted to natural gifts in public speaking, and this would seem also to have been the case with Phocion : but on the whole, even political oratory could not save itself from the inroads of rhetoric, and thus we have in Demosthenes the highest combination of both, but probably a political eloquence inferior to the more pregnant and more poetical, though less elaborated, eloquence of Pericles.

During the period of Pericles' greatness as a political orator, judicial eloquence was shaping itself, as we shall presently see, into an exact science in the hands of Antiphon. But at the same time, the third prominent branch among the Greeks, *epidéictical* oratory, or the eloquence of display, was rapidly developing in the hands of Gorgias. It was of course impossible that these three branches of oratory should keep perfectly distinct, for great distinction in any one of them must naturally lead to the others, as Pericles was called upon to deliver panegyrics, and Antiphon to defend himself by a political speech. Still the parentage of the ' Attic orators ' from Antiphon, and of Antiphon from Korax, is direct and certain ; so is the descent of Isocrates from the school of Gorgias. Equally certain is it, that in Themistocles, Pericles, Alcibiades and Phocion we have a practical kind of public speaking, which did not condescend to rhetorical artifices, and was probably more like the best speaking in the English House

of Commons than anything else which I can suggest. But of
course, from the very nature of this eloquence, which was not
written out by the speakers, and never reported (a device
unknown to the Greeks), we can trace in it no development
or necessary progress.

§ 346. We therefore turn at once to GORGIAS, whom we
merely mentioned (p. 60) in speaking of the philosophic side of
the Sophists, as his real importance belongs to the history of
oratory. Aristotle speaks of Empedocles as his forerunner ; but
does not imply that Empedocles actually prepared a τεχνη, or
devoted himself to rhetoric, but that his reputation in this direction arose both from the splendid diction with which he recommended his physical theories, and from his democratic action
at Agrigentum. If Empedocles was the teacher of Gorgias in
philosophy,[1] this may have been an additional reason for the
remark. But the slight difference of age, as Blass remarks,
between the two men, as well as between Protagoras and Tisias,
makes the relation of master and pupil between any of them
unlikely. For Empedocles seems to have become prominent
about 470 B.C., and the birth of Gorgias, who lived all through
the fifth century, cannot have been much after 490. All our
authorities agree that he lived over 100 years, and that he came
to Athens as a celebrated man in 427, apparently for the first
time, as his speaking then made so wonderful an impression.
He was born at Leontini, the son of Charamantides, and had a
brother Herodicus, a physician whom Plato mentions, and a
sister, whose descendants set up a memorial statue, which
Pausanias describes, to the rhetor at Olympia. His other
remarks in connection with it[2] are curious, but not very trustworthy. Though Gorgias was justly counted a sophist, and
published a celebrated sceptical treatise, he seems to have
preferred to call himself a rhetor. He travelled much about
Greece, and was reputed to have amassed great wealth—yet
he only left a very small fortune, though he was unmarried,

---

[1] The testimony of Plato (*Menon*, 76 C) is decisive that Gorgias and
Empedocles were advocates of the same doctrines, and must therefore have
been in some way connected.

[2] vi. 17, 8 : this inscription has been found lately at Olympia (Blass,
Att. Ber. iv. 324).

and had frugal habits. But frugal habits, as I explained (p. 59), are consistent with luxury and even extravagance in other directions. He seems to have died in Thessaly, whither so many celebrated men of letters resorted.

A great number of eminent men are named among his pupils : Menon and Aristippus in Thessaly, who are mentioned in Xenophon's *Anabasis ;* Likymnius, Polus, Alkidamas and Isocrates, the rhetors, with good reason ; Thucydides, Critias and Alcibiades, on doubtful authority. Though he shared with all the other Sophists the boast that he could make the weak appear the strong, and that no professional man could argue even concerning his profession against a trained dialectician, he seems to have been a man of good moral character and high aspirations, and is said to have designated as a lampoon, and the work of a young Archilochus, the celebrated dialogue (*Gorgias*) in which Plato attacks his theory of rhetoric. He left several technical essays, but they are supposed to have been ready-made commonplaces rather than scientific expositions of principles. He is besides reported to have composed political speeches and harangues ; probably the former were merely accidentally political, and belonged properly to the *epideictic* species, the *harangue*, of which he was the real founder, and in which his great merit lies.

§ 347. The subjects of these oratorical displays are preserved to us. Two of these, called the *Olympicus* and *Pythicus*, were, like Isocrates' *Panegyricus*, intended as a sort of political pamphlet, except that Isocrates was unable to deliver them with effect, while Gorgias evidently trusted to the power and grace of his voice and presence. The subject of the once famous *Olympicus* was an exhortation to the assembled Greeks to give up internal feuds, and combine in attacking and appropriating the territory of the barbarians. This subject was a favourite one with the Rhetors, and gave them opportunity to flatter the Greeks on their national advantages as compared with the surrounding barbarians ; but it is a great mistake to confound this Panhellenism, either in Gorgias or in Isocrates, with the Hellenism of a later age, which sought to infuse Greek culture into the surrounding empires.   Similarly there was an *Epitaphios* of Gorgias, which probably served as a model to succeeding orators, for, in addition to the lost *epitaphios* delivered by Pericles and other leading Athenian citizens, we have five extant—that in Thucydides, that in the *Menexenus* of Plato, that of Hypereides, and those ascribed to Lysias and to Demosthenes, which are late and poor.[1]   We know from these how stereotyped was the form of such harangues, and it is more than probable that it is to Gorgias that we owe its first establishment.   There was also a panegyric on Elis, beginning, we are told, without preface (proem) with the words Ἠλις πόλις εὐδαίμων.   The further allusions in Aristotle's *Rhetoric* to his use of digressions in these harangues make us imagine them not unlike Pindar's odes in a prose dress, wherein the mythical ancestors and former greatness of the victor's family formed the chief ornament of the encomium.

§ 348.   Gorgias' style was far more flowery and poetical than the chaster taste of succeeding generations could tolerate even as a display, for of course the judicial orators, who spoke in court and for a fixed purpose of persuading a jury, must have been from the beginning more ordinary in their language, and tamer in their reasoning.   But in addition to the license of his subject, and the occasions of his display, there seems in our extant fragments a striving after alliteration and riming in sound, and antitheses in sense, which show how prose in his hands still felt afraid to abandon the aids by which poetry seeks to charm the ear.   The composition seems far too attentive to form, and the display of ingenuity in this respect is so conscious and excessive as to be considered childish by the Greeks, who laid him aside, till the Roman rhetors took him up, and studied him afresh.   The grammarians who write about style censure him gravely for this excess of πάρισα and ὁμοιοτέλευτα, just as Plutarch censures Aristophanes for using them, as compared with Menander.

---

[1] Isocrates also mentions that the subject of the *Panegyricus*, so far as it consisted in the praise of Athens, brought him into direct competition with these *encomia*.   His *Evagoras* was often called, though wrongly, an Epitaphios, because it dealt with the virtues of the deceased monarch.

His metaphors also were so frequent as to be tedious. Most of these very superficial devices were called Gorgian figures. I here quote the principal fragment given by Dionysius, as it is not easily accessible, except in Mullach's *Fragmenta* or Clinton's *Fasti*, though a curious and early specimen of Attic prose.[1] For Gorgias appears to have adopted this dialect, and thus in another important respect to have marked an epoch in Greek eloquence.

There are two speeches preserved among the orators under his name, the *Encomium of Helen*, and the *Defence of Palamedes*, which have much exercised critics as to their genuineness. Blass, after a careful examination of them in his first volume, cannot make up his mind to accept them, though they have many likenesses to his certain fragments, and there is no decisive anachronism in style or matter to expose them ; but when he comes to discuss the *Helen* of Isocrates[2] he is so impressed by the arguments in favour of its being a reply to the Encomium, and to a speech of Gorgias, that he decides in favour of its genuineness. Nothing can better prove to us the difficulty of deciding the

---

[1] Schol. *ad Herme*. 412 : Τί γὰρ ἀπῆν τοῖς ἀνδράσι τούτοις, ὧν δεῖ ἀνδράσι προσεῖναι ; τί δὲ καὶ προσῆν, ὧν οὐ δεῖ προσεῖναι ; εἰπεῖν δυναίμην ἃ βούλομαι, βουλοίμην δὲ ἃ δεῖ, λαθὼν μὲν τὴν θείαν νέμεσιν, φυγὼν δὲ τὸν ἀνθρώπινον φθόνον. Οὗτοι γὰρ ἐκέκτηντο ἔνθεον μὲν τὴν ἀρετήν, ἀνθρώπινον δὲ τὸ θνητόν· πολλὰ μὲν δὴ τὸ παριὲν ἐπιεικὲς τοῦ αὐθάδους δικαίου προκρίνοντες, πολλὰ δὲ νόμου ἀκριβείας λόγων ὀρθότητα· τοῦτο νομίζοντες θειότατον καὶ κοινότατον νόμον, τὸ δέον ἐν τῷ δέοντι καὶ λέγειν καὶ σιγᾶν καὶ ποιεῖν· καὶ δισσὰ ἀσκήσαντες μάλιστα ὧν δεῖ. γνώμην καὶ ῥώμην, τὴν μὲν βουλεύοντες, τὴν δὲ ἀποτελοῦντες· θεράποντες μὲν τῶν ἀδίκως δυστυχούντων, κολασταὶ δὲ τῶν ἀδίκως εὐτυχούντων, αὐθάδεις πρὸς τὸ συμφέρον, ἀόργητοι πρὸς τὸ πρέπον, τῷ φρονίμῳ τῆς γνώμης παύοντες τὸ ἄφρον, ὑβρισταὶ εἰς τοὺς ὑβριστάς, κόσμιοι εἰς τοὺς κοσμίους, ἄφοβοι εἰς τοὺς ἀφόβους, δεινοὶ ἐν τοῖς δεινοῖς. Μαρτύρια δὲ τούτων τροπαῖα ἐστήσαντο τῶν πολεμίων, Διὸς μὲν ἀγάλματα, τούτων δὲ ἀναθήματα· οὐκ ἄπειροι οὔτε ἐμφύτου Ἄρεος, οὔτε νομίμων Ἐρώτων, οὔτε ἐνοπλίου Ἔριδος, οὔτε φιλοκάλου Εἰρήνης· σεμνοὶ μὲν εἰς τοὺς θεοὺς τῷ δικαίῳ, ὅσιοι δὲ πρὸς τοὺς τοκέας τῇ θεραπείᾳ, δίκαιοι πρὸς τοὺς ἀστοὺς τῷ ἴσῳ, εὐσεβεῖς δὲ πρὸς τοὺς φίλους τῇ πίστει. Τοιγαροῦν αὐτῶν ἀποθανόντων ὁ πόθος οὐ συναπέθανεν, ἀλλ' ἀθάνατος οὐκ ἀπωμάτοις σώμασι ζῇ οὐ ζώντων.

Σεμνὰς γὰρ (says Dionysius) ἐνταῦθα συμφορήσας λέξεις ὁ Γοργίας, ἐννοίας ἐπιπολαιοτέρας ὑπεξαγγέλλει, τοῖς τε παρίσοις καὶ ὁμοιοτελεύτοις καὶ ὁμοιοκατάρκτοις καλλωπίζων δι' ὅλου πρὸς κόρον τὸν λόγον.

[2] *AB.* ii. p. 222 ; and more decidedly, iv. 326.

question than these doubts and changes of opinion in such a
critic as Blass, who is not, like most German², over-sceptical, or
disposed to make light of all evidence against his own subjective opinions.   Still, as all early critics seem to ignore them,
they are probably clever forgeries, at least on me they produce
that impression, as on most of the German critics.[1]   These
speeches are now printed in the Teubner *Antiphon* (ed. Blass),
but he has unfortunately not added the fragments, which must
be sought in Mullach's *Fragmenta Philosophorum*, vol. ii.   The
MSS. are very numerous for the *Helen*, and in general found
with the speeches of Antiphon.   Their value is discussed by
Blass in his Preface to Antiphon, p. xi, sq.

§ 349. It is unnecessary in this place to make more than a
passing mention of *Polus* of Agrigentum, and of *Likymnius*,
(perhaps the Chian lyric poet cited by Bergk, FLG. p. 1251),
pupils and followers of Gorgias.   For of neither have we any remains, nor do the ancients quote any works of Polus save a rhetorical treatise.   The picture of the man in Plato's *Gorgias* is
disagreeable, forward, and insolent ; but perhaps here too Plato
is playing the Archilochus.   Likymnius is even more obscure,
and only survives in stray allusions of Aristotle and Dionysius
as the inventor of ' Likymnian words' of more sound than
meaning.   The greater pupils of Gorgias, Alkidamas and
Isocrates, belong to a later generation, and a newer epoch of
literature than that with which we are now occupied.

§ 350. We turn to ANTIPHON the orator, the father of Attic
judicial oratory, who may indeed have heard Gorgias, and
learnt from him, as some of the ' Lives ' assert, but who was
nevertheless the founder of a very different and far more solid
branch of Attic prose composition.   Plato in his *Phædrus* (257 D)
says, that distinguished statesmen in Greek cities were ashamed

---

[1] In the preface to his Antiphon (Teubner, 1870), Blass, in recording
his change of opinion on both orations (after Reiske), regards the *Palamedes* as a valuable specimen of early Attic judicial oratory, which is quite
true, so far as accurate dissection of the subject goes.   He adds, that even
if forgeries, these speeches give us as good an idea of the genuine Gorgias
as the Roman copies give us of old Greek sculpture.   Cf. Susemihl,
Gorgias und Att. Prosa, in *Jahn's Jahrb.* for 1877.

to commit to writing and leave behind them speeches, lest they might hereafter be called sophists. Though his evidence as regards the Sophists is always suspicious, it is not unlikely that this sort of teaching was at first classed with other teaching, and the office of schoolmaster or pedagogue (in our sense) has never ranked high among the 'upper ten' of any society. It is probable from Thucydides' expression (though not certain, as Blass implies) that at first Attic counsel, who were not allowed to speak for their clients, aided them with verbal instructions. But it was inevitable that they should come to write down the speeches in full, and practise their clients in delivering them, so that this species of eloquence soon outran the political speeches on the bema, which remained for a long time the composition of mere practical politicians. Hence it was that when a professional rhetor like Antiphon did happen to make a political speech in the course of a judicial debate, the effect of it was so extraordinary. The Germans think that this practice of retaining a professional advocate by litigants was the result of what they call the ochlocracy, which invaded Attic politics about 420 B.C., and which is supposed by them to have rapidly corrupted all morals and principle in the state. But this, as Mr. Grote has long since shown, is a mere servile submitting to the evidence of the comic aristocrats, who traduce and malign the completed democracy. It required no special revolution or degradation of public opinion to produce written court speeches, when the habit of retaining counsel was once sanctioned.

§ 351. Antiphon the son of Sophilus, of the deme Rhamnus [1] in the north of Attica, was born early in the fifth century, about 480. His grandfather was said to have been an adherent of the tyrants, so that his origin was probably aristocratic, as is to be also inferred from his politics. The authors of the 'Lives' are at variance as regards his education, concerning which they evidently knew nothing; his style shows, as might be expected, evident traces of the study of Tisias and Gorgias—the *reasonable presumptions* (εἰκότα) of Tisias, and the

---

[1] Cf. the picturesque description of the district in M. G. Perrot's *Éloquence politique et judiciaire à Athènes*, i. p. 106.

antitheses of Gorgias being prominent in his speeches. He
was evidently a celebrated teacher of rhetoric, as appears
from an allusion in Plato's *Menexenus*, and from Thucydide,'
statement we know that he was the leading advocate at
Athens.   But it appears from the hint of his being self-taught,
from his appellation Nestor, and from other allusions in the
Lives, that he did not become celebrated as a practical orator or politician till he was advanced in years.   We possess
none of his speeches which seem to date before 420 B.C., ex-
cepting possibly the *indictment of the stepmother*, which in my
opinion is not genuine.   He appears, from his traditions, and
perhaps from constant associating with young nobles as their
teacher, to have acquired a profound hatred of the Athenian
demos ; he wrote speeches for the allied cities in disputes
about the tribute, and wrote a violent attack on Alcibiades,
who, as being a renegade, was of course exceptionally hated
by the aristocratic party.   But it is probable that this speech
was spoken by some client, for all through his life this wily and
able man kept in the background, and pulled the strings of
public affairs through weaker men whom he put forward.   He
was in fact a sort of Athenian Baron Stockmar, who made
excursions from education, or perhaps still more a Richard
Wagner, who made excursions from art, into politics.   This is
the picture drawn of him in a famous passage by Thucydides,
who was, according to common tradition, his pupil and friend,
and who evidently regarded him with no common admiration.

The circumstances in which he became a moving force are
a prominent part of Greek history.   After the Sicilian disaster,
when he was now an old man, he undertook the organising
of the oligarchical revolution, which resulted in establishing
the Four Hundred at Athens.   We know from Thucydides'
graphic picture that this was done by a huge conspiracy, which
worked by means of the aristocratic clubs in Athens.   These
clubs, called ἑταιρίαι, were purely political, and may perhaps
be compared to the Orange societies in the north of Ireland,
which while they profess loyalty to the constitution in their own
sense, and to their own order, hardly conceal their hatred of
their political opponents in the very formulæ of their party

creed. We know that these clubs carried out their object by
political assassination, and that they intimidated the populace
by their prompt and daring crimes. For this policy Thucydides makes Antiphon responsible, and if indeed he proceeded
to call him 'second to no man of his day in *virtue*,' we might
well doubt the historian's morality as well as his veracity. But
of course Thucydides meant intellectual ability, as well as a
generous devotion to the oligarchy. Horses or dogs which
performed their allotted functions properly possessed an ἀρετή of
their own quite analogous. After describing the plots and mur-
ders perpetrated by the oligarchical conspirators, he adds,[1] that
Peisander was apparently the chief actor and public head of the
movement; 'but the man who devised the whole thing so as
to bring it to this point, and had watched it longest, was Antiphon, a man second to none of the Athenians of his day in
merit (ἀρετῇ), and abler than any to devise a plan, and to express his thoughts; who never came before the (assembled)
people, nor so far as he could help it into any debate, but (yet)
was an object of suspicion to the masses on account of his reputation for cleverness; for, indeed, he was the one man able
to give most help as an adviser to those who were contending
in debate both in court, and in the assembly.'

It is not our province to detail the fortunes of the leaders
of the Four Hundred; how they despatched a deputation, in
which Antiphon took part, to Sparta, to put Athens completely
in the hands of the Lacedæmonians; how when they returned after the failure of this embassy, the moderate party
with Theramenes obtained the ascendancy, and how most of
the conspirators fled to Dekeleia. Antiphon and Archeptolemus remained, for reasons which have not been preserved.
They were forthwith tried for their treasonable negotiation with
the enemies of the city, and we are fortunate in still possessing
the text of the indictment, as well as of the sentence, which in
Plutarch's *Life* is copied from the rhetor Cæcilius, who found it
in Craterus' collection of state documents.[2] It appears that

---

[1] viii. 68. According to the parallel passages quoted by Classen in his
Introduction (p. lxvii), ἀρετή also implies *unselfishness*.

[2] Both these statements are quoted by Blass, *AB.* i. pp. 88-9, notes.

Antiphon put forth all his strength in his own defence. The veteran rhetor, who had for years been the acknowledged master of judicial eloquence, at last found himself obliged to apply in his own case the arts and arguments with which he had supplied his clients. His speech, which was famous in antiquity, is an irreparable loss to us, as he did not adopt a technical or narrow ground of defence, but reviewed the whole revolution of the Four Hundred, and probably his own political life, in his harangue on the *coup d'état* (περὶ τῆς μεταστάσεως). Thucydides goes on to say, when describing his character as above quoted, that the defence was the finest oration of the kind known up to his day. Agathon is said to have specially praised it to the orator, who replied that the approval of one competent judge atoned for its ill-success with the many. But of course the case was too clear, and the general distrust of the dangerous rhetor must have felt itself thoroughly justified by the evidence of his antidemocratic policy.[1] He and Archeptolemus were condemned to death, their descendants to loss of civic rights; their bodies were refused burial in Attic soil, and their houses razed to the ground.

§ 352. These events happened in 411 or 410 B.C. (Ol. 92, 2). We have no other evidence whatever of the personal character of this remarkable man. The Greek lives have sought to afford it by confusing him with several other men of the same name, first with Antiphon the democrat, whose services in war and politics brought him death at the hands of the Thirty, who were the successors of the Four Hundred in policy at Athens. There was also Antiphon the tragic poet, murdered by Dionysius of Syracuse for an anti-tyrannic joke, and (omitting obscure persons) the sophist Antiphon, already mentioned (p. 61). Didymus ascribed none but the speeches on homicide to the rhetor, to the sophist not only essays on truth and concord, but even what he calls the δημηγορικοί and the πολιτικός— political harangues. This judgment, which Hermogenes quotes from Didymus, is shown to be correct from the careful examination of the fragments by Blass,[2] and they are accordingly

---

[1] See the elegant sketch of the temper and feelings of the Athenian people at this moment in M. G. Perrot's *Éloquence,* i. p. 117, sq.

[2] *AB.* i. 97, sq.

printed as an appendix, under the sophist's name, in his
edition of Antiphon. I have spoken of these fragments in
connection with the Sophists. If the rhetor left no political
speeches, we must understand Thucydides to mean that on
these subjects his advice was given orally, and not by writing
—a probable supposition, as the litigants might be obscure
people, but the politicians already speakers of some experience.

§ 353. We pass to the consideration of the still extant
speeches which are ascribed to him. These are obviously divis-
ible into two classes, the theoretical exercises, and the practical
or actual court speeches. The former are peculiarly interesting
as affording a specimen from early times of the training given
by the rhetors — training of a strictly real and practical tendency, and very different from the idle declamation upon
impossible cases which was fashionable in the later schools.
On the other hand, they show plainly the professional spirit
then disseminated by the Sophists, who advocated the theory,
so naturally acceptable to the over-subtle and not over-con-
scientious Greek, that rhetoric was a sort of magic art, and
that by unlocking its secrets a man could ply at will the assent
and obedience of his hearers. Now a-days, when a great part
of eloquence consists merely in feeling intensely upon a subject,
and letting the heart find its most simple and natural utter-
ance, we cannot easily put ourselves into this curiously artificial attitude, which allows the conviction of the speaker in his
cause to go for little, and makes his eloquence a mere play
of intellectual dexterity. But such was indeed the case in the
days of Antiphon. His exercises, called *tetralogies*, because
they contain a double attack and reply on each case, are all
upon murder cases, as indeed are all his extant speeches ; but
though this branch of them was particularly famous, the unity of
subject in his remains is rather to be ascribed to the accidental
preservation of that portion of his collected speeches in which
this class of cases had been brought together. They are meant
to show how a master of the art could frame arguments with
equal persuasiveness on either side of a given case.

One pair of the first tetralogy will here be sufficient as an example. A distinguished man has been found in the way murdered by night, but his person not plundered. His attendant slave is found lying beside him, mortally wounded. Before dying, he attests that he recognised one of the murderers, the man who is now charged with the crime. Moreover, the latter was known to be at enmity with the deceased, and just engaged with him in personal litigation. As the accused denies the charge absolutely, the case would come for trial before the Areopagus. It should be remembered that as it is an imaginary one, there is no stress laid on the narrative of the facts, which are assumed as undisputed on both sides ; the problem is simply to argue from them in the best possible manner.

The accuser, who is a relative of the deceased, opens with reminding the court how an offender of known talent and mature experience will be sure to commit a crime in such a manner as to avoid easy conviction, and that for this reason, as direct evidence is almost sure to be wanting, the greatest importance must attach to εἰκότα, or probable inferences. He adds a reminder of the public pollution resting upon the state until the murderer has been prosecuted and punished. This is the exordium. The argument opens by rejecting successively all causes for the outrage except that of premeditated murder, and shows that, such being the case, the accused had the strongest motives to prompt him to the act, both from old antipathy, and from the fear of condemnation in the pending suit. Added to this, there is the only possible evidence, that of the dying slave. On these grounds the speaker presses for a verdict of condemnation, repeating in conclusion the religious aspects of the question, and picturing the defilement of all the temples and altars frequented by a blood-stained criminal.

To this very strong case the accused replies by opening with a bitter complaint of his singular misfortune. While others are relieved by a cessation or change from a pressing danger, the defendant, whose property has been ruined by the persecution of the deceased, has not escaped him even now, but has his life still threatened and annoyed, so much so, that it is actually no longer sufficient to establish his own good character, but he is in danger of condemnation if he cannot

discover and convict another man's murderers. He proceeds
at once to show that, granting his hostility to the deceased,
the certainty of being suspected was to him on prudential
grounds the strongest dissuasive from attempting it. But he will
undertake to retort the probable arguments set up against
him. In the first place, the deceased may have been slain by
robbers, who did not strip him because some one approached,
or by some criminal whom he had surprised in the commission
of another crime, or by some other personal enemy. Nor is
the evidence of the slave trustworthy ; for his excitement
must have made it hard to recognise the murderers, and he
would naturally name any person suggested by his master's
relations. Moreover, the evidence of slaves is at all times
doubtful, being never accepted without the test of torture.
But as regards the probabilities of the case, they are clearly
against the accuser, for how could a man in danger of being
condemned to a mere fine risk his life and liberty to avoid it?
and if he did, he would do it through another, and not expose
himself to direct detection. His having strong reasons to
commit the deed rather show that he was suffering injustice at
the hands of the deceased, and it were indeed hard if this
injustice were to entail the still greater injustice of a capital
condemnation. The defendant concludes with retorting the
charge of impiety upon those who leave the real culprit un-
punished, and endeavour to convict an innocent man, who is
also a man of high public character and of blameless life.

Such are the two speeches which open the debate, carried
on through another attack and defence. They are all very
short, in fact mere skeletons to be filled out, as occasion
might suggest, but are so able and subtle as to show us how
natural was the distrust of such an art on the part of the
Athenian public, and how invaluable must have been the help
of such a counsel, if the opposite side was not furnished with
similar weapons.

§ 354. The second tetralogy is on a case of homicide by
an accident in the palæstra, when a lad, throwing a dart in
accordance with all the rules of the school, hit another who
ran across him at the instant. The case is interesting as

showing the Greek sentiment concerning the pollution or blood-guiltiness of any man or thing which was the *cause* of death, whether intentionally or not. Hence the constant subtleties as to the real *cause* of the event which we find here, and in the speech *on the chorister*, and which are reported to have occupied the attention of Pericles and Protagoras for hours together. The third tetralogy is a dispute about a homicide during a quarrel. The question argued is that the accused merely defended himself against the attack of the deceased, who thus succeeded in causing his own death ; and moreover, that his wounds not being mortal, he deliberately, and against professional advice, had himself treated by an incompetent physician, who caused the fatal result. All these curious rhetorical exercises are evidently from the same hand, and there have not been wanting attempts to prove them of later date and inferior authorship than that of Antiphon. But there is no reasonable ground for such scepticism. The faults of over-subtlety and of crudeness attributed to them are exactly those which we should expect from his age and character, and their similarity in style, in spite of a few peculiarities, to Antiphon's certain speeches and to Thucydides' history are satisfactory evidence of their genuineness.

§ 355. I feel much more doubt about the *Charge of Poisoning against a Stepmother*, which comes first in our MSS. This speech has no doubt many features very similar to the acknowledged pieces, such as the προκατασκευή, or short summary *before* the narrative of facts, which was usual with Antiphon, and the artificial antitheses and assonances. But it is certain that other rhetors of the same age used these devices. On the other hand, the narrative of the facts obtains a prominence and a picturesqueness in this speech which are foreign to what we know of Antiphon, while the argument is neither forcible nor ingenious, as his arguments are wont to be. There is, moreover, a predominance of pathos in the speech which seems to me strange to him. But the best modern critic, Blass, is not convinced by these objections to reject the speech, and the reader may therefore regard my opinion as having the weight of authority against it.

§ 356. As the speech about the chorister is on the subject handled in the second tetralogy, so the speech *On the Murder of Herodes* is in character very similar to that of the first. Herodes was an Athenian, and a relation of the accuser, who became a cleruch at Mitylene after its capture in 427 B.C. While on a journey to Ænos, he left his ship at Methymna by night, apparently in a state of intoxication, and never returned, nor could his body be anywhere discovered. His relatives charged with the murder the only companion of his voyage, a Mitylenæan, who was supposed to be incited by an enemy of Herodes called Lykinos, who also lived at Mitylene. As additional evidence there was adduced a letter supposed to be written by the accused to Lykinos, and the declarations of a slave on board, who was tortured by the relatives, and confessed against the Mitylenæan, but was forthwith put to death, having revoked his evidence when he saw that he gained nothing by it. It is in this interesting case, and for a citizen of a subject town, accused with murdering an Athenian citizen, that Antiphon composed his admirable speech. We perceive that the accused had been harshly and unjustly treated. Upon coming to Athens, he had been at once cast into prison, and been refused the alternative of offering bail for his appearance, or of standing a second trial on appeal, though such refusal was illegal. The orator must therefore not only disprove the charge, but overcome a strong bias in the jury, arising from his inferior condition, and the feeling against Mitylene, which had not died away since the memorable crisis described by Thucydides. I will not here pursue the intricacies of the argument, in which there is, as usual, little narrative, but rather a subtle discussing of the probabilities of the case. The trial is interesting in showing the constant and stupid application of torture, and the little faith which was put in slaves' evidence even with this precaution. Moreover, a free man who was on board was also tortured, which seems very strange, and one of the speaker's points is the fact that while the slave confessed and criminated him, the free man would confess nothing.

§ 357. Particularly interesting is the argument which shows that mere probability is an unsafe guide, especially in capital cases, and this is illustrated by several cases of false condemnation, where the truth came out afterwards.[1]   The conclusion is also very characteristic, as showing the religious character of the Athenian public, to which Antiphon perpetually appeals.   The speaker urges that had he been guilty, the gods must have shown their displeasure by unfavourable weather when he was sailing, or unpropitious signs when he was sacrificing with others ; whereas the contrary was the case.[2]   This and other like appeals in Antiphon's speeches have been used with great simplicity by Blass[3] to prove that the orator was a man of antique sanctity, and an advocate of the national and established religion.   We may be sure that the follower of the great sophists, and the master of Thucydides, held no such views. His political career, and the practice of devising clever arguments to sustain the weakness of a bad cause, are anything but the marks of an old-fashioned and conservative piety.   But of course Antiphon, as a skilled rhetor, knew the audience he was addressing, and especially in cases of homicide the religious superstitions of the people were very strong, and sustained by a wholesome instinct.   Hence he takes the utmost care that his case shall not be ruined by disclosing the least irreverence or scepticism on such matters—the least hint of which would have been to an elderly and sedate jury the strongest εἰκός that the speaker was a lawless and guilty person.

---

[1] § 69, sq.   Ἤδη δ' ἔγωγε καὶ πρότερον ἀκοῇ ἐπίσταμαι γεγονός, τοῦτο μὲν τοὺς ἀποθανόντας τοῦτο δὲ τοὺς ἀποκτείναντας οὐχ εὑρηθέντας . . . . αὐτίκα Ἐφιάλτην τὸν ὑμέτερον πολίτην οὐδέπω νῦν εὕρηνται οἱ ἀποκτείναντες . . . . τοῦτο δ' ἐντὸς οὐ πολλοῦ χρόνου παῖς ἐζήτησεν οὐδὲ δώδεκα ἔτη γεγονὼς τὸν δεσπότην ἀποκτεῖναι· καὶ εἰ μὴ φοβηθείς, ὡς ἀνεβόησεν, ἐγκαταλιπὼν τὴν μάχαιραν ἐν τῇ σφαγῇ ᾤχετο φεύγων ἀλλ' ἐτόλμησε μεῖναι, ἀπώλοντ' ἂν οἱ ἔνδον ὄντες ἅπαντες· οὐδεὶς γὰρ ἂν ᾤετο τὸν παῖδα τολμῆσαί ποτε τοῦτο. He adds a curious condemnation of all the Hellenotamiæ on a false charge, when only one escaped through the delay of his sentence.

[2] From the fact of Andocides (*De Myst.* §§ 137–9) urging similar points in favour of his own innocence, I infer that it was a commonplace at Athens to argue that fair weather was a proof of favour from the gods, and that a sea voyage was supposed to afford them a peculiarly convenient opportunity for punishing the guilty.

[3] *AB.* i. 135.

§ 358. Though the subject-matter of Antiphon's speeches is not without interest, there can be little doubt that the most important feature about him, especially in a history of Greek literature, is his form.　For he is the earliest master of that artificial and technical prose, which reached its climax in Demosthenes, and which is one of the most remarkable developments of the genius of the race.　Nor is there any department of Greek Literature so foreign to modern taste or to modern ideas.　We would willingly attribute all the minute analysis of sentences in Greek orations to the barren subtlety of the rhetors of Roman times, and believe that the old orators scorned to compose in gyves and fetters, and study the syllables of their periods, and the prosody of them, as if they were writing poetry.　But all these details seem to have been handed down in the τέχναι which each of them published, and Antiphon's was not the least-known among them.　It seems that every sentence was to be weighed and measured in these orations, which were indeed not long but yet very intricate, and which were constructed with so close an adherence to rules, both in matter and in form, that we cannot imagine any parallel now-a-days.　Not even French prose, the most polished and artificial organ of thought in modern Europe, can compare with Greek rhetoric in this respect.　The Greek orator composed in *periods*, each of which was divided into one or more κῶλα, or members, four being the major limit.　These *cola* implied one another in construction, and were summed up or completed by the last member, which was longer and weightier in sound than the rest.　This is the κατεστραμμένη λέξις, of which Antiphon is the earliest official representative, though Gorgias was probably its originator, and there are not wanting examples of it in Herodotus.　The relative length of the *cola*, their cadence, their ending syllables—all these matters were made subject to rules.　Antiphon, standing at the opening of this peculiar study, has by no means attained all its refinements ; he often offends against the canons of the Roman critics by allowing the natural course of expression to carry him away.　But this is only in comparison with later Attic eloquence.　In comparison with our eloquence, we per-

ceive at once a stiff and artificial tone about him, enhanced by
the antique flavour of his language, wherein he and Thucydides affected the old and unusual, in contrast to the beautiful
spoken Attic of their day.[1]   I will not trouble the reader by
going into more minute details on these technical points, which
rather injure than help our enjoyment of Attic prose, but recommend the full discussion in Blass' chapter on Antiphon,
with the special tracts to which he refers.   In an official history
of Greek oratory these are essential details, however dry and
uninteresting they may be to the general student.

   To us moderns much of the force of Antiphon consists
perhaps in his having not refined his style into complete
accordance with these technical laws.   The *austere harmony*
which we find in him and in Thucydides is far more impressive
than the *smooth harmony* of Isocrates.[2]   This character is sustained by his choice of words, which are dignified and often
poetical without the excess of metaphors censured in Gorgias.
He uses the older σσ, though it had been already replaced by
ττ, and the expression τοῦτο μέν—τοῦτο δέ, so common in Herodotus but abandoned in later Attic prose.   As to the method
of his orations, we notice that the arrangement is simple and
natural.   After a proem, he throws in a sort of προκατασκευή, to
prepare the mind for the narrative of facts which follows.   But
here is his weak point, particularly as compared with Lysias,
while his strength lies in argument, especially in the urging and
retorting of *à priori* probable proofs.   He reiterates, however,
a good deal, and comes back on points already argued.   Besides

----

[1] Thus, while such writers as Dionysius and Demetrius are constantly
showing anacolutha in the use of particles (μέν repeated, or without δέ, or
vice versa, &c.), we are rather struck with such sentences as this : ἐγὼ δ'
ἡγοῦμαι πολὺ ἀνοσιώτερον εἶναι ἀφεῖναι τοῦ τεθνεῶτος τὴν τιμωρίαν, ἄλλως
τε καὶ τοῦ μὲν ἐκ προβουλῆς ἀκουσίως ἀποθάνοντος, τῆς δὲ ἑκουσίως ἐκ προ-
νοίας ἀποκτεινάσης (i. 5)—or this : οὐ γὰρ δίκαιον οὔτ' ἔργῳ ἁμαρτόντα διὰ
ῥήματα σωθῆναι, οὔτ' ἔργῳ ὀρθῶς πράξαντα διὰ ῥήματα ἀπολέσθαι · τὸ μὲν
γὰρ ῥῆμα τῆς γλώσσης ἁμάρτημά ἐστι, τὸ δὲ ἔργον τῆς γνώμης.   And yet this
latter is found fault with by the critics for having the last clause too short,
and nothing corresponding to ἁμάρτημά ἐστι !

[2] We have no better word than *harmony* to use here for the Greek
ἁρμονία, which is not at all the same in meaning.

the *figures of language,* as the rhetors called them, that is to say, balanced antitheses, alliterations at the end of clauses, and such like, he made but sparing use of *figures of thought,* such as indignant questions, invocations of the gods, and such indications of emotion as we should certainly leave to nature, but which these strict theorists had discussed as mere rhetorical devices.   It was remarked that five of these, the *aposiopesis,* the assumed hesitation (διαπόρησις), the emphatic repetition of a word (ἀναδίπλωσις), the *climax,* and the use of irony, were unknown to him.   But this is not true of irony, which is prominent enough in the Herodes speech, when the speaker is refuting the point that, as no murderer had yet been discovered, he is bound to clear himself by making the discovery.

The sum of these remarks leads us to the conclusion, that while the early condition and incomplete development of oratory made Antiphon adhere more closely than his more subtle and variously trained successors to a fixed and symmetrical plan, he did not equal them in the smoothness and grace of their structure, or in the artful simplicity of their narratives. Nevertheless he makes an august and haughty impression, even when pleading in the person of others. His tone is severe and dignified, his language strong and clear, without being fervent or passionate ; and he stands before us not only as the fit organiser of an anti-democratic revolution, but as the master and model of the historian Thucydides.

§ 359. Turning to the external history of Antiphon's work, we note that, though greatly esteemed by his actual contemporaries, he was soon eclipsed by succeeding orators, whose developed graces were more agreeable than the harsh harmonies of the antique rhetor.   His commonplaces are mentioned by Aristotle as of the same kind as those of Gorgias, and it is probable that Aristotle refers to the extant tetralogies, which may have been part of the well-known τέχνη. But the other earlier writers on rhetoric do not seem to have paid any attention to him.   He was not a model for either late Attic or Roman eloquence.   Dionysius often refers to him as being, like Thucydides, a writer of the old rough style, and as being with Lysias and Isocrates a leading orator

of Thucydides' day—as being a fine writer, but not pleasant. Cæcilius of Calacte appears first to have made a special
study of him, and we have many good things cited from his
criticisms in a special treatise on Antiphon and in his *Lives*
of the orators. Hermogenes speaks of him with equal care
and appreciation. The Life in *Plutarch's Lives of the Ten
Orators*, the Greek arguments, and many citations of phrases
in the Lexica show that he was studied if not generally read
in late Greek times. There was even a special book on Antiphon's *figures* by Caius Harpocration, and we have extracts
given by Photius from the orations.

§ 360. *Bibliographical.* As to MSS., Aldus tells us, in the
preface to his *Ed. Princeps*, that Lascaris was sent to the East
to look for Greek books, and brought back one containing the
orators from Mount Athos. This MS. was evidently different
from any of those now extant, but not, I think, superior to
the best we possess, though in some passages it alone pre-
serves the true reading. Foremost is the Crippsianus (A),
used by Bekker as the basis of his text, which is in the British
Museum, and of the thirteenth century. But since Mætzner
collated the Oxford (N), of about the same age, it has been
found, after much controversy, to be a better copy of the same
archetype as A.[1] Others are the Laurentian and Marcian,
(B and L), and a Breslau copy (Z). After the *Ed. Princeps*
(1513), which contains all the orators save Demosthenes, as
well as the speeches attributed to Gorgias and Alkidamas,
and is the first edition of them all save Isocrates, there are
texts by Stephanus and others; but of highest authority, in
our own time, are those of Bekker, Baiter and Sauppe (the
Zurich *Ed.*), Mætzner, and Blass (Teubner, 1871). If these
are not professed commentaries on the author, there is a host
of critical monographs by Sauppe, Franke, Brieglebe, Spengel,
and others, with occasional flashes of light from Cobet in the
Mnemosyne. An exhaustive account of the man is given by
Blass,[2] and F. Ignatius, *de Ant. eloc.* (*Gött. Diss.*, 1882), is a
partial lexicon.

[1] Cf. the discussion in Blass' Preface to his text of Antiphon, which
differs from his earlier history of Attic oratory in some points.

[2] *AB.* i. ch. iii.

§ 361. In connection with the technical development of rhetoric by Antiphon, it may be well to add a word on some contemporary or immediately succeeding men, whose main activity
is to be placed before the archonship of Eucleides, and who are
specially noted in Plato's dialogues, in Cicero's rhetorical works,
and by Dionysius, as marking epochs in the history of Attic
eloquence. The fact that their writings are almost wholly lost
prevents their claiming any considerable space in this short
history. Foremost stands *Thrasymachos* of Chalkedon, who
can be inferred from the extant notices to have flourished during
the later years of the Peloponnesian war. He figures as a leading personage in Plato's *Republic*, where he appears in the character not of a rhetor, but of a bold and vulgar sophist, of
blustering manner, and of low moral tone. But whether this
portrait is indeed a fair one may well be doubted. In the
Phædrus he is mentioned with Theodorus as a cunning rhetor,
and this is more in consonance with our other notices of him.
His technical treatises are referred to as ἀφορμαὶ ῥητορικαί (which
probably do not differ from his *great techne*), as ἐπιδεικτικοί,
and as παίγνια. Perhaps the deliberative speeches, of which
a fragment remains, were also technical models. From his
ἀφορμαί were cited various set proems, ὑπερβάλλοντες, or cli-
maxes, and ἔλεοι, or appeals to pity; Plato[1] speaks of him as
able to excite to rage, and to soothe again the minds of his
hearers, and this praise seems not ironical. But more generally,
Blass has shown from a comparison of the ancient authorities[2]
that he was regarded as the real founder of the newer Attic eloquence, inasmuch as he adopted in *style* the just mean between
poetically artificial diction, on the one hand, and vulgar col-
loquialism, on the other. Secondly, he determined more accurately the rhetorical period, a proper rounding of sentences
for proper effect, where everything is subordinate, and related to
the main thought, no loose or disconnected clauses being admitted. Thirdly, according to Aristotle, he first used the pæonic
rythm, beginning his period with a first pæon, and ending with
a first or fourth—a subtlety which is now of little interest,

---

[1] *Phædrus*, 266-7.　　　[2] *AB.* i. 246.

and, as Blass shows, not verified by the extant fragments, but which tells how profoundly artificial was Greek oratory in comparison with ours. Cicero, however, also observes in Thrasymachus this strict attention to rythm, but observes that both he and Gorgias made their clauses too short, and therefore their rythms too manifest. This Blass illustrates from Gorgias' remains (AB. iv. 331). Thrasymachus seems accordingly to have been a valuable guide to Lysias, and other practical orators of the next generation. Only two short fragments remain.

We have the same sort of praise in Plato's *Phædrus*[1] of *Theodoros* of Byzantium, and of *Euenos* of Paros, who seem to have been fertile in separating each part of an oration into subdivisions, such as προδιήγησις, διήγησις, and ἐπιδιήγησις, πίστωσις, and ἐπιπίστωσις ; Euenus also suggested indirect and, as it were, accidental effects, which he called παρέπαινοι, παράψογοι, and the like. But all these subtleties belong strictly to the history of Greek rhetoric, and require no special treatment in a general history of literature.

---

[1] 266 E.

CHAPTER V.

THUCYDIDES—ANDOCIDES, CRITIAS.

§ 362. THUCYDIDES is said, upon late and doubtful authority, to have been born in 471 B.C., and to have been therefore forty years old at the opening of the Peloponnesian war. This agrees, however, fairly well with the two passages in his work [1] in which he states that he began his study of the war from its commencement, being then of mature age, and having perceived its importance; that he wrote down the events as they occurred, and lived all through it to the close. As to the historian's early life, we can only affirm that, while he is not known to have taken any active part in politics, and yet had sufficient means to permit perfect leisure, he must have studied with care in the rhetorical schools of Gorgias, and still more of Antiphon, as well as in the sophistical schools of philosophical scepticism. He further tells us that he was the son of Oloros, that he himself suffered from the plague at Athens, which he so graphically describes; [2] also that he was appointed general for the protection of Athenian interests in Thrace, and that he was sent for from Thasos, where he was occupied, by his colleague Eukles to save Amphipolis, but that having failed in this object, owing to Brasidas' promptness, he secured Eion. [3] He tells us that, owing to his possession of gold mines in Thasos and on the opposite coast of Thrace, he was of great influence in that country, [4] but that he was banished *after* the affair at Amphipolis (B C. 424) for twenty years, and thus had the opportunity of studying the other side of the conflict, especially the Peloponnesian affairs.

[1] i. 1, and v. 26.   [2] ii. 48.   [3] iv. 104-6.
[4] This circumstance may have caused his appointment as **strategus**, without any expeditionary force, in that region.

These are then the indisputable facts which we possess on his own authority—moreover, we may infer that he outlived the capture of Athens by Lysander in 405 B.C., perhaps for some time, as these confessions occur early in the fifth book, and we must allow him time to complete the remainder. On the other hand, his assertion that he witnessed and recorded the *whole* war is not borne out by the close, which ends abruptly, and shows evidence of being broken off by the death of the author, or some other untoward circumstance. Indeed his observation[1] that the eruption of Ætna in the year 426 was the third recorded, and the last known up to the date of the remark, seems to fix his death, or the limits of his revision of his work, before 396 B.C., when another eruption took place. However, his long absence from Athens, as well as his severe and perhaps surly character, kept him from being affected by the rapid changes of style and taste which mark the later years of the fifth century. Hence, though his work was, in part at least, written after new Attic prose had been developed, and when Lysias was delighting the juries with translucent simplicity, Thucydides kept up certain austerities of style, which make him and Sophocles peculiar among all the extant Greek writers.

According to the most current tradition, he was assassinated in Thrace, where he lived in retirement on his property, and his unfinished work, which passed into the hands of his daughter, was edited either by her or by Xenophon, to whom she entrusted it. As we shall presently see, there are some points of style in the last and unfinished book which make Xenophon a possible editor. There is a great controversy among the Germans, some arguing that he considered the war concluded with the peace of Nicias, and had actually composed the first four and half books when he found that he must continue his task, and so he began again[2] with a new proem. Others, among whom is the latest editor, Classen, consider that the so-called inconsistencies in his work, on which Ullrich based this theory, can be explained away, and that there is a clear proof of the whole work being the outcome of one deliberate

---

[1] iii. 116.   [2] v. 26.

plan, not carried out till the end of the war, though evidence was taken, and notes made, all through its course. The controversy is, however, neither interesting nor profitable, and by modifying our purely subjective opinion as to the degree of completion which the earlier books may have attained before the later were written, we may indefinitely approximate the one hypothesis to the other.[1]

Two other more fanciful inferences are drawn from his work. When he contrasts it with those which are intended for immediate display, and speaks[2] of them as composed by the logographers rather to afford pleasure than profit to the hearer, he is supposed to refer to the recitation of Herodotus at Athens. The earliest possible date for any such performance, and that of only parts of his work, is 446 B.C., which may serve to mark the time when the two historians came in contact, not when Thucydides was a child (according to a current anecdote), but a grown man, and able to criticise. But all this is doubtful, and still more so is the notion of Ullrich, that his remark on Antiphon's defence of himself, being the finest known τῶν μέχρι ἐμοῦ points at the defence of Socrates. This conjecture assumes that Socrates' defence was esteemed an oratorical performance, which it certainly was not.

There is a note of Plutarch, in his life of Kimon, which is of more value, and apparently trustworthy. After detailing the descent of Kimon through his mother from a Thracian king

---

[1] The legends about Thucydides' life have been lately examined (apart from Classen's Introd.) by Petersen, *De Vita Thucyd.*, Dorpat, 1873; by Wilamowitz-Möllendorff in *Hermes* (xii. p. 326, sq.); by O. Gilbert (*Philol.* 38, 2), and by Firmani, *Revista di Filologia*, for 1877, p. 149, sq. But no new facts have been established. The newer tracts on the composition of his history, and the relation of the earlier to the later part, are enumerated by L. Herbst, in the first part of his elaborate *Jahresbericht* (*Philologus*, 38, p. 504). The result of his very dry and intricate discussion is to show that while Thucydides regards and speaks of the first ten years of the war as a separate war, he did not compose its history, nor even his general introduction, without a knowledge of the whole twenty-seven years of its course. Whether the allusions which prove this were originally in the narrative, or inserted on revision, no man can tell.

[2] i. 21 : ἀγώνισμα ἐς τὸ παραχρῆμα ἀκούειν . . . ὡς λογογράφοι ξυνέθεσαν ἐπὶ τὸ προσαγωγότερον τῇ ἀκροάσει ἢ ἀληθέστερον.

Oloros, he adds: 'Therefore the historian Thucydides, being
related to Kimon's family, was the son of an Oloros, called
after his ancestor, and owned gold mines in Thrace. He is
said to have been murdered at Scaptesyle (in Thrace), but the
monument over his remains, which were brought to Attica, *is
shown* among the tombs of Kimon's family, next the tomb of
his sister Elpinike. But Thucydides was a Halimousian as to
his deme, whereas Miltiades' people were Lakiadæ.' There is
also a very explicit and credible statement in Pausanias[1] that
his return from exile was due to Œnobius, son of Eukles (apparently his old colleague in Thrace), who carried through a
decree that he should be restored to Athens, but that having
been assassinated as he was returning, a statue was erected to
him in the Acropolis, and a monument set up to him not far
from the Melitean gate.

§ 363. On a double Herme in the museum of Naples we have
representations of Thucydides and Herodotus, which represent
the former as a somewhat mean, surly-looking person; yet the
type is so unlike an ideal Greek head, and so thoroughly individual, that it was always believed to have some authority.
The printing of photographs of the splendid bust at Holkham,
by the Earl of Leicester (in May 1878), along with a translation
of Prof. Michaelis' essay upon these portraits,[2] proves that the
Naples portrait is a poor and shabby copy of the same (probably bronze) original from which the Holkham bust is taken.
The latter is in splendid condition, and expresses all the stern-
ness and strength, together with the peculiar modernness, which
marks the character of Thucydides. I am of course far from
thinking that a bust which did not express these qualities could
not be genuine; some men are very disappointing in their appearance. But it is very satisfying to have the portrait corresponding to our ideal, and in no conventional way. It is the
opinion of Otto Gilbert[3] that this is a copy of the portrait
statue set up by Œnobius.

[1] i. 23, 9.
[2] I must here record my thanks to the Earl of Leicester for sending me
a copy of this valuable but unpublished contribution to archæology.
[3] *Philologus*, 38, 2, p. 259

§ 364. Turning to a survey of his work as we have it before us, we must adhere to the now received division into eight books, though it is nowhere countenanced by the author, and though we hear of divisions into nine and into thirteen books as known in old days. But the existing arrangement is convenient and well devised. Thucydides intends his work to be a military history of the Peloponnesian war, compiled from original documents, and from a careful record of personal observations, as well as a comparison of the fresh reports of eye-witnesses. That he has carried out this plan perfectly, and that his book is the most complete and careful record of the details of a long war, cannot be for a moment questioned It is a work infinitely more complex, and more difficult than Xenophon's account of his Retreat from Cunaxa, but is like it in being a contemporary history. The chronological method which he prefers, and specially vindicates,[1] as superior to the ordinary plan of quoting archontates and priesthoods, is that of successive summers and winters. Nevertheless, his starting point [2] must be determined on the old method, and his strict adherence to summers and winters leads him at times to break off a connected account of military operations to notice some distant and unimportant, but synchronous transaction. This defect of arrangement has been commented on by Mure and others. Unfortunately it has led the author to record a vast number of petty raids and resultless movements in outlying parts of Greece, while he has omitted the whole of the literary and artistic, as well as almost the whole of the social and political, history of the great epoch on which he wrote. This is the more to be regretted as the few digressions he does make into archæological or political subjects are, in proportion to their extent, the most valuable and interesting parts of his work.

§ 365. But the author himself is by no means of that opinion. His preface opens with the assertion that the Peloponnesian war, as he had from the very commencement expected, turned out by far the most important crisis in Hellenic, and therefore in human, history. It is almost impossible that in making this statement Thucydides should not have had the great work of

---

[1] v. 20.   [2] ii. 1.

Herodotus in his mind's eye, especially if he did not begin to
write, as many critics maintain, till the close of the war. But
whether this be so or not, his proof of the bold assertion as to
the importance of his subject is singularly sophistical. He turns
first to the very ancient times, and in what is called his *Archæ-
ologia* reviews the condition of early Greece, and especially the
resources displayed in the Trojan war, which he holds to have
been but small, for want of the real sinews of empire—χρήματα
καὶ ναυτικόν, money and a navy. The same was in a lesser degree
the case with the states which became prominent under tyrants
from this time to that of the Persian wars, as he shows by a
series of most interesting observations.

But when he comes to this crisis [1] he shirks a fair estimate of its comparative importance with his own subject ; he
gives a very meagre extract to show its effects upon Sparta
and Athens, and concludes [2] by saying that the ancient affairs
were difficult to ascertain on proper evidence, because of the
uncritical way in which people hand down tradition. He
illustrates this by three examples : first, that of the Athenian
misconception about Harmodius and Aristogiton, to which he
again reverts more fully,[3] and then to the popular Greek errors
about two trivial matters, which had not past into oblivion,
the λόχος Πιτανάτης, and the double vote of the Spartan kings,
in one at least contradicting an opinion of Herodotus. 'So
little pains do the many take in seeking after truth, and rather
turn to what is ready at hand !'[4] In c. 23 he returns to the

---

[1] c. 18.   [2] c. 20.   [3] vi. 54.

[4] Herbst, in a very minute examination of this preface (*Philologus*,
38, pp. 534-45), gives a new exposition of the whole argument, and defends Thucydides against the charge of having endeavoured to slight the
importance of the Persian war in the history of Herodotus. He considers
that Thucydides divided his retrospect into two portions, that of the
παλαιά, reaching from mythical times down to the battle of Marathon, and
that of the Μηδικά. The παλαιά, which he reviews in cc. 2-17, embrace
the *Troica*, which have been exaggerated by fables, and the period of
the tyrants, in which a careful examination of facts shows want of the resources of war. He then sketches the Μηδικά in cc. 18, 19. The criticism
which follows (cc. 20-2), and which contains the disrespectful remarks on
the logographers, and the general untrustworthiness of old traditions, is

comparison of the *Medic* affairs, and observes that they were
settled by four battles, whereas the later war was more pro-
tracted, severe, and full of horrors.   He speaks of cities being
now destroyed by barbarians, of which we know only a single
small instance (Mycalessus).   He also asserts that this war
greatly affected barbarians as well as Greeks.   Historically
this is not provable, but I fancy Thucydides' opinion was
rather that any war, however petty, among Greeks was vastly
more important than the most momentous struggle with barbarians.   This is the real cause of his exaggerated estimate of
the Peloponnesian war—a war which was perhaps of less importance in the world's history than any other struggle of
similar length, for it was not a struggle of either opposed races,
or religions, or great ideas ; and had its issue been reversed,
it would not have materially affected the general course of
human history.   But an exaggerated notion of his subject is
a good fault in an author, and only to be blamed when it
leads him to invidious comparisons with his rivals.   With the
twenty-fourth chapter the real history of the war begins, and in
an excellent narrative he tells us of the quarrel between Corinth
and Corcyra about Epidamnus, followed by other preliminary
movements and the discussion at Sparta.[1]   But before entering
upon the actual war, he again reverts to the past, and resumes
the sketch of Greek history—this time Athenian—from the
capture of Sestos to the outbreak of the war.[2]   There follow

directed, according to Herbst, wholly against the historians of the παλαιά—
poets and poetical logographers—and has nothing to say to Herodotus.
Thucydides then turns (c. 23) to a parallel criticism of the really important
Μηδικά, and though allowing their greatness, nevertheless maintains the
greater importance of his own period, because of the brief crisis of the
Persian war, and because of the lesser number of Greeks engaged.   But
this presupposes that he is comparing the Μηδικά with the whole twenty-
seven years war, and not with the Archidamic alone.   I think this general
sense may be read into the passage, but it is certainly not the obvious
one, and I do not believe that Thucydides intended to avoid censuring
Herodotus' method of writing history, as distinguished from the early
logographers.   Cf. A. Bauer's *Themistocles*, pp. 31, sq., since published
(1881).

   [1] cc. 24-55, 56-88.
   [2] cc. 89-118.   This was known among old critics as the Πεντηκοντε-
τηρία of Thucydides.

additional preliminaries to the war, again interrupted by the episodes of Pausanias and Themistocles ;[1] and the book ends with the completion of the preliminary matter.

§ 366. It is remarkable that in the latter chapters Thucydides not only implies a knowledge of Herodotus, but also some respect for him. He starts his second retrospect from the capture of Sestos, where Herodotus had paused ; he says that while the *Medic* affairs had been fully treated, the succeeding period was neglected, even by Hellanicus, who was inaccurate in his chronology ;[2] he, moreover, in his digressions about Pausanias and Themistocles, expressly fills up the points omitted by Herodotus. This seems to me to denote a difference of date in the composition of the early preface and these later portions of the first book. We see, however, that this book is full of digressions and of prefatory matter, all in the author's opinion strictly necessary to the understanding of the Peloponnesian war. I have also omitted all mention of the speeches—a peculiar and somewhat foreign feature in the history, to which we will revert presently with more detail.

Passing on to the succeeding books, we find in every one of them some brilliant piece of narrative ; indeed, wherever the subject is worthy of the writer, his talent for nervous and spirited description responds fully to the occasion. Thus we have in the second book the night attack upon Platæa (at the opening), then the graphic and affecting account of the plague,[3] which has been the model for so many subsequent writers ; and the naval operations of Phormion off Naupactus.[4] We have in the third book[5] the night escape of the Platæans from their city, which has been reproduced in our own day by Sir E. Creasy in his Attic novel, *The Old Love and the New ;* the terrible tumults at Corcyra, with the historian's reflections,[6] and a very interesting chapter[7] on Delos. The fourth book opens with the brilliant Athenian success at Sphacteria, and contains not only the equally disastrous failure at Delium,[8] but the active operations of Brasidas

---

[1] cc. 128–38.   [2] c. 97.   [3] cc. 47, sq.

[4] cc. 83, sq.   [5] cc. 20, sq.   [6] cc. 75, sq.

[7] c. 104.   [9] cc. 77, sq.

in Thrace, including the historian's own failure to save Amphipolis.[1]

This passage, which is curt and stingy in detail, has given rise to much discussion among critics. Most of the Germans, whose enthusiastic reverence for Thucydides will allow no flaw in his character, maintain that he did all that could be done to save Amphipolis, and that his exile, to which he alludes casually in another place, was an unjust sentence, caused by the disappointment of the Athenians at Brasidas' success. The most prominent supporters of this view are Classen (in his Commentary) and Ernst Curtius (in his History). On the other hand, the reticence of the historian on the date and nature of his appointment to the command, and the unconcealed dislike and contempt he shows for Cleon, who probably caused his exile, have led critical English scholars, such as Mure in his chapter on Thucydides' life, and Grote in his *History*, followed (as usual) by Oncken, to declare that the historian was remiss and dilatory up to the last moment, and probably deserving of his punishment. We have not sufficient evidence to settle the question with any certainty. It seems to me that the historian honestly thought he was not to blame, but that the Athenians, perhaps just as honestly, differed with him in opinion. His silence as to the sentence passed upon him is quite in keeping with his usual reticence on the disappearance of leading men from the scene. Thus he merely tells us that Pericles lived two years into the war ; he only lets out accidentally that Phormion was dead, by stating that the Acarnanians applied for his son to be sent to command them.

§ 367. Returning to our catalogue of remarkable passages, we have the celebrated reflections on the close of the Archidamian war, and the new proem to the rest of the work in the fifth book ;[2] and later on, after the long and complicated intrigues of Alcibiades in the Peloponnesus, the description of the battle of Mantinea, apparently from personal observation.[3] The sixth and seventh books, by far the finest portion of the work, are mainly concerned with the preparation and

[1] cc. 104 6.   [2] c. 26.   [3] cc. 64–75.

outfit of the Sicilian expedition, its interruption by the outrage on the Hermæ, its gradual progress, and disastrous close. Indeed, the sustained splendour of the narrative in the seventh book makes it impossible to specify passages. The eighth book, in which we miss the finishing hand of the author, is mainly interesting for its accurate account of the oligarchical revolution at Athens in 411 B.C., a political crisis so closely connected with the war as to form part of it, and thus fortunately to find its way into the narrative.

But it must be remembered that these remarkable narratives are interrupted both by barren chronicles of petty raids and ineffectual campaigns, which are given in most conscientious detail, and by political speeches inserted at intervals, in order to expound the feelings and passions which formed the atmosphere in which the facts occurred. While the former details arise from a too minute and careful registering of the facts, which Thucydides no doubt overrated in importance, the second are of a very different kind, and are rather violations of, than servile submissions to, historical accuracy. I need only say one word about the former. The various raids about Ætolia and Acarnania, among the Sicilian cities before the arrival of the great Athenian armament, or in the Peloponnesus after the peace of Nicias, though they are of little moment, and are now passed over by most readers, nevertheless serve to give us a very living picture of Greek warfare and of Greek politics, with their perpetually shifting intrigues and varying aspects; and although we should gladly have taken instead a few more of his invaluable digressions on antiquities or on changes of constitution, we must acknowledge that they give his narrative of the war great completeness. There is indeed only a single passage in which he betrays weariness of these trivial movements, and says he will not chronicle them concerning Sicily, except when the Athenians were directly concerned.

§ 368. But wherever the facts become important, his narrative is not content with a mere chronicle, it adds the motives of the actors, and describes their most secret thoughts, as if the historian had been present and had heard them declared. This drawing of human character in accordance with the suggestions of the facts, is particularly remarkable in the 8th book, where there are no set speeches, and is a striking example of the dramatic way in which Greek historians identified themselves with their subject. We moderns make our reflections consciously, and separate them from the narrative. Thucydides seldom does so, but lets his subjective opinions come out in the drawing of character, and the attribution of motives as historical facts. As his basis is strictly the *human*, as opposed to the *divine* so often admitted by Herodotus, these motives are general y verified by the results, and are never improbable, but yet they are not history in our sense.[1] This is far more distinctly the case with the speeches, where he absolutely leaves the domain of sober narrative, and assumes the person of a rhetorician, from which point of view he is justly criticised by all competent and complete historians of Attic eloquence. It is indeed most probably his great example which has led subsequent classical historians to interlard their narrative with imaginary harangues, and which gave to Greek and Roman history that rhetorical flavour noted by Mure as the main defect of Attic prose literature. It is generally admitted that these speeches have no claim to any accuracy; and though most historians long to find at least Pericles' Funeral Speech in the second book authentic, Mure has shown in this particular case how the mannerisms of the historian are specially prominent, and how he uses arguments which could not possibly have been spoken by a Greek political leader who possessed the secret of fascinating his audience.

There is even very little *apparent* effort made to preserve character in these speeches. Thus the Lacedæmonian speakers are as voluble and as lengthy as the rest, and their Doric dialect is exchanged for the old Attic diction of the work. Thucydides himself[2] notes the difficulties of preserving accuracy in these speeches, and says he endeavoured to reproduce the general sense *of what was really spoken*, that is to say, really spoken *in his opinion;* but we may be quite sure that no such speeches could ever have had any effect upon a large audience. Ac-

[1] Cf. the excellent remarks of Herbst, *Philol.* 38, p. 556-9.
[2] i. 22.

cordingly he toned them all to the uniform dress required by
his history as a work of art, and only suggests peculiar features
by the short and rude speech of the ephor Sthenelaidas,[1] or
by the lively style of Athenagoras,[2] or by the egotism of
Alcibiades.　But more frequently they are so general and impersonal as to be ascribed to 'the envoys' or 'the speakers' of
a certain city or policy.　The best analysis of them has been
given by Blass, in the first volume of his work on Attic eloquence, in which he follows closely the well-known criticism
by Dionysius of Halicarnassus.

§ 369. Excluding the dialogues, which we shall consider presently, there are forty-one speeches, of various length, inserted
in the first seven books, the eighth being peculiar in possessing
none.　They may be classed as panegyrical, of which the famous
speech of Pericles[3] is the only specimen, juridical, of which
the demurrer of the Platæans and reply of the Thebans[4] are
specimens, and thirty-eight deliberative harangues.　About
fourteen of these are exhortations to soldiers by their general,
and are mostly short and to the point.　There remain twenty-
four strictly deliberative speeches, inserted generally in pairs
or threes, and sometimes even so constructed that the answer
follows a long time after the first speech, and not professedly in
reply to it.　A careful reading of these speeches will show a
gradual improvement in clearness as the work advances ; those
of the sixth book being much more to the point and freer from
obscurity than the earlier ones, the speeches of Hermocrates
especially being very good specimens of the deliberative style.
It seems indeed not unlikely that Thucydides in his exile made
the acquaintance of the great Syracusan, to whom he is everywhere very favourable, and from whom he may have obtained
the outlines of his policy.　Colonel Mure thinks that the same
sort of relations with Alcibiades, when in exile, are to be inferred from the minuteness with which his secret policy is described.　O. Müller has the same idea about Athenagoras, and
most critics about Pericles and Nicias.　These conjectures only
prove how much character Thucydides has succeeded in in-

---

[1] i. 86.

[2] vi. 36.

[3] ii. 35-46.

[4] iii. 53-9 ; 61-7.

fusing into these speeches, though conceived in his own form and diction.

§ 370. Dionysius, whose judgment as a rhetorician is of value, however modern scholars may despise his notions of composing history, gives us a very complete criticism of many of them, with a full appreciation of the glaring defects which require the genius of the author to palliate them. The chief of these is *obscurity*, which most critics think a natural and unavoidable result of the early and undeveloped condition of Attic prose, combined with the perpetual striving of the author to pack his sentences as full as possible with meaning. Hence even his censors have perpetually admired his marvellous power of conveying substance in the smallest amount of words, and of pressing on the reader a new thought before the former one is fully expressed. Next to this compression and consequent obscurity, the historian has been justly censured for many sophistical *mannerisms*, such as the perpetual antithesis of *nominally* and *really* (λόγῳ and ἔργῳ), which in the Funeral oration occurs sixteen times, and nearly one hundred times in the course of the work. There are also needless definitions of obvious words, and subtle distinctions, not to speak of the affected use of neuter adjectives for nouns—a practice for which his latest German commentator finds reasons which will appear, to such as are not pedants, invented to sustain a bad case.[1]   Colonel Mure and Dr. Blass have also noted curiously inappropriate arguments in some places, where an orator of common sense could not possibly have followed the course assigned to him.   Such are the opening words of Pericles' *Epitaphios*, in which he ascribes a spirit of niggardly detraction to his audience, and the speech of the Corinthians,[2] where the changes and chances of war are insisted upon by those whose object was to urge it, and not to dissuade from it.

To these criticisms, which seem to me well founded, I have two remarks to add.   In the first place, when Classen and others speak of the undeveloped condition of Attic prose, and the difficulties of wrestling with an unformed idiom to express

[1] Cf. Classen, i. p. lxxiii, quoting the authority of Hermogenes.
[2] i. 120.

adequately great and pregnant thoughts, they altogether over-state the matter in their efforts to defend Thucydides. Euripides and Cratinus had already perfected the use of Attic Greek in dramatic dialogue. Again, not only was it quite feasible to transcribe into Attic the excellent models in Ionic prose already subsisting, but in Attic prose Antiphon had already attained clearness, as we can see in his extant speeches. Possibly his example may have aided in making the speech of the Platæans and the Theban answer, which are essentially court speeches, the best in the work. But apart from dramatic poetry and oratory, it seems perpetually forgotten that the tract *on the Athenian polity*, which we have among Xenophon's works, must have been published before 415, and more probably about 428 B.C., and therefore years before Thucydides' history, and that whatever faults the tract may disclose, it shows an easy and complete mastery of the Attic prose idiom.[1]

Secondly, when critics, both ancient and modern, reiterate their praise and wonder at the extraordinary compression of thoughts in these speeches and in the descriptions of the historian, and speak of his hurrying on from new thought to new thought without waiting to express himself clearly, they seem to me to misstate altogether the true nature of his eloquence. I cannot find that there is this crowding of ideas in his orations, but rather a crowding of curious and distorted aphorisms about some leading idea, which is reiterated in all sorts of forms.

The real key to his style is to be found in the characteristic description of his Athenian audience which he puts into the mouth of Cleon.[2] There appears, in fact, as before observed in

---

[1] Dionysius notes the same thing in comparison with the prose of Critias, whom he calls one of the new Attic school, but who wrote before Thucydides.

[2] iii. 38 : αἴτιοι δ' ὑμεῖς κακῶς ἀγωνοθετοῦντες, οἵτινες εἰώθατε θεαταὶ μὲν τῶν λόγων γίγνεσθαι, ἀκροαταὶ δὲ τῶν ἔργων, τὰ μὲν μέλλοντα ἔργα ἀπὸ τῶν εὖ εἰπόντων σκοποῦντες, ὡς δυνατὰ γίγνεσθαι, τὰ δὲ πεπραγμένα ἤδη, οὐ τὸ δρασθὲν πιστότερον ὄψει λαβόντες ἢ τὸ ἀκουσθέν, ἀπὸ τῶν λόγων καλῶς ἐπιτιμησάντων· καὶ μετὰ καινότητος μὲν λόγου ἀπατᾶσθαι ἄριστοι, μετὰ δεδοκιμασμένου δὲ μὴ ξυνέπεσθαι ἐθέλειν, δοῦλοι ὄντες τῶν ἀεὶ ἀτόπων, ὑπερόπται δὲ τῶν εἰωθότων, καὶ μάλιστα μὲν αὐτὸς εἰπεῖν ἕκαστος βουλόμενος δύνασθαι, εἰ δὲ μή, ἀνταγωνιζόμενοι τοῖς τὰ τοιαῦτα λέγουσι, μὴ ὕστεροι ἀκολουθῆσαι

the case of Sophocles (Vol. I. p. 316, § 194), a sort of tendency to play hide-and-seek with the reader, and, while expounding an obvious or familiar idea, to astonish him by the new and strange way in which clause after clause is brought out.

§ 371. In support of this opinion, that Thucydides is only condensed in expression but not in thought, a great number of passages could be cited, but I must content myself with a few. The famous picture of the excitement of the land forces during the last great battle in the harbour of Syracuse [1] may serve as the first. It has elicited the profound admiration of Grote, and the ridicule of Mure for the same reasons. And though we cannot but agree with much of Grote's praise—' the modern historian strives in vain to convey the impression of it which appears in the condensed and burning phrases of Thucydides ' —there is real truth in the words of Mure : ' The specification of the modes in which the assembled crowd displayed its emotions ; of the exact position of the groups of which it consisted ; of the precise amount that each saw and heard, with the vicissitudes of their feelings and gestures, even to the nervous " bobbing " and " ducking " of their heads or bodies in sympathetic response to the critical turns of the combat, are overstated to superfluity or triviality.' He shows too in a note the greater tendency to antithetical jingle of structure and sound in this part of the narrative.

I will next refer to an equally well known passage, both as a good specimen of the style, and as an illustration of my position. It is the account of the Athenian character as contrasted with the Spartan by the Corinthian envoys.[2] Now in this passage,

δοκεῖν τῇ γνώμῃ, ὀξέως δέ τι λέγοντος προεπαινέσαι, καὶ προαισθέσθαι τε πρόθυμοι εἶναι τὰ λεγόμενα, καὶ προνοῆσαι βραδεῖς τὰ ἐξ αὐτῶν ἀποβησόμενα· ζητοῦντές τε ἄλλο τι, ὡς εἰπεῖν, ἢ ἐν οἷς ζῶμεν, φρονοῦντες δὲ οὐδὲ περὶ τῶν παρόντων ἱκανῶς. ἁπλῶς τε, ἀκοῆς ἡδονῇ ἡσσώμενοι, καὶ σοφιστῶν θεαταῖς ἐοικότες καθημένοις μᾶλλον, ἢ περὶ πόλεως βουλευομένοις.

[1] vii. 71.

[2] i. 70 : οἱ μέν γε νεωτεροποιοὶ καὶ ἐπινοῆσαι ὀξεῖς καὶ ἐπιτελέσαι ἔργῳ ἃ ἂν γνῶσιν· ὑμεῖς δὲ τὰ ὑπάρχοντά τε σώζειν καὶ ἐπιγνῶναι μηδέν, καὶ ἔργῳ οὐδὲ τἀναγκαῖα ἐξικέσθαι. αὖθις δὲ οἱ μὲν καὶ παρὰ δύναμιν τολμηταί, καὶ παρὰ γνώμην κινδυνευταί, καὶ ἐν τοῖς δεινοῖς εὐέλπιδες· τὸ δὲ ὑμέτερον τῆς τε δυνάμεως ἐνδεᾶ πρᾶξαι, τῆς τε γνώμης μηδὲ τοῖς βεβαίοις πιστεῦσαι, τῶν

not only is the contrast very much over-strained (instead of being qualified by such cases as those of Nicias and Brasidas), but the whole description plays round the single idea that the Athenians are a very enterprising. and the Spartans a very conservative, society. Again, in the fine speech of the Platæans in defence of their lives, the appeals to the generosity of Sparta are repeated all through the argument till they become wearisome. An endless number of similar instances, and of the repetitions of the same ideas and the same phrases, even in different speeches. indicate, if anything, rather a poverty than a richness of ideas.[1]

The fullest and most suggestive is, perhaps, Pericles' *Epita-phios*, though it too has its reiterated antitheses of *in word* and *in deed;* but even here we may perceive one great reason both of the obscurity and of the constant playing with a few ideas which characterise almost all the harangues. It is the fixed purpose of the historian to make them quite general in application, and hence the careful avoidance of all details and all particulars which give point and flavour to every great speech of every real orator. Thus the allusions of Pericles to the art education and æsthetic pleasures afforded at Athens lose much point by the avoidance of every detail concerning the great artists

---

τε δεινῶν μηδέποτε οἴεσθαι ἀπολυθήσεσθαι. καὶ μὴν καὶ ἄοκνοι πρὸς ὑμᾶς μελλητάς, καὶ ἀποδημηταὶ πρὸς ἐνδημοτάτους. οἴονται γὰρ οἱ μὲν τῇ ἀπουσίᾳ ἄν τι κτᾶσθαι, ὑμεῖς δὲ τῷ ἐπελθεῖν καὶ τὰ ἑτοῖμα ἂν βλάψαι. κρατοῦντές τε τῶν ἐχθρῶν ἐπὶ πλεῖστον ἐξέρχονται, καὶ νικώμενοι ἐπ' ἐλάχιστον ἀναπίπτουσιν. ἔτι δέ, τοῖς μὲν σώμασιν ἀλλοτριωτάτοις ὑπὲρ τῆς πόλεως χρῶνται, τῇ γνώμῃ δὲ οἰκειοτάτῃ ἐς τὸ πράσσειν τι ὑπὲρ αὐτῆς. καὶ ἃ μὲν ἂν ἐπινοήσαντες μὴ ἐξέλθωσιν, οἰκεῖα στέρεσθαι ἡγοῦνται, ἃ δ' ἂν ἐπελθόντες κτήσωνται, ὀλίγα πρὸς τὰ μέλλοντα τυχεῖν πράξαντες, ἢν δ' ἄρα που καὶ πείρᾳ σφαλῶσιν, αντελπίσαντες ἄλλα ἐπλήρωσαν τὴν χρείαν. μόνοι γὰρ ἔχουσί τε καὶ ὁμοίως ἐλπίζουσιν ἃ ἂν ἐπινοήσωσι, διὰ τὸ ταχεῖαν τὴν ἐπιχείρησιν ποιεῖσθαι ὧν ἂν γνῶσι. καὶ ταῦτα μετὰ πόνων πάντα καὶ κινδύνων δι' ὅλου τοῦ αἰῶνος μοχθοῦσι, καὶ ἀπολαύουσιν ἐλάχιστα τῶν ὑπαρχόντων διὰ τὸ ἀεὶ κτᾶσθαι, καὶ μήτε ἑορτὴν ἄλλό τι ἡγεῖσθαι ἢ τὸ τὰ δέοντα πρᾶξαι, ξυμφοράν τε οὐχ ἧσσον ἡσυχίαν ἀπράγμονα, ἢ ἀσχολίαν ἐπίπονον. ὥστε εἴ τις αὐτοὺς ξυνελὼν φαίη πεφυκέναι ἐπὶ τῷ μήτε αὐτοὺς ἔχειν ἡσυχίαν μήτε τοὺς ἄλλους ἀνθρώπους ἐᾶν, ὀρθῶς ἂν εἴποι.

[1] Cf., for example, the latter half of iii. 37, iii. 44, and the appendices to Mure's fifth volume, on the rhetorical mannerisms of Thucydides.

or the great works which were within the sight and in the mind of all his supposed hearers. Indeed, throughout the whole work not a single contemporary artist, or poet, or literary man is mentioned, except Hellanicus, and that for his inaccuracy ; not a single public work or monument, save the Propylæa, and that perhaps because it was a needless expense in the way of mere ornament, without the excuse of religion. But if this adherence to generalities has damaged the rhetorical effect of the speeches, it has made them a better and more enduring monument of the philosophy of history as the author conceived it.

Finally as to the form of the speeches, the rhetorical critics have observed that while there is a general attention paid to the rules prescribed in the early handbooks, while there is generally a fixed exordium, a *prothesis*, a narrative of facts, and a formal conclusion, there is no such slavish adherence to them we should expect rather in professional court-speeches than in the deliberative addresses of political leaders. While figures of *diction*, such as rimed endings, artificial antitheses, and the like, are frequent, figures of *thought*, such as indignant questions, irony, aposiopesis, and the like, are rare, as if beneath the dignity of the historian, and chiefly admitted in the harangue of the demagogue Athenagoras ;[1] whereas even in the speeches of Cleon, whom the author hated and despised, no attempt has been made to portray his vulgarity in his language.

§ 372. Passing to the dialogues, the first to be mentioned, on account of its length and prominence, is the so-called Melian dialogue at the close of the fifth book. The form of this passage is that of a court-speech interrupted by replies to each point, and is an ingeniously constructed method of expounding the brutal policy of the Athenians as expressed in a private conference. Grote has raised special objections to its historical value, and thinks it rather a sort of tragic climax of insolence, intentionally dramatised before the disastrous *peripetia* of the

---

[1] They are, however, much more frequent than is to be inferred from Blass's account, who speaks of Athenagoras' speech as affording the only examples.

Sicilian expedition. While agreeing fully with his objections, I think he need not have contrasted it, as less genuine, with the speeches, many of which rest on just as little evidence, and have just as little internal probability. But in any case the obscurities and outlandish contortions of expression in the discussion have struck all commentators, and elicited from Dionysius special censure. It is properly ranked with the speeches on account of its rhetorical and sophistical tone, and may be regarded as one of the weakest points in the great history. The other two examples, the dialogue of Archidamus with the Plataeans,[1] and that of the Ambraciot herald and the Acarnanian soldiers of Demosthenes,[2] are both admirable, the former being formal and stately, the latter very brief and dramatic ; and it is to be regretted that there are not more such passages in the work.[3] For on the whole this dramatic quality is a feature which we miss in Thucydides, after perusing the more picturesque Herodotus : the genius of the Father of history has not been here equalled by his great Attic rival.

§ 373. The absence of both speeches and dialogues from the eighth book has caused much discussion in ancient and modern times, and is generally considered to be due to the accident of the work being unfinished at the author's death. There are several summaries of opinion throughout the book which would, it is thought, have been expanded and transformed into speeches had he lived to revise and complete it. Cratippus, his contemporary, is reported to have said that Thucydides deliberately omitted them, finding that they did not suit the prevailing taste. But this seems to imply that the earlier books were published by the author himself, unless we interpret Cratippus to mean that Thucydides observed such a change in Attic eloquence with the rise of Lysias that he felt what he had already composed was becoming antiquated. On the other hand, Xenophon, in the first two books of the *Hellenica,* which are a professed continuation of Thucydides, inserts several speeches—a proof

---

[1] ii. 71–4.   [2] iii. 113.

[3] Perhaps i. 53 should be added as another case, but there is here only a single protest and reply.

that he at least did not consider the eighth book showed a
change of style in its author. The later books of the *Hellenica*,
written years subsequently, have no speeches in them, so that
there seems really to have been a change of fashion, but not
in Thucydides' time. There are, moreover, a good many
peculiarities in this book, a good many words not elsewhere
occurring in the history, but common in Xenophon, and a
prominence of personal expressions of opinion, which have been
sufficient to suggest its spuriousness to many ancient critics,
and which have led some moderns to believe that the editor,
probably Xenophon, had some share in reducing it to its present
form. The reader will see most of the peculiar phrases in an
appendix to Mure's fifth volume. I would especially add the
violent sentence about Hyperbolus,[1] which is so different from
what the historian says even about Cleon, and so historically
false and misleading when we consider the real circumstances
(preserved by Plutarch) of Hyperbolus' ostracism, that I wonder
how Grote can quote it in a foot-note[2] without perceiving that
it either overthrows his own theory of ostracism or the trustworthiness of his infallible guide. So also the emphatic com-
mendation of the Athenian Five Thousand[3] seems to me too
personal and explicit for the usual manner of the historian.

The last discussion of this question is in Classen's introduction to the eighth book, in which he of course adopts the
theory most honourable to Thucydides, and most favourable to
the dignity of the text on which he has spent so many years of
his life. He has pointed to the peculiar recension of the text of
this book in the Vatican B, as showing an early feeling that it
had not received the author's final revision, but this recension he
attributes (at earliest) to some Alexandrian grammarian, though
he joins Bekker in accepting it, as approaching what Thucydides would have produced had his labours not been cut short
by death. This may be reasonable enough, but when he goes

---

[1] c. 73 : καὶ Ὑπέρβολόν τέ τινα τῶν Ἀθηναίων, μοχθηρὸν ἄνθρωπον,
ὠστρακισμένον οὐ διὰ δυνάμεως καὶ ἀξιώματος φόβον, ἀλλὰ διὰ πονηρίαν καὶ
αἰσχύνην τῆς πόλεως, ἀποκτείνουσι μετὰ Χαρμίνου (a strategus).

[2] vii. 145.   [3] c. 97.

on to argue (p. x. sq.) that the historian deliberately omitted speeches here, as in a large part of the fifth book (which, by the way, also shows want of a final revision), he will not carry conviction to any unprejudiced mind. It is all very well to say that the political movements were too fleeting and intricate for set declarations, but surely nowhere in the work can we see better scope for a great harangue than in the stirring events at Samos (c. 76), where the fleet became in fact the Athenian democracy. Classen thinks that Thucydides only inserted speeches where they had really been made. I do not agree with him that Thucydides was restrained by any such considerations, but even taking up Classen's ground, does he imagine that the events both at Samos and at Athens were carried out without both vigorous and plausible speeches at every meeting? But there is endless room for this not very profitable subjective criticism.[1]

Mr. Jowett's Translation and notes to Thucydides have now supplied the English reader with a fine edition of this great author. Unfortunately, that part of the work which would have been of inestimable service in the literary estimate of the man is for the present delayed. But it is clear from the tone of the Preface and Commentary that Mr. Jowett's forthcoming Essays will be far more conservative than the general review in this volume, and that they will present to the reader in the best and most attractive form that account of Thucydides which refuses to adopt the newer German *Quellenkritik* altogether. This already appears in the case of Antiochus of Syracuse, who is the only earlier writer on Sicilian antiquities known to have discussed the foundations of the various towns, and whom it is almost certain that Thucydides, if he consulted any authorities at all, must have consulted. There seem to be even traces of Ionic diction, possibly transferred from Antiochus by Thucydides. If Mr. Jowett is not convinced that Antiochus was an authority used by Thucydides, still

---

[1] Cf. another ingenious attempt by Cwilinski in *Hermes*, xii. pp. 23–87.

less will he accept the arguments of Adolf Schmidt (*das peri-kleische Zeitalter*), that the estimate of Themistocles, and many other points, were borrowed from Stesimbrotus, or those of Müller-Strübing, on the deliberate omissions of important facts in the History. The *Thukydideische Forschungen* of the latter contain some acute essays on deep and ancient corruptions of the text, recently reinforced by Mr. Rutherford's researches.[1]

It is very common to allege that, because Thucydides was dependent on his own enquiry for his account of contemporary affairs, and because he is silent about his authorities, that in his digressions on past history he trusted altogether to tradition and his own sagacity. Mr. Jowett, for example (Preface, p. xvi), quite underestimates the amount of obligation he owed to previous writers. He certainly knew Herodotus' history ; he can hardly have avoided Antiochus' archæology in speaking of what happened centuries before his day in a country not known to him as Athens was : it is equally probable that he had before him Stesimbrotus' memoirs of Themistocles. To assume that he did not use these authorities is to assume a great improbability, and indeed to lower his authority as a historian of past generations.

Similarly, the excuse for his obscurity, that Attic prose style was as yet unformed, is met by the answer that Antiphon, Lysias, Critias, and the author of the Tract on the Athenian State, do not show this feature. To admit both charge and excuse together, as Mr. Jowett does (Preface, p. xv), is surely to halt between two opinions. If any writer be great enough to have his faults freely admitted, it is Thucydides. But it is surely uncritical praise to say that we have no right to borrow lights on this period from later and inferior writers, because he 'stands alone among the historians, not only of Hellas, but of the world, in his impartiality and love of truth.' The means of proving such a statement do not exist, as he is our sole authority for most of what he tells. If we had good contemporary evidence to control him, I venture to say his standard of impartiality and truth,

---

[1] Cf. his ed. of the 4th book (Macmillan, 1890).

though very high for his day and his nation, would not
stand one moment's comparison with such a history as Thirl-
wall's.   But it is the undying reward of his literary genius
to produce this strong confidence in his readers.   This is
the *Thukydidescultus* of which Adolf Schmidt speaks with impatience, but which we should rather respect and reckon
with as a natural consequence of the writer's isolation and
greatness.

§ 374. It remains for us to gather up the details, and to form
some general estimate of the genius and character of the great
historian.   Whatever faults of style, whatever transient fashion
of involving his thoughts, may be due to a sophistic education,
and to the desire of exhibiting depth and acuteness, there cannot be the smallest doubt that in the hands of Thucydides the
art of writing history made an extraordinary stride, and attained
a perfection which no subsequent Hellenic, and few modern
writers, have attained.   If the subject which he selected was
really a narrow one, and many of the details trivial, it was
nevertheless compassed with extreme difficulty, for it is at all
times a hard task to write contemporary history, and more
especially so in an age when published documents were scarce,
and the art of printing unknown.   Moreover, however trivial
may be the details of petty military raids, of which an account
was yet necessary to the completeness of his record, we cannot
but wonder at the lofty dignity with which he has handled
every part of the subject.   There is not a touch of comedy,
not a point of satire, not a word of familiarity throughout
the whole book, and we stand face to face with a man who
strikes us as strangely un-Attic in his solemn and severe
temper.

This dignity was, perhaps, even more strongly shown by his
reticence on topics which excited the interest, and filled the
thoughts, of ordinary men.   We can hardly think that he despised the great artistic and literary life at Athens, which was so
dear to his ideal hero, Pericles ; yet, as already remarked, he
never turns aside, except in a passing clause, to mention it, or to
notice any of the great rival intellects which were fascinating the

Athenian public of the day. It would have been strictly to the point, when he insists upon the elastic and irrepressible hopefulness and energy of Athens, which astonished all her enemies, to have noticed that even during the invasions of the land, and the long dolours of siege and of sickness, not only did Sophocles, Euripides, and their many tragic rivals continue to hold the attention and the interest of the Attic public, but even the buffoonery and broad farce of the Old Comedy found in war and distress a subject for fun and banter, and a people ready to enjoy and delight in it. All this would have enhanced his argument, but he merely mentions this side of Athens in passing, and by the mouth of Pericles, who probably made a far different use of so great and fruitful a topic.

§ 375. Far more distinct and unmistakeable is his contempt for the social gossip and scandal of the day, which encompassed the two prominent Athenians of the period—Pericles and Alcibiades—with a perfect cloud of anecdote. The older comedians —we hear the echo of it in Plutarch and Athenæus—were aristocratic and conservative, and never ceased attacking in Pericles his policy, and his private life. The attacks on Alcibiades, who seems to have either bullied or cajoled the comic writers, still remain to us in the form of orations which are very libellous accounts of his private life, but are corroborated by the allusions of Thucydides and other good authority. The later aristocratic thinkers also were adverse to Pericles' policy, and it seems to me as if Thucydides, in composing his history, had among other objects this in view, that he should vindicate from these objections the statesman whom he regards as the ideal leader of Athens. But concerning the private scandals told about the life of Pericles, concerning the very existence of Aspasia, concerning the heresies of Damon and Anaxagoras, and their persecution as Pericleans, on all these topics he is contemptuously, perhaps indignantly, silent. Indeed, as regards women, he seems to have summed up his views in a single sentence at the close of Pericles' speech, when he said that 'she was best who is least spoken of among men, whether for good or for evil.' It is not unlikely, indeed, that a conscious antagonism to Herodotus led him to a faulty reserve in this respect, and we cannot but regard it as a defect of over-dignity, when he leaves us to discover from a late epigram of Agathias, that a jury of the same Athenian assembly which condemned the whole population of Mitylene to death, forced Paches to suicide for violating the honour of two of the women who had been condemned to slavery by the same decree.   It is not, indeed, his habit to allude to the death of any leading men unless it took place in battle, but it was here the duty of an impartial observer, who disliked the democracy, and often records things against it, to mention the example of a just and upright feeling.[1]   It has been very common to praise Thucydides for the wonderful impartiality of his statements ; it is not at all so certain that he was strictly impartial in his reticence.   This question has been discussed with great ingenuity by M. Müller-Strübing in his works on Aristophanes and Thucydides, and he has made out a case against the historian or against the purity of our text.[2]

§ 376. Parallel to this dignity of reticence on social matters and on political scandal, is the historian's neglect of religious matters, and his somewhat contemptuous allusions to oracles and other manifestations of Providence.   This may be referred to the strictly modern character of his history, in which it differs strongly not only from that of Herodotus, but from the subsequent histories of Xenophon and others who relapsed into a religious attitude.   The age and society in which Thucydides grew up were probably the most sceptical in all Greek history ; it was a period like the close of the eighteenth century in France, from

[1] I am bound to add that Mr. Bury has since led me to doubt the whole story in Agathias as a late invention.

[2] The arrogance of this author, who professes to have learned political insight by long residence in England, but who is certainly in every other respect un-English enough, has elicited from Classen a vigorous reply, as regards Thucydides, in the Introduction to his Commentary on the fifth book. But to attack Thucydides is such high treason with Classen, that even the strongest arguments of this kind could have no effect upon him. Nevertheless his rejoinder, though short, is valuable, though Mr. Strübing has shown many fresh reasons for his views in his *Thuk. Forschungen* (Vienna, 1881).

which society afterwards recoiled, and returned to the more
natural condition of either belief or acquiescence in the national
faith.   But Thucydides will only admit religion where the fears
or the hopes it raises become moving springs of human action ;
there is no trace in his work of any positive faith, no hint of
ruling power in the world beyond that of human intellect.
Appeals to Divine aid are only the appeals of the weaker side,
who have no solid argument at their back, and are contemptuously set aside as idle by those who insist on the motives of
self-preservation and of self-interest as the real guiding principles of society.   He uses indeed frequently the term ἀρετή
apparently for a moral quality in men, or at least for that
generosity and unselfishness [1] which obtain a good report in
society, sometimes perhaps for that reputation itself.   But
when he applies it to a deliberate political assassin—Antiphon
—we feel that he must have meant it in some widely different
sense from its later use, and that even this word must be applied
in an intellectual way, and mean generally ability or reputation.
Of course no man has ever been able to banish the notions of
right and wrong from his language or his thoughts, and perhaps
it fared with ἀρετή [2] as with the terms ἀγαθός and κακός, which
Mr. Grote asserts to have had at first a political meaning
only, whereas the moral meaning is really the ground of their
application in politics.   However this may be, it is more than
likely that with the belief in the religion of his day, and the
belief in rewards and punishments from on high, Thucydides
abandoned the belief in the intrinsic worth of moral excellence,
and that he especially points to the fate of Nicias to show that
these qualities availed nothing when combined with want of
vigour and ability.   Hence the clearness with which he ana-
lyses motives and explains policy from the single ground of
selfishness and a regard to material interests.   It was left
indeed for Classen, his latest commentator, to discover in
Thucydides a hidden wealth of piety and virtue, which leads

[1] Cf. the list of passages given in Classen, i. p. lxvii.

[2] It is specially noted by Suidas that Thucydides and Andocides used
ἀρετή in the sense of εὐδοκία, and this seems to me true in several places
throughout both authors.

him to set forth the evil results of passion and selfishness, and
to show the fatal consequences of impiety and neglect of the
gods. There is no use in arguing the point with a man who
after long and laborious study, perhaps owing to this study,
adopts such views. But it is one more instance of the simplicity
of mind and partial appreciation of evidence for which the
Germans are no less remarkable than for their industry and
their enthusiasm. I trust that in refuting this undue glorifying
of a favourite author, I have not detracted aught from the great
and enduring merits of the historian who has taught us to know
more of Greek interpolitical life than all other Greek authors
put together. In acuteness of observation, in intellectual force
and breadth, in calmness of judgment, in dignity of language,
there has never been a historian greater than Thucydides.

§ 377. As regards the historian's trustworthiness, it has been
so universally lauded that it is high time to inquire how far his
statements are to be accepted as absolute truth. We may be
confident, I think, that on contemporary facts his authority is
very good, and so far there has been no proof of any inaccuracy brought home to him. The discovery three years ago of
the original text of the treaty, which he reproduces in v. 47,
has indeed shown that our MSS. differ considerably from the
actual wording of the original. I agree with Classen that these
variations were probably due to an originally inaccurate transcription, and not with Kirchhoff, that they prove a great corruption of our texts. But what is more important for us to
note is this, that the variations, though many (thirty-one in all),
are very trifling, and do not in a single case alter the sense.
This is the outcome of Kirchhoff's careful discussion in the
twelfth volume of *Hermes*.[1] So far then the authority of

---

[1] This is not Kirchhoff's opinion. He cannot believe for one moment
that such a man as Thucydides would make or insert in his work a
'slovenly copy' of a document. I think that is exactly the difference between the most accurate of ancient historians and the moderns. Thucydides, whose speeches were no doubt very wide of the mark, and represented very vaguely what the various orators really said, was not in my
mind the least disposed to quarrel about trifling details in the transcription
of any document, and I think we are very fortunate to find it done as accurately as it has been done. Cf. the later article of Kirchhoff on the
documents used by Thucydides in *Sitzbcr. Berlin Acad.* xxxiv. p. 829, sq.

Thucydides is unassailed.   But when he goes into archæology,
the case is very different.   His admirers have not indeed ventured to establish the reality of the Trojan war on his authority,
but they all assume that his Sicilian history is as accurate as
his history of the war in his own day, though it reaches back
300 years, nay even to 300 years 'before the advent of the
Greeks.'   It is only lately that his sources for this early history
have been examined, and it appears that he copied from
Antiochus of Syracuse, a λογοτοιος of the stamp of the forerunners of Herodotus.   Hence in this portion of his work he
has really no more authority than Antiochus, and the whole
tradition requires careful reconsideration.   But this would lead
us too far from our subject, and I will refer the reader to the
second appendix of my first volume, where I have discussed it
in relation to the knowledge of western geography shown in the
Odyssey of Homer.

§ 378.   Turning to the external history of the text, we find
that though it is not mentioned by any of the writers of the succeeding generation, it must have at once attained a high reputation, for several historians—Xenophon, Cratippus and Theo-
pompus—set themselves to continue or complete it, without
venturing to handle over again the epoch treated by the master
hand.   The later encyclopædists of Greek history refer to
him as the best authority.   In Roman times we know from the
manifest imitations of Sallust, from the praise of Cicero and of
Quintilian, that they admired the man, and were offended at his
obscurities, just as we are.[1]   But the Alexandrine critics had
declared him the highest model of the older Attic dialect, and
commented copiously on his text.   So also the schools of rhetoric established at Rome turned their attention to him ; and we
have already frequently made mention of the judgments of
Dionysius of Halicarnassus, whose remarks upon our author
are full of acuteness, and often very just, though he judges altogether from a rhetorical point of view, and therefore fails to
comprehend the higher merits of Thucydides as the first philosopher in historiography.

§ 379.   *Bibliographical.*   The body of scholia which we pos-

[1] Plutarch, *De Gloria Ath.*, is full and appreciative on his merits.

sess, and which, in contrast to those on Herodotus, are often
very full, seem to be derived from a variety of commentaries
(ἐξηγήσεις) by Asclepius, Antillus, Evagoras, Phœbammon,
Sabinus and Didymus, most of them of unknown date, but
some very old and of value. From these we have excerpts of
various value, and often contradictory, so that the study of them
is one of difficulty. They are to be found in most of the MSS.,
which are many, and by no means of ascertained value, Poppo,
Bekker, and Arnold differing broadly as to their relative importance. Nor do the MSS. seem all as yet collated, and we may
expect new results from a critical appendix to Classen's edition, which would form the proper conclusion to the work. Thus
Haase (in the Didot ed. 1842) says that a twelfth century copy
with good scholia had just been acquired at Paris, but too late
for his edition. There is preserved at Monte Cassino a fine
and early MS., which I cannot find mentioned in any of our
editions. So far as I can make out, a Laurentian codex (69, 2)
is the earliest, but the Vaticanus (B) is the best. A lost ' Italus '
(Bekker's A), a Cassel MS., an Augsburg (Augustanus), now in
Munich, and a Clarendonius at Cambridge, are all about the
twelfth century in age, and all of value for the recension of the
text. The Vatican (B) is peculiarly valuable for its recension
of the eighth book, in which it constantly differs from the other
copies, but whether these variations are early and clever
emendations, or due to an originally purer text, is difficult to
determine. The former is the opinion of Classen, and the
German critics generally. Hence Schöne still proposes to
make the Laurentian (C) the basis of the text, but Classen
prefers the Vatican recension.

The editions are very numerous. The *princeps* is that of
Aldus (1502), then there is a Juntine with scholia (1526), but
they had already been printed with Xenophon by Aldus in
1503. The edition of Stephanus (1564, and often reprinted)
gives the scholia round the text, and Valla's early translation.
Hudson's folio of 1696 (Oxford) is a handsome book. Then
we have Duker, Poppo, Göller, Haack, and in our own time
Bekker, Arnold, Haase, Krüger, G. Boehme, and Stahl (re-ed.
Poppo). The most recent commentary is that of Classen, a
careful and scholarly work, but sadly in want of an index and

of a critical preface on the MSS. and older editions.   Messrs. Bigg and Simcox have given us four books, Shilleto a learned edition of two.   The recent edition of Book IV. by Mr. G. Rutherford (Macmillan, 1890) opens up a new line in criticism, and shows great corruption in the text.

The translations of Thucydides are in themselves a curious study.   The earliest Latin version was that of Valla (1485), corrected by Portus (1594), then Casa (Florence, 1564), and Baron Hoheneck (1614).   There are two very early English renderings, that of Nicholls, ' citizen and goldsmith of London,' in the fourth year of Edward VI. (1550, who mentions the older French edition of Claude de Seysell, Archbishop of Turin), and that of Thomas Hobbes, about 1670.   We have since, Smith (1753), Bloomfield (1829), Dale (ed. Bohn, 1848), Crawley (1874), and also the speeches done separately by Wilkins.   All are now eclipsed by Mr. Jowett's Translation and notes (2nd ed. Oxford, 1881).   There are Italian versions by Cellario (Verona, 1735), and Strozzi (Venice, 1735), who calls the book, as might be expected at Venice in those days, ' the war of the peoples of the Morea with the Athenians.'   The German version by Boehme, and the French by Bétant and by Zévort, are in good repute.   The Lexicon of Thucydides (London, 1824) seems to me of little value,[1] and that of Bétant is out of print (Geneva, 1843-57).

§ 380.   It seems fitting to close the splendid epoch of Attic literature which has so long occupied us with two very distinct and characteristic names—one of whom sums up in his single person almost all the literary tendencies of his age, but was too strong and ambitious in character to rest content with such glory, and who accordingly lived and died in the violent conflicts of party politics the notorious Critias.   The second, Andocides, was involved in public affairs from apparently the very opposite cause, a certain weakness and instability of character which would not let him rest content with an ancient name and an ample fortune, but which involved him in troubles and wanderings, and in the bad repute of being an uncer-

---

[1] The review of Thucydidean literature up to 1887 in Bursian's *Jahresbericht* (vol. lviii. pp. 65 sq.) by Franz Müller gives all the recent literature.

tain friend and, under pressure, a betrayer of his party. But in another way he shows the results of Attic culture in that he attained, under these circumstances, a place in the Attic Ten who were models for subsequent eloquence, and that although, like Critias, he was thought an amateur by professionals, he was quite a first-rate professional among amateurs. The life of Critias ends with the second restoration of the democracy, as that of Antiphon with the first, but, as beseemed his more violent character, on the field of battle, and not by the verdict of the court. Andocides, whose activity and whose eloquence are concerned with the same period, prolonged an inglorious life after the Restoration. But he is in no sense a connecting link between the old and the new. He was not, like Thrasymachus, a stepping-stone beyond Antiphon leading to Lysias. He was rather a weak echo of the school of Antiphon, modified by the subjects which he treated, or perhaps owing to these subjects, different from Antiphon, and interesting as the earliest specimen we have, along with Thucydides, of the deliberative as contrasted with judicial style of Attic eloquence.

But we must first gather the facts known to us concerning the life of Andocides. In this case we are not in want of full information, at least on the important moments of his career, but unfortunately our information is untrustworthy from the fact of its being conveyed either in the bitter attack preserved among the speeches of Lysias, or the impassioned defence of his character by the orator himself. On both sides we can even now detect exaggerations and inaccuracies, so that it is not easy to say how far the rest may not be equally vague or misleading. Thucydides, for example, will not assert many things which Andocides claims to have been clearly proved. The following sketch has accordingly been compiled by modern historians from the somewhat conflicting evidence of lying or at least prejudiced witnesses.

§ 381. ANDOCIDES was an aristocrat of ancient family, deduced by the genealogist Hellanicus from the god Hermes through Odysseus, which belonged to the Kydathenæan deme, and the tribe Pandionis. The orator asserts that his great-grandfather Leogoras commanded an attack upon the Peisistratids, which we find it hard to verify.   This man's son (the elder) Andocides was employed as strategus with Pericles and Sophocles against Samos, also at Korkyra, and in the negotiations for the thirty years' peace previous to this time.   These facts are corroborated by Thucydides.[1]   The elder Andocides' son was Leogoras (the younger), a man of luxurious and hospitable habits, who begat the orator, and a daughter, married to Callias, the son of Telekles.   Thus the boast of the orator that his family had been celebrated both in war and peace, and was well known and respected at Athens, is fairly justified.

The pseudo-Lysian attack upon him, which seems a genuine speech delivered in 399 B.C., states that, though some forty years old, he had never done any public state-service.   This assertion, while attributing to him a character inherited from his father rather than his remoter ancestors, contradicts the date of his birth (467 B.C.) given in the Greek *Life*, which is a most untrustworthy compilation, and probably confounds the elder and younger Andocides.   The orator seems rather to have been born about 440 B.C.   We know nothing of his training, but can hardly conceive him not to have profited by the teaching of Antiphon, then the foremost sophist of the day, and, moreover, of known aristocratic sentiments.   Having joined the political club of Euphiletus, he became involved in the affair of the Hermæ, and hence in various troubles, which lasted most of his life.   The details of the affair belong rather to Greek history than to literature.   It is certain that after several inferior persons — slaves and metics— had informed, a certain Diokleides informed against the family and friends of Andocides, who were all thrown into prison, and were in the utmost danger of immediate execution.   Under these circumstances, Andocides, pressed by his relatives, and under promise of a free pardon gave such informations as satisfied the public and restored public confidence.[2]   Our authorities vary widely as to how many they embraced, and what credit they deserved.   His opponents said he accused his own father and himself.   The orator asserts that this is false, and that he only added four names to those already implicated, and these he specifies.

---

[1] i. 51.   [2] Cf. the quotation below.

He confessed to have known of the plot, but to have opposed it, and so accounted for the escape of the Hermes before his own door, which Euphiletus had given the conspirators to understand would be mutilated by Andocides, while he was in bed with a broken collar-bone, both unable to stir and opposed to the conspiracy when he first heard it broached. Thucydides says[1] that the real truth was never ascertained, but, as many commentators observe, he wrote before the speeches of Andocides could have been known to him, and may thus have been less well informed than we are. Of course this informing made the orator an object of hatred to his companions, and presently, by a decree of Isotimides, entry into the agora and temples was forbidden to those who had committed sacrilege, even though freed from penalties in consequence of the Hermæ affair.

It is plain that as soon as the high premium for informing about this matter was offered, a perfectly distinct set of informations was given concerning the violation of the Eleusinian mysteries, and in these Alcibiades was involved, when his enemies failed to connect him by any evidence whatever with the mutilation of the Hermæ. The two charges were accordingly intentionally confused, and the man who had escaped the one was implicated in the other. Thus Andocides, who merely confessed some knowledge of the latter, was assumed by his adversaries to have admitted guilt concerning the former. This he steadily denies; but the decree of Isotimides compelled him to leave Athens and wander abroad, where he made his living by mercantile speculations. His adversaries told ugly stories of his dangers and adventures in Cyprus. Then he brought various supplies to the Athenian army at Samos in 412 B.C., in the hope of working out his return by conferring solid benefits upon his countrymen, but upon venturing to Athens he was seized by the Government of the Four Hundred, and only escaped death by their fall. So he returned to Cyprus, where he is said to have been again imprisoned by Euagoras, and having managed the despatch of a corn fleet for Athens, returned about 409 B.C., when he delivered the extant speech

[1] vi. 60.

concerning his return.   But failing in his object, he again went into exile. and is said by his accuser to have visited almost all Hellenic lands ; he himself confesses that he made friendships with various kings and strangers, and probably acquired by trade a considerable fortune. After the capture of Athens by Lysander, he returned with the other exiles about 402 B.C., and found his paternal property gone, and his house, after his father's death, occupied by the demagogue Cleophon, though now probably empty. He then began his career as a rich citizen, performing public duties, of which a tripod commemorating a victory with a cyclic chorus was long extant. But after three years he was attacked by the demagogue Kephisius for his old complicity with the profanation of the Mysteries. The pseudo-Lysian speech against him seems to have been delivered by one of Kephisius' fellow accusers, Miletus or Epichares. Being supported by the respected democrats Anytus and Kephalus, Andocides gained the cause.

Once more he appears on the political scene. The speech *concerning the peace,* if genuine, asserts that during the Corinthian war, he was sent with full powers to treat for peace with Sparta. He brought back terms, and an embassy of Spartans, and pressed on the people the arrangement he had negotiated, but in vain. The *Life* says he was again banished in consequence of his failure (about 391 B.C.) ; but the whole story of these negotiations, on which Xenophon and Diodorus are silent, is very doubtful. Blass believes it because Philochorus is cited in the argument of the speech as asserting the fruitless visit of a Spartan embassy at this time. Of Andocides' death or of his posterity we hear nothing. Thus this lengthy summary of the facts of the orator's life shows him to have been an aristocrat who moved in political circles, and spoke either on public or on personal matters, but did not compose speeches for others or teach the art of rhetoric as a professional.

§ 382. The extant speeches and fragments of Andocides can be classified chronologically with tolerable certainty, and fall into the following order : (1) the fragment πρὸς τοὺς ἑταίρους, before 415 B.C., and with it, perhaps identical, is the συμβουλευτικός, from which we have two fragments ; (2) the speech *on his*

Return, sometimes called περὶ τῆς ἀδείας, 409 B.C. ; (3) *on the Mysteries*, also called περὶ τῆς ἐνδείξεως, 399 B.C. ; (4) *concerning the peace with the Lacedæmonians*, 390 B.C.   The attack on Alcibiades, though handed down as Andocidean, and spoken in the person of Phæax, is now generally believed to be the composition of a later sophist, as shown both by his ignorance of history and his polished style.   It is hardly necessary to analyse these speeches individually, as they are not very important specimens of Greek oratory, and their loose and disconnected structure makes a brief abstract impossible.

If we take up the speech *on the Mysteries*, which is far the longest and the most characteristic, we can frame from it a perfectly adequate idea of his style, which in the other orations is less marked and striking, though of the same complexion.   He opens with a proem, which reappears in the nineteenth oration of Lysias, and which both orators seem to have adopted from some collection of commonplaces by an earlier sophist.   But when we compare both versions, we find that Andocides inserts matter of his own, and reverts again to his model, whereas Lysias seems to have used it with hardly any modification.   In Blass' text (Teubner, 1871) the quotations from the proem are printed in special type, so that the reader can easily see the use made of it by our orator.   He then proceeds, after expressing a doubt what line he will follow, to a long narrative of his share in the affair of the Hermæ, and the various informations tendered concerning it.   He shows that his informing only touched the Hermokopidæ, and had nothing to say to the profanation of the Mysteries, with which he was now charged.   The whole narrative is very lively and picturesque, and full of a natural charm rarely to be found amid the artifices of Greek orators.   The scene in the prison (§ 48) is very pathetic, and worthy of special note.[1]   He is at

---

[1] ἐπειδὴ δὲ ἐδεδέμεθα πάντες ἐν τῷ αὐτῷ καὶ νύξ τε ἦν καὶ τὸ δεσμωτήριον συνεκέκλειστο, ἧκον δὲ τῷ μὲν μήτηρ τῷ δὲ ἀδελφὴ τῷ δὲ γυνὴ καὶ παῖδες, ἦν δὲ βοὴ καὶ οἶκτος κλαιόντων καὶ ὀδυρομένων τὰ παρόντα κακά, λέγει πρός με Χαρμίδης, ὢν μὲν ἀνεψιός, ἡλικιώτης δὲ καὶ συνεκτραφεὶς τῇ οἰκίᾳ τῇ ἡμετέρᾳ ἐκ παιδός, ὅτι ᾿Ανδοκίδη, τῶν μὲν παρόντων κακῶν ὁρᾶς τὸ μέγεθος, ἐγὼ δ᾽ ἐν μὲν παρελθόντι χρόνῳ οὐδὲν ἐδεόμην λέγειν οὐδέ σε λυπεῖν,

great pains to contradict the charge that he confessed any personal guilt, or brought any charges whatever against his father and relations, whom he claims, on the contrary, to have saved from an unjust sentence. The legal portions of the speech, in which he discusses the various kinds of ἀτιμία, and the subsequent restoration not merely of ἄτιμοι, but of exiles, are not so clear, and evidently not so much to the taste of the speaker. But when he reverts again to personal matters, and attacks the motives and private character of his accusers, especially Callias, son of Hipponicus, he becomes very lively and striking. A very full and accurate analysis of this and the other orations is given by Blass.[1]

§ 383. The criticisms upon his style are, however, all based on the formal and technical ideas of the rhetoricians, and seem to me to do little justice to the orator. They call him simple, unadorned, irregular, and wanting in method and vigour. They notice that his periods run frequently into abnormal constructions, and end in anacolutha. They mark his frequent digressions, and the want of due proportion in the parts of his speeches. They complain that, although he generally uses the language of common life, and is even vulgar and comic in his pictures, he nevertheless often employs poetical idioms, which violate the strict notions of Attic prose. But if we remember that his speeches must have been published, not as models of style, but as pamphlets vindicating the character and policy of the author, who was no rhetor or sophist, but merely a cultivated aristocrat, most of these charges fall to the ground. In fact Andocides stands nearest of all the Attic orators to our modern conception of a public speaker. We do not admire too

νῦν δὲ ἀναγκάζομαι διὰ τὴν παροῦσαν συμφοράν. οἷς γὰρ ἐχρῶ καὶ οἷς συνῆσθα ἄνευ ἡμῶν τῶν συγγενῶν, οὗτοι ἐπὶ ταῖς αἰτίαις δι᾽ ἃς ἡμεῖς ἀπολλύμεθα οἱ μὲν αὐτῶν τεθνᾶσιν οἱ δὲ οἴχονται φεύγοντες, σφῶν αὐτῶν καταγνόντες ἀδικεῖν . . . . εἰ ἤκουσας τι τούτου τοῦ πράγματος, εἰπέ, καὶ πρῶτον μὲν σεαυτὸν σῶσον, εἶτα δὲ τὸν πατέρα, ὃν εἰκός ἐστί σε μάλιστα φιλεῖν, κ. τ. λ. λεγόντων δὲ ὦ ἄνδρες τοῦ Χαρμίδου ταῦτα, ἀντιβολούντων δὲ τῶν ἄλλων καὶ ἱκετευόντων ἑνὸς ἑκάστου, ἐνεθυμήθην πρὸς ἐμαυτόν· ὦ πάντων ἐγὼ δεινοτάτῃ συμφορᾷ περιπεσών, πότερα περιίδω τοὺς ἐμαυτοῦ συγγενεῖς ἀπολλυμένους ἀδίκως, κ. τ. λ.

strict or logical a frame, we like the language of common life, adorned occasionally with flowers of poetic ornament ; we enjoy digressions and personal attacks as giving life and point to political debate. It is moreover confessed that by his dramatic habit of introducing the very words of other speakers, he has attained a very striking amount of *ethos*, in the sense of character-painting, which lends a great additional charm to his narrative. But we can understand how this orator was always despised by the formal and technical writers, to whom we owe all our information on this side of Greek literature. Yet it is hardly creditable to modern critics that they should blindly follow this judgment, and ignore the very interesting and modern features in this remarkable man, who alone represents to us the amateur and non-professional eloquence of the higher classes at Athens.[1]

§ 384. The external history of the text is bound up with that of Antiphon, both authors being handed down to us together, except that the good Oxford MS. (N) omits Andocides. Otherwise what has been said above of the MSS. and the Aldine *princeps* on Antiphon may be consulted. A. G. Bekker has published a translation and commentary on the orator (Quedlinb. 1832). Without producing special editions, Sluiter, Meier, Vater, Kirchhoff, Hirschig and others have elucidated many points in the text.[2] Baiter and Sauppe's, and Blass' are the best texts.

§ 385. Widely different in character from Andocides was his contemporary and relation, CRITIAS, born also of a noble family, which had been known and celebrated as far back as Solon's

---

[1] Perhaps I should add that in the *Phædrus* of Plato, an amateur speech on Eros is composed by way of contrast with the formal *epideixis* which he professes to quote from Lysias. There is, moreover, a long attack on formal rhetoric, and an exposition of the conditions which moderns would think proper for an orator, though the standard of Plato is too high. Possibly the speeches of Phocion, if we had them, were similar protests against artificial rhetoric from the practical side. But the dissent of Socrates and his school, and of such men as Phocion, were ineffectual in stopping the tide of public opinion in favour of professional and technical eloquence.

[2] Cf. Blass's Preface to his Ed. (Teubner), p. vi.

time. Indeed, both Solon and Anacreon celebrated the beauty
of the ancestors of Critias.[1] We hear through Xenophon and
Plato that Critias applied himself much to mental culture, and
attended the teaching of Socrates, but would not be dissuaded
by him from pursuing immoral objects, and hence quarrelled
with the philosopher.[1] Nevertheless it is very remarkable that
a man who made literature only a stepping-stone to political
influence should have attained so high a point in various kinds
of writing.

He may have been born about 450 B.C., but showed little
prominence up to the time of the Four Hundred, of whom
his father Callæschrus was a prominent member. Of course
he was always an oligarch, but he probably spent his earlier
life in study, and did not see a proper scope for his energies.
It is remarkable that he took no strong side with the Four
Hundred, so that he not only remained at Athens, but proposed decrees about the recall of Alcibiades, and the enquiry
into Phrynichus' death, which show a desire to agree with the
democracy. Yet he roused the suspicions of Cleophon, who
had him banished. It was during his exile, in the dissolute
society of Thessalian nobles, that he developed that strong
hatred of the democracy, and that general lawlessness and violence, which make his name a byword among later Athenians.
His career as one of the Thirty, and his death in battle against
Thrasybulus, are matters of notoriety. He was evidently a
man of strong clear head and logical consistency, but probably
a sceptic in morals, and an advocate of the worst theories of
the sophists whom Plato brings up as opponents to Socrates.

Though highly cultivated in music and literature, though a
good artist in various kinds of poetry and prose, he was a ruth-
less and cruel man, upon whose nature the refinement of aristocratic birth and good society had no effect. His political
misdeeds have, however, probably obscured his literary merits ;
for he sums up in himself all the forms and kinds of Attic
literature, and in all of them he attained a certain eminence.
We have spoken above (§ 137) of his poetry, of his elegiacs and
hexameters, which were political and aristocratic in tone, and of

---

[1] Xen. *Memor.* i. 2, §§ 12, sq.

his tragedies (§ 232), which seem to have quite outdone Euripides in preaching scepticism and a contempt for received dogmas. Nevertheless, the frequent attribution of his plays to Euripides shows how high was their poetical merit. In prose he wrote descriptions of the polities of Sparta, Thessaly, and other states; lives of celebrated men, such as Homer and Archilochus; and philosophical discussions, of which Galen quotes one on the nature of love. Hermogenes quotes as to oratory his προοίμια δημηγορικά. His prose works are said to have been the best, but, being long neglected on account of the deep hatred which his life inspired, were first revived and praised by Herodes Atticus, and then criticised next to the Ten by Hermogenes, by Philostratus and others. It excites some surprise that he did not supplant Andocides in the Canon of the Ten orators. Unfortunately we only possess a few trifling fragments of his prose, and need not therefore discuss the judgments of the critics. They praise his taste and purity, and remark that he rather belonged to the new Attic writers, having none of the harshness of Thucydides, who nevertheless survived him. He was subtle and persuasive, but not, say they, fiery or vehement.[1] His political violence was, we may fear, rather the result of deliberate selfishness and cruelty than of wild passion, for even in his poetry this latter quality seems absent, or under strict control. But from his manysidedness, and from his strictly aristocratic tone, he would have been a very good representative of Periclean culture, and of the older bloom of letters at Athens, which passed away or changed with the Restoration.

---

[1] Cf. Philostratus' interesting critique of his style, *Vit. Soph.* p. 213.

CHAPTER VI.

ATTIC LITERATURE OF THE RESTORATION—
LYSIAS AND ISÆUS.

§ 386. FROM this time onwards the aristocrats, as a party, seem to have been absorbed or destroyed, and though Plato shows plainly enough his tendencies, he lives apart from the people, and seldom attempts to influence the politics of his day. Charges of hostility to the demos are indeed still common in the quarrels of the day ; there is hardly a speech on public matters in the collection of Lysias in which it is not urged by the speaker against his adversary, and likewise pressed as a counter-charge. Even Thrasybulus does not escape it. But parties had been so broken up and confused by the disorders of fifteen years ; the adherents of the Four Hundred were so often enemies of those of the Thirty ; so many aristocrats had been exiled as too moderate ; so many time-servers had changed sides, that we cannot show any definite aristocratic party after this date. But it was a time of sad memories and of poignant regrets ; in spite of the amnesty voted, and honestly enough observed by the demos, every private accusation, every charge of peculation or violence, gave occasion for hints of former treason, and for suggestions that the over-indulgence of the state might now be rectified by condign punishment on another score.

§ 387. It is of course not easy to draw lines of distinction in an epoch where a great number of literary men of various kinds were working collaterally, and where no year or decad could be wanting in intellectual work. But yet it seems, by some curious coincidence, that the lives of most of the great older lights of Attic literature closed during the dark troubles towards the end of the Peloponnesian war. Beginning with

Antiphon, we can enumerate Sophocles, Euripides, and Agathon in poetry ; Critias, Socrates, and Thucydides—all of whom died within a few years of the archonship of Eucleides.   It does not appear indeed that among so many authors more than two—Aristophanes and Andocides—of those whom we know, wrote before this crisis, and also after it.   Andocides, as I have explained, is not of much importance.   The later work of Aristophanes is perhaps the strongest evidence we have of the altered tone of literature after the year 399 B.C.   Attic life was no longer the stormy existence of a tyrant demo-cracy, ruling a great dominion, and occupied with imperial interests—a society keen and intellectual, but rude withal, and in some respects coarse and cruel.   The Athens of Isocrates and Plato is a tamer and more refined city, in which for a generation political interests sink into a secondary place, and in which intellectual and moral culture come into the fore-ground.   This is really the time in which the change took place from the Periclean to the Demosthenic citizen.[1]   The Athenians of the Restoration, excluded from empire by the predominance of Sparta, sought material wealth and social refinement ; they paid mercenaries to perform the military duties which had no vital importance in their eyes.   And for awhile all enterprise, even in art, paused.   The glories of Pheidias found no rival till the schools of Scopas and Praxiteles, a generation later, re-kindled the torch.   Attic poetry decayed, and never recovered. The New Comedy gained its greatness at the expense of all the higher flights of fancy, and cannot rank higher than the genteel comedy of Sheridan.

It cannot, however, be held that the years immediately following Eucleides were merely days of rest and weari-ness, for, as if to mark the epoch of the Restoration, several eminent men, who attained maturity some years before, now enter the field of literature, and perfect the development of Attic prose.   Of these four stand pre-eminent above the rest—Lysias, Isocrates, Plato, and Xenophon.   These men, historians, pamphleteers, philosophers, court advocates, occupy the field till circumstances again brought Athens into the

---

[1] Grote's *Hist.*, vol. xi. p. 390, and my *Social Life in Greece*, p. 269.

position of asserting Hellenic interests against foreign do-
mination ; then political oratory revives with Demosthenes
and his compeers. The lighter literature of the epoch—the
many anecdotists whom later compilers quote, the Middle
Comedy, which gave a picture of the society of the day, are
unfortunately lost, and though fragments of comedies survive
in hundreds, we can form no adequate notion of the merits of
even Antiphanes and Alexis. The dramatic side of Plato and
of Xenophon only gives us a glimpse into aristocratic life, a few
realistic pictures in Lysias' speeches show an ugly counterpart
in the poorer ranks. But if the social aspects of Athens are in
this period but partially preserved, her intellectual development
stands before us in a very clear and instructive way, for we
have ample specimens of the style—the way of thinking—of all
the great prose writers of the age.

§ 388. We will commence with LYSIAS, the oldest of
them, whose technical education must have been completed
in the earlier epoch, but whose literary activity, though late
in development, starts with peculiar freshness and vigour
at the very opening of the Restoration. With him, moreover,
we enter upon a new phase of oratory, and that which is
the most characteristic of old Greek thought and culture. I
have sketched in the last page the general condition of Attic
society after the return of Thrasybulus, how external peace
and an enforced amnesty left many private feuds, and em-
bittered many new disputes. I may add that the Athenians,
who had no longer a great empire to control, turned to a
closer scrutiny of domestic affairs and of home finance. The
state was now poor, and the citizens unable to bear heavy
taxation ; it is not unlikely that many men of doubtful character, who had made money abroad, came to Athens, and
were allowed to obtain or regain civic rights (like Andocides),
because they would undertake liturgies and other expensive
state burdens. On the other hand, there were constant com-
plaints of peculation and waste among public servants—one
man is charged with embezzling the revenues in the administration of foreign affairs, another is capitally accused for
squandering the public chest in adding to the public sacrifices

by false statutes, and thrusting upon the state religious burdens too great for it to bear. Thus this period of external quiet at Athens was prominently an age of litigation. It was not unlike the crisis at Syracuse which was said to have produced the earliest masters of rhetoric, Corax and Tisias.

But at Athens Antiphon had already domesticated the art. We can therefore expect only a new development with the rise of more favourable conditions. This new development is distinctly and prominently set before us in the oratory of Lysias. Let it be remembered that the Athenian theory of public life and of citizen duties required every man to appear personally and transact his own business; as the assembly must not be made up of elected representatives, but of the free citizens in person, so in the law courts it was abhorrent to Athenian notions of the personal dignity and importance of citizenship that any man should hand over his affairs to a pro-fessional advocate, and sit by as a mute. Far less would any Athenian judge have ventured to insult or perplex the litigant who endeavoured to plead his own cause, and escape from the heavy expense of employing a professional pleader. All this trade union feeling which marks the judges and the bar of modern days was unknown at Athens. There was rather an opposite feeling in the Attic courts. The jury suspected and feared the devices of an art which professed openly to confuse the right and the wrong, and to give the victory to the worse over the better cause. As it was nevertheless inevitable that feeble or inexperienced litigants should seek the assistance of those who made the law their study, we find the profession of paid advocate, or professional speech-writer, in this curious phase at Athens, that the orator must conceal himself, that he must assume not only the *person* but *character* of his litigant, and avoid all that the jury might suspect as too perfect for an average citizen.

Thus the *logographer* of the Restoration was strictly a dramatic author,[1] differing from the poet in this, that while his plot was given him by the case in hand, the arguments, the diction, nay even the particular emotions to be expressed were

---

[1] My colleague Mr. Gray reminds me that Demosthenes laid down act-ing—ὑπόκρισις—as the soul of eloquence; a strong corroboration of my text.

devised by the advocate, and put into the mouth of an
actor, who, however poor in forensic gifts, had at least a deep
interest in the performance, and a personal knowledge of the
circumstances of the case.   It had been said by older rhetors
that what was probable (εἰκός) was more valuable in argument
than what was true, as such ; this principle was carried to a
far finer point by the so-called ἠθοποιΐα (conveying of character) and the πρέπον—two hardly distinguishable qualities [1]—
of the school of Lysias.   Thus when critics, old and new, note how
like to comedy are many of the details in Lysias' speeches, they
have caught only particular cases of these ' comic graces ' which
are really of the very essence of this artistic logography.   It is a
matter of common remark how dramatic genius seems to have
faded out at Athens after the days of the three great tragedians
and the old comic poets.   Perhaps it would be truer to say
that this talent became diffused through a wider area, and
through branches of literature apparently foreign to it.   Dramatic speech-writing and dramatic dialogue (as with Plato)
occupied the attention of great artists who might in an earlier
generation have held a foremost place among writers for the
stage.   There was a reality about the courts, and a freedom
about the schools, which suited various complexions of mind.
But the talent, though disguised, is there still ; we are still in
the presence of Attic thought and Attic culture of the highest .
type.   With this preface we turn to the details.

§ 389. Lysias, an Athenian by birth, was the son of the Syracusan Kephalus, a man of respectability and fortune, who was
persuaded by the influence of Pericles to settle in Athens as a
metic, where he carried on a thriving manufacture, chiefly as an
armourer.   He is introduced as a very old man, living in
refined and elegant society, at the opening of Plato's *Republic*.
It appears from the house property owned at Athens and the
Peiraeus by both Kephalus and by his sons, that they must

---

[1] Dionysius speaks of the πρέπον (appropriateness) in three respects ; as
regards the character of the *speaker*, as regards the character of the *audience*, and as regards the character of the *speech itself*, which should change
according as narrative, argument, or appeal become necessary.   The first
of these is ἦθος.

have all been of the privileged class of aliens called *isoteleis*, who were assessed the same state-burdens as citizens, though they enjoyed no full political rights. The date of Lysias' birth seems to be wrongly stated in the *Lives* of him as 458 B.C., in which case he would have been nearly sixty years old before he made his first essay as an orator. For other critical reasons the date of his birth has been brought down by recent scholars to about 435 B.C., but this is merely a matter of inference, and depends on our denying the accuracy of Plato's picture of the family in his dialogues. We are told that as a boy of fifteen he, and at least one of his brothers, went to Thurii, and the assumption that they went among the original settlers was the main cause of the orator's birth being fixed at the now rejected earlier date. But there is no reason to sustain this view. It seems that at Thurii he came in contact with Tisias or his pupils, and studied under them the art of rhetoric, in which he became known as a theorist, probably at an early age.

We hear from Aristotle that he kept a school of rhetoric, but that finding himself outdone as a theorist by Theodorus, he took to practical oratory, in which he was without any dangerous rival. This story, repeated for us by Cicero, is I think suspicious, because, as Lysias seems to have adopted speech-writing for a profession owing to his loss of fortune, we need not conceive his adopting rhetoric from any other motive, and we find him coming out as a great practical orator immediately after the catastrophe which deprived him of his fortune. Moreover, Plato in his *Phædrus*, which is supposed to be a discourse between Socrates and Phædrus, when Lysias is a young and rising man, speaks of him already as a celebrated orator.[1] However this may be, it seems certain that he sojourned at Thurii from the age of fifteen till the Sicilian disaster brought troubles on the democratic party through most cities of Magna Græcia, and he was among the 300 citizens banished

---

[1] Grote (*Plato*, i. p. 200, note) makes this allusion in the *Phædrus* an argument for his view that it was not written till after 399 B.C. He thinks that Lysias, according to his own statement of his want of experience in the opening of the speech against Eratosthenes, was not famous before that date.

by a revolution which sent him back to Athens in the archonship of Callias (412, B.C.).   Here he and his brother Polemarchus carried on their business, and apparently without incurring
the general impoverishment which affected Athens at the close
of the Peloponnesian War.   For when the Thirty were in
power, and were looking out for convenient persons to plunder,
these brothers, with other resident aliens, were chosen as
affording the best booty.   In the striking narrative of his
speech *against Eratosthenes*, an adherent of the Thirty, Lysias
has told us the story of this cruel and violent proceeding,
in which his elder brother, Polemarchus, was put to death without cause or trial, the property of both seized by the Thirty,
and Lysias only saved by presence of mind and accident from
their hands.   When in exile at Megara he seems to have worked
actively in aid of the democratic party.   Plutarch's Life, apparently quoting from his lost speech *about the benefits he had con-
ferred* (on Athens), states that he presented Thrasybulus' soldiers
with all the rest of his property, 2,000 drachmæ and 200 shields,
which must have been invested in business far from Athens.
He, moreover, collected mercenaries, and persuaded the Elean
Thrasydemus, his own great friend, and a strong democrat in
politics, to give two talents in aid of the undertaking.   It was
in consequence proposed by Thrasybulus, as soon as they succeeded, that civic rights should be accorded to Lysias ; but the
proposal, though carried, was indicted by Archinus, a companion,
perhaps a rival of Thrasybulus, as illegal, because proposed
before the council who should have prepared it were properly elected, and in consequence Lysias remained for the rest
of his life an *isoteles*.   Several somewhat hostile allusions to
Thrasybulus in the extant speeches have puzzled the critics,
who think that the orator ought to have been a staunch adherent
of his democratic friend—as if it were not part of Lysias' art to
assume the person of his client, and perhaps by such very allusions to lull the suspicions of the jury that he and not a simple
citizen was pleading the cause.   But we do not know how far
this disguise was possible, or whether it was not as transparent
as that of the assumed authorships which we noticed in the Old
Comedy of the previous generation.   For we hear that Lysias

having lost his fortune, and having revealed to both himself and others his practical power in prosecuting the murderers of his brother, became so popular a professional speech-writer, that at least 200 of his speeches (not to mention spurious attributions) were preserved. Among the many rivals who may have written some of the speeches assigned to him, none approached him in celebrity. We hear nothing further concerning his private life, save that he stood in intimate relations to a certain Metaneira, though married to his niece, the daughter of his youngest brother, Brachyllus, according to a common fashion at Athens. He does not seem to have lived to an advanced age, his latest extant speeches not reaching, I think, below 380 B.C. The epigram or poem of Philiscus upon him cited in Plutarch's *Life* is so corrupt as not to be worth quoting ;[1] but there is a fine bust of him in the Naples Museum, which seems to be genuine, and shows a strong, clear, somewhat hard face.

§ 390. The speeches of Lysias are upon so great a variety of subjects, that it is extremely difficult to classify them. The great majority are very short pleadings in private disputes, some on trifling subjects, but even here constantly touching on public affairs, and discussing the general character both of the litigants, and of the public men of the day. But before entering on this side of the orator's work, we may dispose briefly of his rhetorical and political speeches—I mean political as opposed to mere court arguments. Of his earlier works, his technical treatise, which is alluded to, and his erotic and panegyrical efforts, which were extant both in the form of speeches and of letters, we know almost nothing. But a curious sketch or specimen of his rhetorical essays on erotic subjects is preserved in the *Phædrus* of Plato, where Socrates insists on Phædrus reading out to him a composition of the kind which he has just heard Lysias, the famous orator, deliver. There is considerable controversy as to the genuineness of this document, most English and French critics, such as Mr. Jowett and M. Perrot,[2] holding it to be a

---

[1] Cf. Bergk, *Lyr. Fragg.* p. 640.

[2] Mr. Grote, in his admirable chapter on the *Phædrus* (Grote's *Plato*, ii. cap. xxiv.), seems never to have suspected the genuineness of this docu-

mere satirical imitation of the orator by Plato, many Germans, and among them Blass, asserting it to be a real transcript. Blass, indeed, goes so far as to say that even such a stylist as Plato could not have produced so characteristic an imitation of the graces and turns of Lysias, whose speech is here, as he well observes, *formally* far superior to Socrates' answer. But surely the imitation of Agathon's style in the *Symposium* shows how clever a counterfeiter Plato could be. I confess myself not convinced by these arguments, nor by others such as this, that the direct assertion of its being read from a written copy precludes its being the invention of Plato. The historical impossibilities in the Dialogues show plainly how far Plato considered his dramatic license to extend, and it seems more likely that he closely parodied some kindred speech of the orator, than that he introduced real quotation of such length into his compositions—a practice which would have inestimably increased their value for the history of literature. From Lysias' *panegyricus* we have, on the contrary (in Dionysius), a genuine fragment, that of a speech delivered at the ninety-eighth Olympiad, when the elder Dionysius of Syracuse sent a pompous embassy to contend at the games. The subject is the increasing danger to Greece from the great king on the one side, and the Sicilian tyrant on the other, with strong exhortations to harmony among Hellenes, and a firm resistance to the encroachments of both. The mob at Olympia, as we are told, in consequence of this address, hooted the poems of Dionysius. plundered his gilded and embroidered tents, and insulted his deputation, but this was the only effect produced. The critic Dionysius says it was inferior in weight and dignity to similar compositions of Isocrates and Demosthenes. The fragment, however, as far as it goes, seems quite equal to the more diffuse rhetoric of the former, and must have been fully as exciting to the hearers, though Dionysius says it is not so.

§ 391. The *Epitaphios* [1] appears to be spurious, and I will

---

ment. But he was a man strangely easy of faith concerning the alleged authorship of Greek documents, and in the same chapter (p. 256) implies his belief in the authenticity of the *Epitaphios* of Lysias.

[1] Or. 2. Mr. Rutherford tells me that many more are wholly un-Attic.

therefore postpone the consideration of it to another place, where we can bring it into comparison with other displays of the kind. Of the imaginary speech for Nikias before the Syracusans, we have only a sentence or two, and though it was accepted by Theophrastus, it is likewise of doubtful authenticity. But a genuine and interesting fragment of a ἐημηγορί,[1] or deliberative speech, has been preserved by Dionysius, in which the speaker urges a complete restoration of the democracy after the expulsion of the Thirty, against the proposal of Phormisius to limit civic rights to landholders. In this, as in many other speeches, Lysias spoke his own strong sentiment against every form of government except that of the whole people. This sentiment is practically illustrated by the longest and best known of his court speeches, that *against Eratosthenes*, delivered in his own person, and generally stated (after his own exordium) to be the first essay that he made in court. It falls after the fragment just mentioned, which must have been delivered in 403 B.C. The only other document in the collection of earlier date is the speech *for Polystratus*, which may be as early as 406, but which all good critics refuse to consider genuine.

I may remark that spurious speeches like this, if really delivered at the time they profess, and not the work of later sophists, are a most valuable index of the general condition of Attic oratory apart from the great masters who towered above the average crowd.

§ 392. The speech against Eratosthenes is in every respect a very fine oration, full of point and of vigour, but only exhibiting a certain number of Lysias' perfections. The narrative of his brother's murder and his own escape is admirable, and the pressing of his proof by questioning of the accused irresistible. But far more interesting to us is the sketch of the political acts of Theramenes, who at the moment was somewhat rehabilitated in character by his enmity to Critias and his tragical death. The whole speech seems intended to have a larger scope than the condemnation of Eratosthenes, who is too contemptible an adversary to have his motives dissected, or his character painted

[1] Or. 34.

at full length. Neither does Lysias seek to convey his own character to the jury, a device chiefly useful to a defendant, but not to a plaintiff who merely sought to fasten his charge upon the adversary.

The speech *against Agoratus* is very similar in character, except that both plaintiff and defendant are lower in the social scale, so that while there is less of general political argument, there are more copious details, especially of the wretched conduct of Agoratus, who after becoming a tool to the Thirty and doing to death a large number of honest citizens, escaped to Phylæ, and attempted to join the democrats.[1] Though saved from instant death by Anytus, who nobly reminded his soldiers that this was not the time or place to take vengeance on their enemies, he was shunned as an accursed outcast, and when attempting to join the solemn procession on the return of the exiles from Peiræus, was disarmed and driven off with scorn by Æsimus, the chief of the ceremony. Thus if this oration is remarkable for Lysias' dramatic power or character-drawing, it is in the drawing of the adversary. This feature recurs in several of the lesser orations spoken by plaintiffs, of which I may refer the reader to that *against Alcibiades* (the younger), a dissolute young debauchee, who is depicted as having inherited only his father's vices ;[2] that against Philon,[3] in which a mean and selfish creature, who profited by his neighbour's misery, is brought before us in strong colours ; that against Diogeiton,[4] who was a false guardian, and an oppressor of helpless orphans, according to his accuser ; and that against Nikomachus.[5]

§ 393. Far more striking, however, and more artistic than these portraits of adversaries, are the portraits conveyed by Lysias of the characters of defendants in their own speeches. Here character was of great importance, for in answer to the allegations of the prosecutor, the defendant, without boasting

---

[1] §§ 77, sq.

[2] The authorship of this oration, which is evidently a genuine speech, is doubted by Blass and others, chiefly because they think the character-painting not delicate enough for Lysias (Blass, i. 406).

[3] Or. 31.   [4] Or. 32.   [5] Or. 30.

or insolence, was bound to let the jury know his past history, his services to the state, and his general blamelessness of life. This is more strictly the *ethopœia* for which the orator was so celebrated. His defendants are all personages distinct enough for a drama or a modern novel. The most remarkable examples are those found in the speech for Mantitheus,[1] that of the accused, a political character, in or. 25, that of the speaker in or. 21 (very similar, with delicate distinctions, to that of Mantitheus), and that of the defendant charged with cutting away a sacred olive on his estate.

Let us pause for a moment at this group; it consists of people of consideration, who come forward to speak with confidence and dignity in their own behalf. The speech of Mantitheus, whose name is preserved in the superscription, is the most remarkable. He is a young aristocrat, whose ancient family and good traditions have prompted him not to only to seek danger in the van of battle, and retire from action more slowly than the mighty Thrasybulus, but to ascend the bema without waiting for the sanction of mature age, and to advise the people on public affairs. He chooses, moreover, to adopt a style of dress and of life suited to his aristocratic station, though no one has ever seen him joining in the revelries and the misconduct of other young men of the same class. He thanks his present adversary, who has questioned his fitness for the council, for having given him a fitting opportunity in the scrutiny (δοκιμασία) of exhibiting his life. Though somewhat self-assertive for our notions of good taste, the speech is admirably suited to a young Greek aristocrat. The other discourses of the same class, being delivered by older men, are calmer and less confident, but each of them conveys a strong and clear impression of the speaker's respectability, dignity, and superiority to any vulgar crime.

§ 394. Passing to a lower condition of society, we may cite the oration *on the property of Aristophanes*, in which the speaker's father, who was already dead, was charged with having made away with the money of Aristophanes, confiscated after his execution by public decree. Here the speaker, touching lightly

---

[1] Or. 16.

on the dreadful fate of Aristophanes (who was executed without trial, and even his body refused to his relatives), endeavours to show that his own father and he himself were quiet, unpresuming people, his father having maintained a good character to the age of seventy, when he died, and he himself having been too young to share in such a crime. Still more characteristic is the first oration, *on the killing of Eratosthenes*, whom the speaker found in his wife's chamber, having discovered her infidelity by a slave, and having summoned various friends to be witnesses of the outrage. The picture of the innocent and unsuspicious husband—a man of the poorer class ; of all the suggestive circumstances which he overlooked from thorough confidence in his wife; of his sudden awakening to a knowledge of her guilt—all this is drawn in homely detail, and with masterly power.

Similar in some respects, though contrasted in not asserting complete innocence and justification, are the speeches *in reply to Simon*, and *in answer to the charge of malicious wounding*.[1] The speakers, who had quarrelled with rivals in somewhat disreputable love affairs, while admitting their folly, and the reality of the brawl, assert their own efforts to keep things quiet, and the fury and unreasonableness of their opponents. All three orations are very interesting in opening to us views into the inner life of the lower classes at Athens. To take them as specimens of public morality, as is done by most Germans and the English critics who follow them, is to make the Newgate Calendar an index of average morals. As this has been done for Ireland in the last century by a distinguished historian, we must protest against its being done for Athens.

§ 395. Last in this class of speeches I will mention the very interesting speech *on behalf of the Invalid Pauper*, whose allowance of an óbol *per diem*, according to the Athenian poor-law, was challenged, and who shows that his case is a fair one for public charity. The old grammarians, who could not understand how the great Lysias should plead in such a case, where the issue was trifling and any remuneration impossible, rejected it as spurious. Most moderns are of the opposite

---

[1] Or. 3 and 4.

opinion, justly.   But they seem hardly to have appreciated the
circumstances of the case, which are easily to be deduced from
the speech.   The alleged pauper was evidently what we call
' a character,' with a small shop close to the agora, the common resort of many people far above him in means and station, who were doubtless attracted by his wit or his drollery.
These people, moreover, seem to have lent him horses to
ride, and this fact, together with the distinguished company
which thronged his shop, led the accuser to believe that he
was not ἀδύνατος, without means of helping himself.   It is
indeed more than probable that his influential friends got him
put on the relief list in preference to more deserving appli-
cants.   This created envy against him, and he found himself
in danger of losing his pension.   We can imagine him appeal-
ing with comic pathos to Lysias, who probably frequented his
shop with other strollers in the agora, and we can imagine how
the company would join in entreating the great advocate to
help so useful and popular a character.   Thus half in charity,
half in fun, Lysias writes him a defence, which could only have
had effect when spoken by a well-known and original character,
and which gains or loses almost all its point by the delivery.

There is all manner of fun in the speech, comic pathos,
parody of serious arguments, unexpected turns ; but it must
be *acted* to produce any effect.   Most of the arguments are
not serious, and the impression produced is that the speaker
was by no means so badly off as he pretends ; yet the defence
would be very telling, when a trifling sum was at issue, and
would be sure to carry the Council by its cleverness and its
racy humour.   This tendency to the humorous is very apparent
in two other speeches, that *against Theomnestus*,[1] who endeavoured to evade a charge by adhering to the letter of the law
in contempt of its spirit, and the fragment against the Socratic
Æschines, which draws a picture of the defendant worthy of
Aristophanes.   Allied, as usual, to this talent, is the power of
pathos, which, though kept in restraint by the taste of the day,
and sparingly admitted in early Greek oratory, is very prominent in the prison-scene drawn in the speech against Agoratus,[2]

---

[1] Or. 10.   [2] § 39, sq.

which strongly resembles that already noted in Andocides (above, p. 131). Still finer and unique in our remains of Lysias is the narrative in the speech *against Diogeiton*, which indeed Dionysius cites as a model, where the appeal of the mother of the orphans to her father, who was their guardian, is not inferior to the finest speeches in Euripides. I will quote it here, as being little known to ordinary students.[1]

§ 396. I have endeavoured to bring together these general features because the particular analysis of so many short speeches, on so many various subjects, would detain the reader far too long, and occupy a disproportionate space in this history. The argument, the authenticity, and the literary features of each speech have been fully discussed in Blass' *Attische Beredsamkeit* and in Mr. Jebb's *Attic Orators*, to either of which the special student of Lysias may turn for fuller information. I am likewise bound to pass by in silence the many political and social lights on the history of Athens afforded by the allusions of his speakers—many of them not creditable to the public morality of the Restored democracy, and showing how vague suspicions, political changes, and even the poverty of the public purse, were made the handles of private accusations.

---

[1] § 15: 'ἔπειτα σὺ ἐτόλμησας,' ἔφη, 'εἰπεῖν, ἔχων τοσαῦτα χρήματα, ὡς δισχιλίας δραχμὰς ὁ τούτων πατὴρ κατέλιπε καὶ τριάκοντα στατῆρας. ἃ παρ' ἐμοὶ καταλειφθέντα ἐκείνου τελευτήσαντος ἐγώ σοι ἔδωκα; καὶ ἐκβαλεῖν τούτους ἠξίωκας θυγατριδοῦς ὄντας ἐκ τῆς οἰκίας τῆς αὐτῶν ἐν τριβωνίοις, ἀνυποδήτους, οὐ μετὰ ἀκολούθου, οὐ μετὰ στρωμάτων, οὐ μετὰ ἱματίων, οὐ μετὰ τῶν ἐπίπλων ἃ ὁ πατὴρ αὐτοῖς κατέλιπεν, οὐδὲ μετὰ τῶν παρακαταθηκῶν ἃς ἐκεῖνος παρὰ σοὶ κατέθετο. Καὶ νῦν τοὺς μὲν ἐκ τῆς μητρυιᾶς τῆς ἐμῆς παιδεύεις ἐν πολλοῖς χρήμασιν εὐδαίμονας ὄντας· κο᾽ ταῦτα μὲν καλῶς ποιεῖς· τοὺς δ' ἐμοὺς ἀδικεῖς, οὓς ἀτίμως ἐκ τῆς οἰκίας ἐκβαλὼν ἀντὶ πλουσίων πτωχοὺς ἀποδεῖξαι προθυμῇ. καὶ ἐπὶ τοιούτοις ἔργοις οὔτε τοὺς θεοὺς φοβῇ, οὔτ' ἐμὲ τὴν σὴν θυγατέρα τὴν συνειδυῖαν αἰσχύνῃ, οὔτε τοῦ ἀδελφοῦ μέμνησαι, ἀλλὰ πάντας ἡμᾶς περὶ ἐλάττονος ποιῇ, χρημάτων.' τότε μὲν οὖν, ὦ ἄνδρες δικασταί, πολλῶν καὶ δεινῶν ὑπὸ τῆς γυναικὸς ῥηθέντων οὕτω διετέθημεν πάντες οἱ παρόντες ὑπὸ τῶν τούτῳ πεπραγμένων καὶ τῶν λόγων τῶν ἐκείνης, ὁρῶντες μὲν τοὺς παῖδας, οἷα ἦσαν πεπονθότες, ἀναμιμνησκόμενοι δὲ τοῦ ἀποθανόντος, ὡς ἀνάξιον τῆς οὐσίας τὸν ἐπίτροπον κατέλιπεν. ἐνθυμούμενοι δὲ ὡς χαλεπὸν ἐξευρεῖν ὅτῳ χρὴ περὶ τῶν ἑαυτοῦ πιστεῦσαί τινα, ὥστε, ὦ ἄνδρες δικασταί, μηδένα τῶν παρόντων δύνασθαι φθέγξασθαι, ἀλλὰ καὶ δακρύοντας μηδὲν ἧττον τῶν πεπονθότων ἀπιόντας οἴχεσθαι σιωπῇ.

Associated with these disagreeable features is the want of confidence in testimony shown through all his orations.   After a preamble, and the prothesis, or first short statement of the case, the orator proceeds (where it is possible) to a narrative of the facts, in which he seeks in the clearest order and the simplest language to convey his client's view of the case.   Then follows the citing of witnesses, who swear to the truth of the narrative. But, instead of being content with this, the speaker generally goes on to general *à priori* arguments, based on the character or the interests of the litigants.   Indeed, general character seems to have weighed far too much in the Athenian law-courts, as it will ever do where a trained judge is not present to guide and control the feelings of the jury.

The *attack on Alcibiades* (or. 14, 15) is generally regarded as spurious, but by an early if not contemporary author, and bears curiously close relations to the speech of Isocrates *de Bigis*, to which it seems to be a reply.   But the speech attributed to Lysias is not from so masterly a hand as the defence by Isocrates.   Another speech in the Lysian collection, that *against Poliochus*, has likewise distinct references to the same defence, which, though in form a court speech, is really an encomium on Alcibiades, and may have been a good deal modified after its delivery for the purpose of publication.

§ 397. The general merits of Lysias have been implied in the above review of his extant speeches.   It is perhaps important to add that the pettiness of many of the causes pleaded, and the consequent shortness and dryness of the argument, especially when delivered in support of the main speech ($\delta\epsilon\upsilon\tau\epsilon\rho o$-$\lambda o\gamma\iota a$), have much injured his reputation among modern students of Greek.   Did we possess a few more of his great efforts, like those against Eratosthenes, Agoratus, and Diogeiton, we should better appreciate the praises of the ancient critics.

But with this pettiness of particular causes seems connected the criticism of Plato, that Lysias, in contrast to Isocrates, or to Pericles, among his forerunners, did not seek to deduce his special arguments from general philosophical principles.   This was no doubt true ; we also find, as Plato says, his arguments strung together without logical nexus, and even repeated need-

lessly.   On the other hand, this close adherence to the individual case gave him that wonderful variety which the ancients
admired, observing that among 200 genuine speeches no fixed
use of any commonplaces, even in the proem, could be found.
But his occasional repetitions of arguments are probably intentional, and meant to bring important points before the court in
an artless way, and as a simple man might do who could not
give weight or importance to a single statement by lofty diction
or sounding periods.   For, above all things, Lysias aimed at
unaffected simplicity, the *tenue dicendi genus*, the ἀφελὴς λόγος
of the critics, in which he was always considered the un-
approached master.   This character he attained by the use
of plain words, having been the first to perceive that elegant
and even dignified prose did not require poetical diction to
exalt it—and here he broke loose completely from the traditions
of Gorgias.   Secondly, he attained it by clear statement, there
being seldom the least obscurity when we know the whole of
the case, and where the text is not corrupt.   Thirdly, by
brevity—a feature which strikes us very much in most of his
speeches, and which can only be fully understood by regarding
many of the shortest as mere auxiliary statements to the main
argument.

§ 398. Of course a great writer like Lysias does not bind
himself slavishly by such rules.   There are passages of deep
emotion where unusual words and phrases occur, and where
they are more natural than common diction.   There are cases
where, for the sake of pathos, he repeats an idea, and holds it
before the audience with great effect ; again, for the sake
of point, he introduces those parallelisms and balancings
of clauses, which were then so common in Attic eloquence
that to avoid them was perhaps more affected than to use
them.   These ornaments are what give Lysias' speeches the
archaic complexion which has been compared to the stiff curls
and conventional smile of the older Attic sculpture, even in its
high development under the hands of Calamis.[1]   But all these

---

[1] Dionysius uses the parallel illustration of the old simple paintings with
few colours and little perspective. Cf. Plutarch, *De rect. rat. aud.* 9 : ὥσπερ
ἐν τρίβωνι Λυσιακοῦ λόγου λεπτῷ καὶ ψιλῷ καθήμενος, ἄπρακτος καὶ ἀκίνητος.

things are distinctly exceptions to his rule of extreme simplicity, which would often degenerate into dryness or meagreness but for the exquisite *grace* (χάσις) which is the most brilliant feature of his genius. This quality, which cannot be analysed, has been extolled by all critics, and is equalled, especially in his narratives, by Herodotus alone of Greek prose writers. Indeed, as Antiphon stands close to Thucydides, and is strong on the argumentative or dialectical side, so Lysias approaches Herodotus, being far superior in the historical or narrative part of his oratory. His style seems at first sight, as Dionysius observes, so simple and natural that anyone might hope to imitate it, whereas it is really the most exquisite and unattainable gift to copy nature artistically and yet with perfect accuracy. For this purpose he often deserts the rounded period, and uses, like Herodotus, an easy and lucid λέξις εἰρομένη, which makes his story wonderfully plausible and persuasive. Thus he steals upon his hearers, as the ancients observed, instead of coercing them by power and grandeur. He also abandons his periods for an opposite purpose, when in passages of great excitement he adopts short unconnected clauses, as in the famous conclusion of his speech against Eratosthenes, and in the mother's description of her orphans before Diogeiton. All these peculiarities make it easy for us to understand how his critics thought him inferior in those panegyrical or deliberative harangues, where a periodic style was peculiarly effective. Thus a plain and forcible speaker in our own day might find great difficulty in composing a congratulatory address, which is expected to run in long and rounded sentences. Of course rhetors and grammarians have always preferred Isocrates, but if it were only as an antidote to that over-artificial and watery eloquence, the remains of Lysias are of inestimable value.

§ 399. Turning to the external history of his works, I have nothing to add to what has already been said about Plato's criticism, except that he may have been biassed by Lysias' democratic views, which led him constantly to attack and expose with great severity men with whom the philosopher had great sympathy. Aristotle very seldom mentions Lysias in comparison with Isocrates, and Theophrastus, though regarding him as the type of the ' genus tenue,' seems to have thought Thrasymachus more important in the history of rhetoric. Deinarchus, Charisius, and Hegesias are spoken of as imitating his style in contrast to that of Demosthenes. There were treatises composed upon him, as upon the other orators, by the Alexandrian critics, but these are unfortunately lost, nor do we possess any scholia upon this author. But in Roman days, when there was a reaction against the florid Asianism, Lysias found many admirers and students who aimed at old Attic simplicity and purity : of these C. Lic. Calvus is the most important. Cicero, who was attacked by this school, holds the balance very fairly between Lysias and his supposed opponents. He grants Lysias all the merits due to him, but prefers Demosthenes as a model on account of his power.

In the Augustan period, when Atticism triumphed, there were very full appreciations and discussions of Lysias by Dionysius and Cæcilius, both of whom wrote special works on him, besides the extant tract of Dionysius, and many judgments of both these and of Hermogenes in relation to other orators. Various later commentators, such as Zosimus of Gaza, Zeno, Paulus Germinus, are cited in the Lexica. In fact, throughout all Greek criticism, his place seems fixed as next in importance to Demosthenes and Isocrates. Of the 233 speeches declared genuine by Dionysius and Cæcilius, of all these comments and explanations, we have only the critiques already cited, a good many special points in Suidas and Harpocration. the titles of about 170 speeches, and a single collection of 34 speeches, some of them imperfectly preserved, with about 100 lesser fragments.

§ 400. *Bibliographical.* The speeches (with the exception of the spurious *Epitaphios,* which was copied separately also) are handed down to us through one codex,[1] the Palatinus X, preserved at Heidelberg, which is the parent of all other copies, particularly of the Florentine, once esteemed of higher authority. Not only was X copied from an archetype already

---

[1] Written in the twelfth century, and brought from Nicæa to Europe. Cf. a special article upon it by Schöll in *Hermes,* vol. xi. pp. 202, sq.

mutilated, but it has itself lost several pages, and is, moreover, the work of a careless and inaccurate scribe, so that our text has afforded critics ample scope for emendation and correction. Eight of the extant speeches (whole or partial) are attested by Dionysius, the ablest and most careful of the authorities on this question. Five he rejects ; others are doubtful. The selection seems made from two collections of Lysias' speeches, or else there are two selections from his whole works brought together. This is inferred from speeches on murder appearing in the first and twelfth places, the latter of them (*against Eratosthenes*) being evidently the first in order both of time and merit. But all closer classifications are complicated and unsatisfactory, owing to the great variety of the cases treated, as the reader will see from Blass' discussion of the point.[1]

The first edition (Aldus, 1513, with other orators) is taken not from the Palatinus, but from the Athos MS., which Lascaris brought over, and which is now lost, but it was evidently an inferior copy of the same archetype. In our own day, besides the Zurich editors, and the Teubner edition of Scheibe—both excellent—this author has received inestimable aid from the critical labours of Cobet, both in his *Novæ Lectiones*, and in a special school edition (Amsterdam, 1863), which is of course the best text. There are many good essays, and many selections with notes by the Germans, of whom I may mention Hoelscher, Francken, Frohberger, Rauchenstein. There are German translations by Falk (Breslau, 1842) and F. Baur (2nd ed. Stuttgart, 1869). Excellent general estimates will be found (besides that of Blass and Mr. Jebb) in Perrot's and Girard's—the latter specially on Lysias—writings on Greek literature.[2]

§ 401. It is usual to pass from the consideration of Lysias and his court speeches to that of Isocrates and his epideictic displays, and then to return to Isæus as the special forerunner and master of Demosthenes. But as the evidence of this latter relation is not very clear, and in any case only applies to a special class of Demosthenes' speeches—those against his

---

[1] i. 348, 368.

[2] G. Perrot, *Éloquence politique, &c., à Athènes*, vol. i, and J. Girard, de *l'Atticisme dans Lysias, passim.*

guardians—it seems preferable to take up the works of Isæus in close connection with Lysias, to whom he affords many points of resemblance and of contrast. This will enable us to form a better estimate of the legal eloquence of Athens before we turn to her philosophers and pamphleteers, who were also, according to the fashion of the day, orators and special students of rhetoric.

§ 402. The darkness which shrouds the life of ISÆUS is hardly an accident ; it is rather the mark—I had almost said the distinguishing mark—of the developed profession to which he belonged. While Antiphon's apparent privacy of life only concealed an active and constant interference in public affairs, as was clearly shown when he came to lay aside the mask ; while Lysias' speeches contain several discourses of public interest and on public affairs in which he was personally concerned, the works of Isæus, not only as we have them, but as they were known to the ancients, were λόγοι ἰδιωτικοί, not merely for private individuals,[1] but on private suits, and in these they approach more nearly to what we should call Chancery practice than any other Attic eloquence preserved. Accordingly as our Chancery lawyers do not even attain the notoriety of those engaged in criminal or nisi-prius actions, far less that of political speakers, so Isæus remains personally unknown, and even his speeches, remarkable though they be, have seldom been studied except by special enquirers into the principles of Attic jurisprudence. Hence the dates of his birth and death are not known. His origin is said doubtfully to have been of Chalcis, and his father's name Diagoras. He may have been an Eubœan cleruch, driven back to Athens by the loss of the island to Athens, or a *metoikos*, a resident alien,

---

[1] The Greek argument of the fourth oration (concerning Nicostratus, &c.) says that Isæus was related to Hagnon, nephew of the testator, and spoke this speech in aid of them personally. As there is no hint of these facts in the course of the speech itself, they must have been derived from some old authority, and are not improbable, though Blass thinks (ii. p. 506) that this is alleged *wohl lediglich aus thörichter Vermuthung.* But, unfortunately, the people in question are obscure, and the speech gives us no light concerning Isæus' life or connections. Cf. for a careful review of the facts, Blass, *AB.* ii. p. 454.

who settled and practised at Athens without the social position of Kephalus and his son Lysias. The dates of the
extant speeches, so far as they can be determined, range from
389 to 352 B.C. This, and his alleged instruction of Demosthenes, show his activity to have extended through the first
half of the fourth century B.C. Of his education equally little is
ascertained. He is called a follower of Lysias, a pupil of
Isocrates. But his speeches only show the general influence
which these great contemporaries must have exercised upon a
man of his ability. The absence of closer likenesses even
suggests that their education of him was not more direct.

§ 403. The subjects of the eleven speeches, and of the considerable fragments quoted as specimens by Dionysius, have no
special literary interest, nor is there any one of them which is
worth analysing in this place.[1] The most elaborate and Demosthenic in tone is the eleventh, that *on the bequests of Hagnias.*
Concerning this lawsuit, which lasted many years and underwent many trials, we have among the speeches of Demosthenes
that *against Macartatus*—a performance not only below the
usual level of the great orator, but inferior to the speech of
Isæus, which is far more logical and better constructed. The
eighth, *on the succession to Kiron's property,* is similarly interesting in having been considerably used by Demosthenes in
his speeches against his guardians, but the free and independent
way in which he modifies the commonplaces or quotations from
it, shows that he was even then no mere ordinary pupil, but an
original and powerful rhetor. All the speeches of Isæus are
about questions of succession, about the validity of wills, or of
the evidence on which they are established and impugned, and
upon the rights of relationship. They show us very clearly,
like the speeches of Lysias, the grave defects of the Athenian jury system. These juries were not a small group of
men, sworn to enquire into questions of fact, guided on points
of law by a professional judge, and intended to protect private
individuals from an abuse of power on the part of the government. They were rather the sovereign people broken up

[1] From a collection of sixty-four speeches, of which fifteen were rejected by old critics, we only have a scanty remnant of about one-sixth.

into divisions of 500, and bringing into court all the powers of the sovereign, without responsibility or control of any sort. Accordingly, while the great numbers of the jury made Attic court speeches to be practically harangues to a large assembly —a point seldom adequately insisted upon—its absolute and despotic power turned advocates to aim at persuasion rather than sound argument, to appeal to passion and not to reason, to flatter and not to convince by fair means.

All the court eloquence of Athens is vitiated by this fundamental unsoundness of the tribunal which it addressed, and nowhere is the result more apparent than in the speeches of Isæus, which were on subjects settled by strict law, by established custom and precedent, by traditions as old as any in Aryan civilisation. As regards the right and limits of testamentary bequest, the strict line of succession among collateral branches, the consequences of intestacy, the disturbing elements of mental incapacity and undue influence—in all these matters the system of Attic jurisprudence was very complete and carefully constructed. But, however desirous an advocate of Isæus' legal turn of mind might be to confine himself to the strict law of the case, the jury were averse to such dry discussions. Moreover, they seem to have laid far less stress on positive evidence than we do, probably on account of the mendacity of the nation ; we also find the preparation of documents, and preservation of them in proper archives, strangely neglected. Hence in no case is the advocate content with proving a point by positive evidence, or producing a document establishing it ; he always goes on to the *εἰκός*, the probabilities of the case ; and indeed most of Isæus' speeches are arguments *against* the evidence on the ground of these probabilities. The produced will is argued to be a forgery, because the testator was on bad terms with the legatee ; the alleged adoption of a son is denied on similar grounds. Is it likely a man in his senses would do such a thing? is the perpetual plea of the litigants. It is easy to see how such a state of things stimulated court eloquence, and how the ingenuity of a trained rhetor was required to put a fair face even upon a case which should have stood upon its own merits. The dicasts thought nothing of breaking a will, or even of deciding in the teeth of sworn evidence.   Indeed, from the number of cases of conviction for perjury known to us, we may infer that the swearing in Attic courts was not more conscientious than it is in the Irish county courts of the present day.

§ 404. Hence we see the point of the remark upon Isæus in the Greek *Life*, that he was thoroughly unfair to his opponent and out-generalled his jury.[1]   But this very reputation injured his efficiency, for while Lysias seemed artless when charging the guilty, Isæus was suspected even when clearing the innocent.   Indeed a comparison with Lysias is the best means of showing the peculiar characteristics of Isæus.   In the first place, his speeches are as a rule much longer and more elaborate, and this especially by reason of the many summaries and recapitulations which Lysias would have considered tedious, and which are in any case violations of *ethos*, if the speaker be an inexperienced debater.   But in Isæus the mask seems falling away ; the position of the logographer was too notorious and well established to be denied, and he either disdains, or he fails, to assume the personality of his client.   Hence he abandons the simple structure upon which all Lysias' speeches are based, and affects variety and power of treatment.   He breaks up his narrative into parts, and introduces argumentation between them, he omits the exordium or the peroration, or rather weaves in these preambles and appeals into the body of his speech.   He even begins or ends with the reading of laws —in fact, a study of variety is one of his chief objects.   This is as obvious in the diction as in the arrangement of his speeches. In some of them, and in some parts of them, his periods are almost as grand as those of Isocrates or Demosthenes ; in others he affects, perhaps with less success, simplicity of narrative ; in others he presses the adversary with close questioning, and with a rapid urging of short points.   But while his eloquence is more sustained and logical, and while he forces home his arguments by dint of clever restatement and recapitulation, he does not attain to the grace of Lysias nor to the sustained power of Demosthenes.   Nay, even in spite of the studied

---

[1] καὶ πρὸς μὲν τὸν ἀντίδικον διαπονηρεύεται, τοὺς δὲ δικαστὰς καταστρατηγεῖ.

attempts at variety, there is a certain sameness of character about his speeches which makes them tedious in comparison with those of Lysias.   This may be in some measure due to the uniformity of subjects in Isæus.   Yet even apart from this, the want of ethos and the assumption of rhetorical power naturally produce an unpleasant effect.

§ 405. The influence of Isocrates' rhetoric is to be seen in the avoidance of the hiatus in some speeches, as well as in the general finish and smoothness of many of his periods, but we cannot trace any gradual adoption of these features, or their predominance in the later speeches, so that it is more likely he used this, like other devices, merely to produce variety and novelty.   He certainly never adopted the avoidance of hiatus as a fixed principle.   His *figures of thought*, such as indignant questions and the like, are more frequent than those of Lysias, whose natural gifts he endeavoured to rival by better training.   Thus the old parallel clauses of the Gorgian rhetoric, which give Lysias his antique flavour, are hardly ever to be found in Isæus ; but his composition is not the less careful and artificial, though he seeks to avoid these obvious ornaments.   And thus with all his archaic mannerism Lysias is far the more easy and natural.   It is not necessary to pursue this comparison, which, after the model of Dionysius, has been worked out by Blass and Perrot.

§ 406. *Bibliographical.*   We may add a word on the history of the text.   Beyond the fact of his being Demosthenes' educator, there is little mention of this orator till Dionysius and Hermogenes, who speak very favourably of him.   The notes of Didymus are only once cited (by Harpocration, γαμηλία).   The Greek arguments are very complete, but no scholia, so far as I know, have come down to us.   As to MSS., we are dependent upon the same which have been already noticed under Antiphon.[1]   The *princeps* of Aldus (1513) and the edition of Stephens (1575) were followed by that of Reiske (1773), which were based on no new collation, but all rest on the lost codex of Lascaris.   The translation and legal notes of Wm. Jones (Oxford, 1779) are highly commended by Schömann.

[1] Cf. also Buermann in *Hermes*, xix. pp. 325-68.

The eleventh speech (on Menecles' bequests) was first edited from the Laurentian MS. by Tyrwhitt (London, 1785). The large fragment of the speech on Cleonymus' bequests was added by Mai from an Ambrosian codex in 1815. Of later editors the texts of Bekker and Scheibe and the complete edition and commentary of Schömann (1831), who has also given us a German translation (2nd ed. 1869), are best worthy of mention.

§ 407. We have now followed out Attic court oratory to its completeness under the hands of Isæus ; for any superiority which some of Demosthenes' speeches of this kind may possess, seems rather due to the exceptional genius of that orator than to the discovery of any new principles, or new method of rhetoric. And as Demosthenes' ' private orations ' can hardly be discussed apart from his life, we may pause here, and turn to collateral fields of literary activity. But, instead of taking up Isocrates, who was at this time the leader of the epideictic rhetoric, or oratory of display, and whose merits were altogether stylistic, I prefer to proceed to that branch of Attic prose which forms the strongest contrast to the practical advocacy in the law courts— I mean the dialogues of Plato and other companions of Socrates. These men despised such a trade, and kept aloof from actual politics ; they will therefore afford us a welcome respite from the practical oratory which has occupied us so long. But as thoroughgoing thinkers, and philosophers in the strict sense, their work deserves an earlier and more important place than the idle and empty compromise attempted by Isocrates, of combining a shallow philosophy with equally shallow theoretical politics. Thus this eminent rhetorician, but feeble statesman, will be brought into closer comparison with his proper contrast —Demosthenes.

CHAPTER VII.

PLATO.

§ 408. PLATO, whose proper name was Aristocles, was born either 429 or 427 B.C.,[1] at Ægina, where his father held property. His father, Ariston, son of Aristocles, and his mother, Peristione (sister of Charmides), were both of ancient and noble descent, and though later writers represent him as a poor man, this seems only from the desire of making him a closer copy of Socrates, and of the ascetic type fashionable in Greek philosophy. Several indications may be quoted to show that he was a man of wealth and consideration. He studied gymnastics in his youth, when he was surnamed Plato in the gymnasium from his broad shoulders, and he is reported to have won a prize at the Isthmian games. As his age of military service coincided with the grievous days of the closing Peloponnesian war, he must have been employed in the army; but upon this point, as well as upon his education in music, gymnastic, poetry, and philosophy, we are left to conjecture, and to vague legends, which were no doubt widely circulated about him, but which have no solid foundation. Diogenes says he studied the writing of poetry, and essayed dithyrambs, songs, and tragedies, but that, upon meeting Socrates, he burnt his poems. The epigrams attributed to him in the *Anthologia*, though trifling, are very elegant, and some of them may be genuine. Lastly, Aristotle[2] says that Cratylus had instructed him in the doctrine of Heracleitus before he came under the influence of Socrates.

[1] Cf the conflicting authorities cited in Zeller's *Plato*, p. 2, note (Eng. trans.).

[2] *Metaph.* i. 6.

The whole impression conveyed by these stories is confirmed by his works, and shows him to have been a young
Athenian gentleman in contact with all the current science
of the day, and influenced by all the social and artistic
culture of that matchless city in its matchless period. But
his conversion by Socrates marks the great turning point of
his life. Plato must have met him at an early age, for Socrates'
conversations were very fashionable among his aristocratic
friends—probably the age of twenty, which is reported to us, is
too late. At all events, he became a constant and favourite
pupil, and was with the great master at his trial and condemnation. According to Plato's own statement in the *Apology*, he
endeavoured to persuade Socrates to assess the fine which
the dicasts might impose at thirty minæ, which he and other
friends were ready to pay. This large sum (for those days)
implies that they had means. After Socrates' death he left for
Megara, and stayed for a time with Euclcides, another pupil
of the same school, who became afterwards the head of a
distinct sect. From Megara Plato made voyages to Egypt,
Cyrene, Magna Græcia, and Sicily ; but it is more than probable that he returned at intervals to Athens. The dates of
these journeys, even of those to Sicily, which are best known,
are involved in obscurity. He is said to have studied mathematics with Theodorus of Cyrene, and to have made closer
acquaintance with the Pythagoreans in Magna Græcia. But, in
addition to these theoretical matters, he gained his first practical experience of the effects of irresponsible monarchy from
the elder Dionysius. Though introduced by Dion, the tyrant
was so offended with his views, which were then probably a
reflex of those of Socrates, that he delivered him up to the
Spartan ambassador Pollis, who had him sold in the market of
Ægina. He was, moreover, well-nigh put to death by the
Æginetans, who at this time (about 390 B.C.) would permit no
Athenian to touch their shore. Being ransomed by one Anni-
keris, he returned to Athens, and set up a school at the well-
known Academy, in the western suburbs of Athens.

§ 409. We unfortunately know nothing of the details of his
oral teaching, which he avers in his written dialogues to be far the

most important. We hear that his discourses were very dry, and that in lecturing on the good he by no means adopted the homely style and illustrations of Socrates, but brought in mathematics, astronomy, and finally so abstract an idea of the Good that no one but his special pupils would listen to him. This we have on the report of Aristoxenus, who professes Aristotle's authority, and it agrees with some sneers to be found in the Middle Comedy. At all events, Plato took no part whatever in the politics of Athens, which were thoroughly distasteful to him, and opposed to all his principles. His notions of the proper State and its government are clear enough in the three works he has left us on the subject, the *Politicus*, the *Republic*, and the *Laws*. But when his old friend Dionysius died, he was persuaded by Dion, and also by the younger Dionysius, then under Dion's influence, to revisit Syracuse (367 B.C.) in the hope that, by converting the new tyrant to his views, he might at last have an opportunity of realising his theories of state reform. The experiment turned out exactly as might have been anticipated. After a few days of novelty and of politeness Dionysius grew weary of Plato, and jealous of Dion, so that he banished the latter, and Plato soon departed. But he actually was induced to return to Syracuse about 361 B.C., perhaps chiefly in order to reconcile his friend Dion with the tyrant. After escaping again from the tyrant's displeasure, he returned to Athens, where he spent the remainder of his old age respected by a large society of admirers. He died peacefully at a marriage feast, according to the legend, in 347 B.C., having exceeded the age of fourscore years.

§ 410. Plato is one of the very few Greek authors of whose works nothing has been lost. On the contrary, the catalogue we possess is rather redundant than defective, and one of the main duties of modern criticism as regards him has been the sifting of his writings, and the rejection of what is unworthy or unauthentic. Before approaching the dialogues, we may say a word concerning the lesser and more obscure writings, which were once ascribed to him. There are the epigrams already mentioned, which most critics reject, but one or two of which seem to me probably genuine : there are certain *Distinctions* (ὅροι) to which Aristotle refers more than once ; but as they are never mentioned in any catalogue of his works, they seem to have been some collection of maxims from his oral lectures preserved in the school of the Academy.　There are, moreover, a collection of *Epistles,* which are still printed in the editions of the text, and which Grote, in his great work on Plato,[1] accepts as genuine, and bases upon them many statements about the life of the philosopher.　One of them (the seventh) is so interesting and circumstantial about his relations with Dion and Dionysius, that all critics have longed to have it regarded as genuine, and even those who reject the Platonic authorship think it an almost contemporaneous composition by a writer thoroughly informed on Plato's life.　But I agree with Mr. Jowett and with all the German critics, that none of these epistles are genuine, and am disposed to look on the information derived from the seventh epistle as very suspicious.　It may be all true. but no point unsupported by other evidence should be accepted without the greatest caution.　We hear, moreover, of about ten dialogues which were of old considered spurious, and most of which are mentioned as such by Diogenes Laertius.[2] There remain thirty-five dialogues,[3] of which four (the second *Alcibiades, Anterastæ, Hipparchus,* and *Epinomis*) have been

---

[1] *Plato and the other Companions of Socrates,* i. p. 220, sq.

[2] iii. 62.

[3] Here is the list :—Dialogues of

(a) SEARCH,	(β) EXPOSITION.
Theætetus	*Timæus*
Parmenides	*Laws*
Alcibiades I.	* *Epinomis*
* *Alcibiades II.*	*Critias*
* *Theages*	*Republic*
Laches	*Sophistes*
Lysis	*Politicus*
Charmides	*Phædon*
Menon	*Philebus*
Ion	*Protagoras*
Euthyphron	*Phædrus*
Euthydemus	*Symposium*
Gorgias	*Cratylus*
* *Hippias I.*	*Criton*
Hippias II.	

doubted by the Greek critics,[1] and many more by the school of Ast and Socher, which grew out of the Wolfian controversy in the second decade of this century.

§ 411. The connection of these isolated compositions, and their relation, both logically and chronologically, have ever been, and will remain, a subject of controversy, unless the view of Grote is adopted, that Plato deliberately intended them as perfectly distinct works, and consciously laid aside in each all reference to the rest as regards theory. This Grote distinctly asserts to be the case, at least as regards the two classes of dialogues, into which the Platonic compositions must be divided. We will first discuss the logical order. Plato himself is of course the main authority to be consulted. The same characters who have met in the *Theætetus* meet again expressly in the *Sophistes*, though they do not take up the unfinished thread of the discourse. The *Politicus* proclaims itself a third colloquy of the same party (with a new respondent). The *Republic*, *Timæus*, and *Critias* are similarly connected, and a fourth dialogue, the *Hermocrates*, though apparently announced, was never composed. But I am not sure that Plato did not merely assume the same personages for the sake of dramatic convenience, without meaning to assert intimate relation. I do not know that the author himself gives us any further clue. The earliest attempt at a logical classification of which we know is that quoted by Diogenes,[2] as laid down by Aristophanes of Byzantium. He arranged five trilogies :—1. *Republic*, *Timæus*, *Critias ;* 2. *Laws*, *Minos*, *Epinomis ;* 3. *Theætetus*, *Euthyphron*, *Apology ;* 4. *Sophist*, *Politicus*, *Cratylus ;* 5. *Criton*, *Phædon*, and *Letters*. The rest of the dialogues he placed singly and without any fixed order.

(α) Search,	(β) Exposition.
*Clitophon	*The Apology*
* Hipparchus	*Menexenus.*
* Eraste	
* Minos.	

These last two are not properly dialogues, but the one a dicastic, the other an epideictic exercise.

[1] Cf. Zeller's *Plato and the Older Academy* (Eng. tr.), p. 49, note.
[2] iii. 61.

Several important remarks here suggest themselves. Aristophanes does not utilise the hints just mentioned in the dialogues themselves. He does not follow any scientific order on any conceivable theory of Platonism. He seems also to have recognised as genuine, not only works now rejected, but even those doubted of old, such as the *Epinomis.* Diogenes next mentions the arrangement of Thrasylus, two centuries later, into nine tetralogies—a dramatic connection often forced and absurd, and of no real value. It was probably suggested, as Grote observes, by the really close bond which unites the *Euthyphron, Apology, Criton,* and *Phædon.* It is Thrasylus' full catalogue of thirty-five dialogues (including *Apology* and *Menexenus*) which Grote thinks based upon the safe traditions of the Academy and the critical work of the χωρίζοντες, or critical sifters, of Alexandria, and therefore perfectly trustworthy. But Thrasylus implies another cross division which is of far more value—that into Dialogues of Search (ζητητικοί) and of Exposition (ὑφηγηματικοί).[1] It appears also from the statement of Diogenes that essays of classification in old times were almost as numerous and various as among the modern Germans, for nine dialogues which he mentions were each put first in the list by divers critics. I am very far from agreeing with Zeller's inference, that these attempts imply a trustworthy tradition or belief in some fixed and definite order. But to those who are sceptical as to any other logical nexus between the dialogues, or of the possibility of tracing a gradual philosophical progress throughout them, this distinction at least is salient and quite unmistakeable, that in some of them a discussion is raised, which results in no conclusion, while in others principles are laid down, and a whole system of law or of philosophy dogmatically expounded.

§ 412. Next after the labours of the Alexandrian and Augustan grammarians, who seem not to have attempted any deep sounding of the mind of Plato, but were content with distinctions of form, we come to the neo-Platonists, who went into

---

[1] Cf. the list on page 165, note 3. His subdivisions under these heads I need not repeat. The same principle underlies the classification of Albinus (in his *Isagoge* to Plato), though he differs in his subdivisions, as may be seen in Zeller's note (p. 97).

the opposite extreme, and sought to find mystical revelations and divine allegories at every turn in the dialogues. This method of criticism, along with the attempts to show Plato's agreement with the religion of Moses, and his consequent inspiration as an 'Attic Moses,' is now so universally discredited that it may suffice to refer the reader (with Grote) to the prefaces with which Ficinus, the great Renaissance Platonist, introduces the Dialogues in his Latin version (Florence 1494). Serranus, in Stephens' edition of 1578, goes back to the old external way of classifying, and makes out six groups according to the general subjects treated (Ethics, Physics, Politics, &c.). From this time on till the end of the last century speculation on the internal relation of the dialogues seems to have been suspended. With Schleiermacher a new era commences, and since his day Germany has been flooded with theories based on the internal consciousness of the theorist, ascribing a necessary and natural order to the writings of Plato, together with rejections of all those which will not suit the theory, and bold assertions that all opponents and objectors are ignorant of the true spirit of real Platonism. The combatants may be divided into three camps, that of Schleiermacher—now rather waning in influence, though he was the originator of the whole discussion, and still supported by Ritter, Brandis, and Ribbing, which holds that Plato consciously composed his dialogues in a fixed and logical order, which anyone can ascertain who attains to a thorough knowledge of the Platonic system. Next comes that of K. F. Hermann, with a large following, who denies any conscious arrangement in the mind of Plato, but holds that the dialogues show the necessary growth and development of his mind. Various attempts are now being made to reconcile these theories, and to assert this necessary growth, accompanied with a conscious expression of it in certain pieces. Lastly, there is the English school, of which Grote is the leader, and Mr. Jowett the present representative. and to which we may almost add the German Ast, had he not been so illogical as to reject numerous dialogues, though holding the view which most easily admits differences of style and treatment. This school is perfectly sceptical as to the possibility of proving any large plan or sequence in the dialogues, and not only holds each to be complete in itself and isolated, but even careless of contradicting the rest, and often openly inconsistent with them. It follows logically that all dialogues not discredited by *external* evidence must be accepted, such a thing as internal improbability being seldom admissible.

The great and continuous divergence of opinion among the German Platonists, who have now for 100 years exhausted all possible combinations without establishing any sure results, almost compels us to adopt the third theory in the main. A few general guide-posts are perhaps not denied by anybody. These are, for example, that the purely Socratic and questioning dialogues were written when Plato was fresh from the converse of Socrates ; that after his travels in Italy and Sicily he approached Pythagorean metaphysics, and thus brings out principles perfectly foreign to Socrates under his authority. Furthermore, dialogues like the *Euthydemus* show a polemical antagonism to Antisthenes and Isocrates, or some such persons, who were rivals as heads of schools ; these are to be referred to the more active period of his life, while such didactic and dogmatic dialogues as the *Laws*, which was certainly written in Plato's old age, seem to indicate the latest form of his teaching, and the temper of his decaying years. With the exception of these, and perhaps a few more such generalities, nothing certain ever has been ascertained as to the logical order of the Platonic writings.

§ 413. For convenience' sake, and in order to afford some frame wherein we may arrange the diverse pieces, the plan of Zeller,[1] put forth without much dogmatism, may be followed as reasonable, and fairly probable ; but the great work of Grote has for ever destroyed the hope of any surer results. Following this division, we may regard the first, a purely Socratic group, as consisting of the *Lesser Hippias, Lysis, Charmides, Laches, Protagoras, Euthyphron, Apology,* and *Criton.* In these there is no Pythagoreanism, no attempt at a philosophy of nature ; they are purely ethical, and concerned with virtue in the Socratic sense, as one and reducible to knowledge.

----

[1] *Plato,* pp. 115, sq.

Next come the *Gorgias, Menon, Theætetus,* and *Euthydemus,* in which the doctrine of Ideas, moral theories of the state after death, the theory of Reminiscence, and sundry Pythagorean elements begin to appear. The *Phædrus,* about whose date the widest diversity of opinion exists, may have been an introduction to this group. Next come the dialogues, which, while presupposing both Pythagoreanism and the theory of Ideas, introduce us to Eleatic and Megarian philosophy, abstruse and dry in character : these are the *Cratylus, Sophist, Politicus, Parmenides,* and *Philebus,* and to these Zeller appends the two most celebrated of all, the *Symposium* and *Phædon,* which latter is often placed shortly after the death of Socrates, though its doctrines show a large advance on Plato's earlier works. Towards the end of his life come the *Republic, Timæus, Critias,* and *Laws.* Zeller, in this list, omits the *Ion* and *Menexenus,* as well as the *Epistles* and first *Alcibiades.* I think the former two are not spurious, or at least proved spurious, and feel the danger of determining such matters without very strong evidence. I venture to assert that no modern German critic would have admitted either the *Lesser Hippias* or *Laws,* and that their spuriousness would now be an accepted fact, had not Aristotle chanced to allude to them in passages of still remaining works. While such mentions of Aristotle are of course conclusive (if precise) as to the authenticity of a dialogue, nothing can be inferred from his silence. Thus the *Protagoras,* one of the most universally accepted, has no early guarantee whatever. The extant allusions of this kind, both direct and indirect, are collected with great care by Bonitz in his valuable *Index Aristotelicus,* and are discussed by Zeller,[1] who will not, however, admit the *Menexenus,* in spite of a direct reference in Aristotle's *Rhetoric,* on account of ' internal improbabilities.' So indelible is the habit of preferring *à priori* speculations to external evidence !

§ 414. I must add a word on the chronological order of the dialogues, which need not be the same as the logical order, for Plato may have composed a prior composition, *dramatically,* as an afterthought or introduction to an already

---

[1] pp. 54-77.

existing dialogue.   Again, such a dialogue as the *Phædo*, which in dramatic propriety should follow immediately on the *Apology*, is supposed with good reason to be a very distant afterthought to an early group.

There is no direct evidence that any dialogue whatever was published during the lifetime of Socrates, except the anecdote in Diogenes,[1] that Socrates, on hearing the *Lysis* read, exclaimed, ' Herakles, what a number of lies this youth has told about me ! '   This Grote rejects, and argues with great force that Plato published nothing till after the death of Socrates, and when he had at least reached his twenty-eighth year. We have no evidence to decide the question, though Grote's argument is rendered probable by the fact that several of the apparently earliest dialogues are written about the accusation and death of Socrates, and must therefore fall after this date. So also the group called the second in Zeller's list, above given, alludes to events which happened 395–4 B.C., and is later than that date.   We have hardly any other chronological data, unless we argue that striking inconsistencies imply a lapse of some years for their growth. Thus the theory of the *Protagoras*, that virtue is the intelligent pursuit of happiness, and the balancing of lesser pains against greater rewards—this theory is contradicted in the *Gorgias*, where the identity of the good and the pleasant is distinctly controverted as an immoral doctrine.   Again, Pericles and Isocrates, who are greatly praised by name in the *Phædrus*, are rudely handled and severely censured in the *Gorgias* and *Euthydemus*, if indeed Isocrates is the philosopher-politician alluded to in the latter.   If the *Ecclesiazusæ* of Aristophanes were directed against Plato's *Republic*, we should obtain a minor limit (391 B.C.), which is contrary to all probability, as that dialogue has unmistakeable evidences of maturity in views and dogmatism in tone.   The absence of all direct mention of Plato in the play permits us to reject it as positive testimony.   The author of the seventh Platonic Letter speaks as if the *Republic* were an early work, but probably upon this very evidence, whereas the play itself[2] shows many reasons for believing that Plato is not in view.

---

[1] iii. § 35.   [2] Cf. Zeller, p. 139, note.

§ 415. It seems hardly necessary in this general sketch to give a particular abstract of each of the dialogues, for purely metaphysical discussions are foreign to our plan, and the actual texts are easily accessible, not to speak of the admirable and classical versions of Schleiermacher, the Stuttgart translators (40 vols., 1869), and Mr. Jowett. I shall therefore confine myself to general indications of their contents, while in a few typical cases a fuller treatment will include the broad features which recur in divers discussions. And first let us consider the form adopted by Plato and other followers of Socrates—the philosophical dialogue.[1]

§ 416. It is in no sense true that Plato was the originator of this literary form, though most of his commentators attempt to add this to his other merits. But it is certain that he was the greatest artist of this kind which Greece, or perhaps the world, ever saw, and that as he drew into one all the partial truths of earlier philosophy, so he united in his works all the various kinds and attempts of his forerunners in the use of dramatic prose. His early biographers asserted that he studied carefully the *mimes* of Sophron, which were apparently prose and city idylls, portraying character and manners among the lower classes at Syracuse.[2] In the *Poetic*, indeed, all similarity between these mimes and Plato's dialogues is flatly denied ; but the assertions of the *Poetic* are so inaccurate and conflicting, that I attach little weight to them, and think this denial, if true, refers to the subject-matter only. At all events, it is certain that in this school of Sophron and Xenarchus character-drawing was attained by prose dialogue, perhaps the truest forerunner of the Roman satura or medley. I turn next to another model, which must have been before Plato's eyes, and in which dialogue must have played an important part —the *Memoirs* of Ion of Chios, and Stesimbrotus of Thasos.

---

[1] The definition given by Albinus (*Isagoge*, c. i.) is very complete, and each member of it reasoned out : Ἔστι τοίνυν οὐκ ἄλλο τι, ἢ λόγος ἐξ ἐρωτήσεως καὶ ἀποκρίσεως συγκείμενος περί τινος τῶν πολιτικῶν καὶ φιλοσοφῶν πραγμάτων. μετὰ τῆς πρεπούσης ἠθοποιίας τῶν παραλαμβανομένων προσώπων, καὶ τῆς κατὰ τὴν λέξιν παρασκευῆς.

[2] Cf. Vol. I. § 240.

These works are not known, or not quoted, by writers of this period, and are, as I have above said,[1] liable to suspicion on this account ; but if they existed in Plato's day, as is alleged, he must necessarily have known them, and the extracts in Athenæus show us how essential dialogue and character-drawing must have been to them.   The use of rapid question and reply is fully understood by Herodotus, who perpetually enlivens his history with dialogue ; and even by Thucydides, who in two or three striking passages[2] exchanges the tameness of his narrative for this more striking form.   I am here speaking of the shorter and simpler dialogues in both historians ; for the more elaborate discussions, such as that of Xerxes and Artabanus in the one, and the Melian dialogue in the other, are rather upon a tragic model than upon that of any earlier prose dialogue, nor indeed do they aim at any special character-drawing, as Albinus points out.   Of course the great influence and popularity of tragedy and comedy must have stimulated all contemporary literature in the same direction.   Most young authors of the day—Plato among the number—aspired to be dramatic leaders of thought, like the great poets, who had remodelled all Greek poetry.   We even saw how the legal oratory of the day assumed the dramatic tone, and how the orator composed his speech according to the very *character* of the client who spoke it.   This dramatising of court speeches is perhaps the closest parallel we can find to the philosophical dialogue, as a piece of ἠθοποιία or character-painting.   Along with all these indirect antecedents, we are distinctly told that the form of dialogue had been already employed for philosophical teaching by Alexamenos of Teos—to us a bare name— and the Eleatic Zeno.   We see plainly in the antinomies of the latter how dialogue, with prompt question and answer, was the most natural and almost necessary form for his writings to assume.   But this was pure dialectic, dry metaphysical subtlety and counter-subtlety, and was doubtless devoid of all grace and poetry.   Perhaps in the *Philebus*, the *Sophistes*, and the *Parmenides*, Plato copied this dry and unattractive, but scientifically invaluable, method of enquiry.

[1] p. 42.   [2] Cf. above, p. 115.

But there is no evidence that Plato, in assuming this form, led the fashion, or turned the minds of men to its advantages. Some of the spurious documents may be as old as the genuine, and it rather seems that the fashion grew up with the age and society of Socrates, and that Plato outran and obscured many rivals and competitors by his genius. We can perceive at least four distinct and important objects attained by adopting it. First, it was the best and most natural way of giving a full and lively history of the life, character, and conversations of his master Socrates, thus producing from another mind, and from a different standpoint, a grander, if not so faithful a memoir of the inimitable master. Secondly, it exhibited most clearly the most Socratic and valuable point in Plato's philosophy—the principle of searching after truth, and of resting in this search as a great intellectual end, whether any conclusion was attainable or not : the raising and discussing of all the objections to, and difficulties in, any theory, could in no other way be brought so vividly before the student. Thirdly, it enabled Plato to put forth opinions tentatively, without assuming any responsibility, and of ventilating a new theory before adopting it as a dogma. In the infancy of philosophy this is no unimportant object, and both in this and the last-named points we may justly compare Plato's dialogues with the disputations of the mediæval schools—a great engine of real culture, and of real education, lost in the hurry and crowding of our modern instruction. Lastly, we must not forget that Plato satisfied a keen dramatic and literary instinct by drawing these personal sketches. He gave rein to a satirical and critical spirit also ; and if, in that strangely modern statement of Socrates at the close of the *Symposium*, we are told that the genius for tragedy and for comedy (of old dissociated) is really one and the same, in no Greek author is it so clearly exemplified as in the author of the tragic *Phædon* and of the farcical *Euthydemus.* Gorgias called him an *iambist*, and most critics a *dithyrambist* in prose.

§ 417. While admitting all these advantages in Plato's dialogues—a literary form which has survived to the present day, and of which he was practically, if not strictly, the originator—it

ought not to be overlooked that they have certain faults inherent in themselves, and perhaps some arising from the peculiarities of their author.   A conversation which exhibits character
on both sides must always command attention, but there are
many long passages in which the respondent is a mere answer-
ing machine, and in which his perpetually repeated, 'Yes, certainly,' 'It seems so,' 'By all means,' excite great *ennui* in the
modern reader. Hence comes the undoubted fact, that this great
author is far more talked about, and lauded to the skies, than
honestly read, and that even diligent scholars find it a task to
read a dialogue of Plato honestly through.   Very often the
questions and answers are minute and trivial, containing no
further interest than the persistent assertion of the importance
of the search after truth as such.   Often, again, the points made
by Socrates are really sophistical and unsound, and we feel
annoyed that Plato will not let the respondent give him the
true and embarrassing reply.

There is, moreover—there cannot but be in modern minds
—a strong feeling that Socrates and his school wasted time in
disputation, and induced habits of idleness, cloaked under the
garb of philosophic research.   It is here that the conditions of
old Attic and of modern life are widely in contrast.   The
Athenian gentleman, with slaves to do his work, with no home
occupation, and living about the city as in a huge club, had
apparently no notion that he could waste his time, when it
was not required in the public service. The modern gentleman thinks very differently.   His work lies in reading and
writing, in the transaction of professional or public business,
his amusement in games and field sports ; so that he seldom
regards conversation as a serious pastime, or a means of ac-
quiring new truth or deeper culture.   This is no doubt much
to be regretted, and we should be reminded that a great deal
of our best knowledge is learned by conversation.   But the
Athenians of Socrates' school surely went into the opposite
extreme.   Even all the literary skill and the nameless charm
of Plato's style cannot conceal from us the fact that his dialogues are tedious in the minuteness and elaboration of their
conversations.   This will be admitted by any candid reader of

Plato who does not belong to the scholastic trade union which thinks that all great Greek authors are to be lauded as perfect, and that even the mildest detraction is to be set down as want of taste, or want of real appreciation or of sympathy for the classics. Verily the merits of such an author as Plato do not need to be supported by a suppression of his weaker points.

§ 418. We might hazard even a further word of criticism as to the form of dialogue he has adopted in some of his greatest works, such as the *Parmenides* and the *Symposium*, in which the main conversation is reported *in indirect narration* by one of the speakers. This prolonged obliqueness of construction, with its crowded infinitives, always appears awkward, not to speak of the dramatic absurdity of making any man repeat from memory a set of speeches or an intricate dialogue. This absurdity is only *artistically* tolerable where the speaker reports a conversation in which he himself took a leading part, as is the case with Socrates in the *Lysis, Charmides*, and *Protagoras*. Zeller [1] quotes Weisse and Schöne as making this distinction of direct and indirect dialogues a fundamental one, and ranging them accordingly—another example of perverse ingenuity in forcing the facts to fit into a preconceived theory. There is no reason whatever for classing together the *Charmides* and *Parmenides*, because Plato chanced to make both of them (dramatically) repeated and not direct conversations. The point is as old as the Alexandrian days, for Diogenes Laertius mentions it,[2] remarking that it is a dramatic rather than a philosophic principle.

The anachronisms in the dialogues, on the contrary, are not disturbing to our enjoyment, though we can imagine sober and critical Athenians sharing in the impatience of Grote, who thinks the historical blunders in the *Menexenus* prove that Plato had never read Thucydides ! This judgment is rendered positively comical by the fact that Socrates, in making his speech on the glories of Athens, actually alludes to events as late as the peace of Antalkidas (387 B.C.), whereas he himself died in 399 B.C. The author of such an anachronism would hardly have recoiled from historical

---

[1] pp. 107-8, note.   [2] ii. § 50.

inaccuracies in older times ; and yet the dialogue is quoted as genuine in Aristotle's *Rhetoric.*

§ 419. I will proceed to analyse a very few of the dialogues, each as representative of a class, though it is necessary to add, and to insist, that there are not any two of them strictly upon the same model, nor is there any one of them in which there are not many fruitful and original remarks. Laying aside the *Apology* and *Criton,* which are intended as special pictures of the speculative and of the practical sides of Socrates' life, we will first approach that group which the commentators call purely Socratic. In most of these, after a dramatic introduction, where the passionate relations of young men at Athens are the leading feature, someone makes a remark implying some moral idea, which is not clearly defined, but used by the public with vague and varying associations. Such are the notions of Valour (*Laches*), Friendship (*Lysis*), Chastity (*Charmides*), Religiousness (*Euthyphron*). Socrates, in the dialogues mentioned, immediately fastens upon this vagueness, and proceeds to sift the connotation of the term in the minds of those around him. He refutes the first crude answer easily, by cross-examining the respondent, and showing him inconsistent with himself ; then other answers are suggested, and in their turn refuted. But Socrates himself generally offers no solution of his own, and where (in another class of dialogues) he does attempt to do so, he often proceeds to refute himself, and show that so far o ly a negative result can be attained, and that it will require a deeper philosophy to establish consistent and scientific definitions of even the most ordinary terms. It is quite plain that this negative dialectic, this sceptical cross-examining, was Socrates' great feature, and that (like Bishop Butler) he was far weaker as a constructive philosopher ; for we may be quite certain that the great system or series of theories put into his mouth in Plato's later dialogues contain not his, but his pupil's notions.

The fragment entitled *Cleitophon,* which most critics assert to be spurious, on account of its cogent criticism on the barrenness of positive results in Socrates' teaching, deals altogether with this point. After a negative discussion on justice, in which various definitions are rejected, Cleitophon turns upon

Socrates, and presses for a positive answer. ' It is not once or twice,' he says, ' that I have endured these perplexities, and have importuned you to clear them up. At last I am wearied out, and come to the conviction, that you are doubtless a consummate proficient in the art of stimulating men to seek virtue ; but as to the ulterior question, how they are to find it, you either do not know, or you will not tell. I am resolved to go to Thrasymachus, or anybody else who will help me, unless you will consent to give me something more than mere stimulating discourses. To one who has not yet received the necessary stimulus, I repeat that your conversation is of inestimable value ; but to one who has already been stimulated, it is rather a hindrance than a help to his fully realising the acquisition of virtue, and with it of happiness.' Such is the summary of these negative and sceptical dialogues, to which Socrates here makes no reply, but which the ancients considered a sort of introduction to the *Republic*, in which the notion of Justice is formally and positively considered.[1]

In selecting a specimen, one is at first strongly inclined to cite the *Lysis* or *Charmides*, in both of which the dramatic introduction—which is laid in a palæstra, among a crowd of fair youths with their passionate elder friends—is peculiarly striking and peculiarly Attic. The excitement at the entrance of Charmides, the reigning beauty, and the intoxication felt at his presence even by Socrates, are among the strangest features in old Greek life, as compared with that of modern Europe. But the questions raised and discussed—What is friendship or affection ? What is chastity or self-control ?—are by no means so important as that in the *Euthyphron*, where a permanent moral difficulty is started.

§ 420. Socrates is going to put in his formal plea of defence against the charge of impiety laid against him by Meletus, when he meets Euthyphron, a man of religious life, and an authority in theological matters—perhaps a Greek pharisee—who is coming to the same archon's office to indict his own father for homicide. This strange situation arose from the following circumstances. A free dependant of the father had

[1] Grote, ii. p. 18.

killed a fellow-servant in a drunken quarrel at Naxos, where-
upon his master threw him bound into a ditch, and sent to the
Exegetes at Athens to know what should be done with him.
Meanwhile, the prisoner died in the ditch of cold and hunger.
For this barbarity, Euthyphron indicts his father as guilty of
homicide, which in the Attic law implied a pollution upon the
house, of the same kind as we should consider murder.   But
though we should feel so deeply this outrage on common
humanity that we might feel disposed to sympathise with
Euthyphron, the Greek public, who were well accustomed to
barbarous treatment of slaves (and this wretched θής is regarded as hardly better), and who did not set the absurd
value we do on human life as such, were of a different opinion.
With them family ties were so sacred and binding, that the
feeling of all Euthyphron's relatives was one of horror at his
proceeding.   'Your father,' said they, 'did not kill the man
(who was in any case a wretched hireling) ; if he did, was not
the man a murderer? and, in any case, to indict one's father
is simply monstrous.'   Such, then, was the verdict of public
opinion.   To this Euthyphron opposes his clearer and better
knowledge.   Either his father's act was just or unjust ; if the
former, let it be so proved ; if not, the murderer is tainted
with a curse, and so is his family.   It is, therefore, an obligation of the strictest kind, on the ground of piety, to remove
this curse ; and so far from being impious to indict him, it
would really be impious to omit doing so.

Here Socrates joins issue.   He professes ignorance on the
merits of the dispute ; for he is ignorant of the general feature
which constitutes piety, and in which all pious acts must par-
ticipate.   What, he asks, is this general feature or quality?
Euthyphron answers by giving the particular case in point : it is
holy to bring to justice him who commits impiety, whoever he
may be.   The examples of the gods—Kronos punishing Uranos ;
Zeus, Kronos—show this.   'Do you really believe these stories,'
says Socrates ; 'I can hardly bring myself to do so, and
this is probably why I am indicted for offending against ortho-
doxy.   But if you insist, of course I must admit them, for I
have no evidence against them.   But to return.   The answer

given is tco special; there are other pious acts to be done. What is the general type or standard that a man should know and apply to all actions, and determine them as pious or the reverse?' The second answer of Euthyphron is : 'That which is pleasing to the gods is holy. But the gods, as you just now said, are often at variance, so that the same act may please one and displease the other. Well, then, what all the gods love—and there are such acts—is holy, and what all hate is unholy and impious.' Here Socrates begins to subtilise, and touches dialectically a great theological question—that of immutable morality. 'Do the gods love an act because it is holy? or is it holy because they love it?' Euthyphron declares himself for the former alternative. 'Well, then, the gods loving it is only an accident, by reason of its essential feature, which has not yet been described.' Here Euthyphron confesses himself puzzled, and Socrates suggests that it may be a subdivision of the Just, viz. our duties to the gods, as ordinary justice is our duty to men. But after a short excursion into this field,[1] Euthyphron impatiently returns to the old orthodox answer, that piety is to do in prayer and sacrifice what is agreeable to the gods, which Socrates shows to be identical with one of the already rejected answers. Here Euthyphron breaks off on the plea of other business, and thus no positive solution is attained.[2]

§ 421. Such are the apparently earlier and simpler *Dialogues of Search*, to which may be added the greater and lesser Alcibiades and Hippias, if we accept them as genuine—which critics are agreed to do in the case of the lesser Hippias, but are doubtful as regards the rest. In all of them Socrates is represented as seeking to purify and deepen a popular notion, by showing vague-

---

[1] Plato is here on the verge of another great modern question : whether piety consists in gratitude to the gods—an act of right traffic between gods and men, as he calls it—or in the love of God as the ideal of perfection. The Xenophontic Socrates held the former ; in Plato's later dialogues the latter is expounded with great loftiness and splendour. But whether this latter doctrine be truly Socratic may well be doubted.

[2] The reader will not forget that a particular phase of this very moral difficulty—the conflict of the most sacred obligations—had occupied all the great tragic poets from Æschylus onward.

nesses and inconsistencies in its application, and by comparing various special meanings, with a view to fixing its general character or essence. In an age when formal logic was in its infancy, and the now well-understood processes of generalisation and specification had not been analysed, it was not only useful, but all-important, to insist upon the conscious use of them ; hence we may well excuse Plato for making these logical processes metaphysical engines, and setting up the results attained by them as laws or principles of the nature of things. Such a mistake was peculiarly likely to overtake the first speculators in formal Logic, who were at the same time ignorant of all languages save their own, and came naturally to think distinctions of language must correspond to differences in things. No confusion was more permanent in Greek philosophy than this double meaning of λόγος, ratio and oratio, as if the Greek language were a necessary and natural manifestation of the reason, and through it of the nature of things.

§ 422. These reflections lead us naturally to a second group of the dialogues, those which are supposed to have been written under the influence of the dry logic of Eucleides of Megara, when Plato went to sojourn there ; nay, by sceptical Germans some of them are even supposed to have been written by thinkers of this school. These are the *Theætetus, Sophistes,* and *Politicus,* which are dramatically intended as a trilogy, and the *Parmenides, Philebus,* and *Kratylus.* The references, however, of the *Sophistes* and *Politicus* to each other and the *Theætetus* are merely dramatical ; for the difficulties raised and left unsolved are not touched in the sequel, nor is there any logical connection in these extended conversations, in which a new speaker, an Eleatic stranger, is introduced in the *Sophistes* as taking up the leading part. Of all the dialogues of this group, the *Theætetus* is probably the most valuable ; for while it is, like the earlier group, strictly a dialogue of Search, without any official result, it discusses all the difficulties, and suggests the solution, of the problem : What is knowledge? What is the relation of a varying subject towards varying objects, which can result in universal and necessary truths? What, again, is opinion? How is false opinion possible?

What is the process and what the criterion of knowledge? This dialogue, like the rest of this group, shows an important advance in philosophising, in that it is not so much popular or vulgar beliefs, but the theories of antecedent thinkers, which are subjected to the Socratic *elenchus.* Thus in the present case it is the Protagorean theory that all truth is subjective, that varying man is the measure of all he can know, and hence of the universe, which is canvassed and criticised. And this theory is very properly regarded as the subjective form of the older objective ' flux of all things ' maintained by Heracleitus.

It belongs to the history of Greek philosophy to discuss the metaphysical aspects of such enquiries ; but it is our duty to call attention to the famous literary passage of the piece, in which the rhetor, who speaks before a tyrannical audience to gain a fixed object, and is accordingly a slave, is contrasted with the philosopher, who spends his leisure in the search after truth, unincumbered by any control or coercion from the outer public. This remarkable passage, which shows a dignity and self-assertion somewhat different from that of the historic Socrates, is worth quoting as a specimen.[1]

[1] *Theaetetus,* p. 172 C : καὶ πολλάκις μέν γε δή, ὦ δαιμόνιε, καὶ ἄλλοτε κατενόησα, ἀτὰρ καὶ νῦν, ὡς εἰκότως οἱ ἐν ταῖς φιλοσοφίαις πολὺν χρόνον διατρίψαντες εἰς τὰ δικαστήρια ἰόντες γελοῖοι φαίνονται ῥήτορες. ΘΕΟ. Πῶς δὴ οὖν λέγεις ; ΣΩ. Κινδυνεύουσιν οἱ ἐν δικαστηρίοις καὶ τοῖς τοιούτοις ἐκ νέων κυλινδούμενοι πρὸς τοὺς ἐν φιλοσοφίᾳ καὶ τῇ τοιᾷδε διατριβῇ τεθραμμένους ὡς οἰκέται πρὸς ἐλευθέρους τεθράφθαι. ΘΕΟ. Πῇ δή ; ΣΩ. Ἧι τοῖς μέν, τοῦτο ὃ σὺ εἶπες, ἀεὶ πάρεστι σχολὴ καὶ τοὺς λόγους ἐν εἰρήνῃ ἐπὶ σχολῆς ποιοῦνται · ὥσπερ ἡμεῖς νυνὶ τρίτον ἤδη λόγον ἐκ λόγου μεταλαμβάνομεν, οὕτω κἀκεῖνοι, ἐὰν αὐτοὺς ὁ ἐπελθὼν τοῦ προκειμένου μᾶλλον, καθάπερ ἡμᾶς, ἀρέσῃ, καὶ διὰ μακρῶν ἢ βραχέων μέλει οὐδὲν λέγειν, ἂν μόνον τύχωσι τοῦ ὄντος. οἱ δὲ ἐν ἀσχολίᾳ τε ἀεὶ λέγουσι · κατεπείγει γὰρ ὕδωρ ῥέον, καὶ οὐκ ἐγχωρεῖ περὶ οὗ ἂν ἐπιθυμήσωσι τοὺς λόγους ποιεῖσθαι, ἀλλ' ἀνάγκην ἔχων ὁ ἀντίδικος ἐφέστηκε καὶ ὑπογραφὴν παραναγιγνωσκομένην, ὧν ἐκτὸς οὐ ῥητέον · οἱ δὲ λόγοι ἀεὶ περὶ ὁμοδούλου πρὸς δεσπότην καθήμενον, ἐν χειρὶ τὴν δίκην ἔχοντα, καὶ οἱ ἀγῶνες οὐδέποτε τὴν ἄλλως ἀλλ' ἀεὶ τὴν περὶ αὐτοῦ · πολλάκις δὲ καὶ περὶ ψυχῆς ὁ δρόμος. ὥστ' ἐξ ἁπάντων τούτων ἔντονοι καὶ δριμεῖς γίγνονται, ἐπιστάμενοι τὸν δεσπότην λόγῳ τε θωπεῦσαι καὶ ἔργῳ χαρίσασθαι, σμικροὶ δὲ καὶ οὐκ ὀρθοὶ τὰς ψυχάς. τὴν γὰρ αὔξην καὶ τὸ εὐθύ τε καὶ τὸ ἐλεύθερον ἡ ἐκ νέων δουλεία ἀφῄρηται, ἀναγκάζουσα πράττειν σκολιά, μεγάλους κινδύνους καὶ φόβους ἔτι ἁπαλαῖς ψυχαῖς ἐπιβάλλουσα. οὓς οὐ δυνάμενοι μετὰ τοῦ

The *Sophistes* is by no means so uniform and consistent. It begins with an exercise in logical division, so as to determine in what exact place of the predicamental lines descending from the genus *acquisitive art*, the position of the *angler* should be placed among those who live by catching their food. As Grote remarks, such exercises were of great value and interest in the infancy of logic, though now of little importance. Plato goes on to speak of the sophist as a man who palms off falsehood for truth, but then passes on to the difficulty : how can you speak falsehood—how can you assert non-being, which has *ex hypothesi* no existence ? This question had already occupied him in the *Theætetus*, and is here discussed against the materialists, who assert as real objects of sense only, and against the idealists, who hold that real being is confined to Forms or Ideas. Plato argues that some mediation must take place when we assert unreality. He then, after a long and tedious discussion, returns to the sophist, whom he paints in dark colours ; though, as Grote justly says, his picture is more suitable to Socrates than to any of the professed sophists we know.

Of the *Politicus* I will speak in connection with the state theories in the *Republic*. It would lead us too far to speak at length of the other three dialogues I have grouped here : the *Parmenides*, which puts into the mouth of that venerable philosopher an exposition to the youthful Socrates of the famous antinomies of the Eleatic school ; the *Philebus*, which discusses the nature of pleasure ; and the *Kratylus*, that curious first essay at derivation of words. In this latter Plato shows plainly

δικαίου καὶ ἀληθοῦς ὑποφέρειν, εὐθὺς ἐπὶ τὸ ψεῦδός τε καὶ τὸ ἀλλήλους ἀνταδικεῖν τρεπόμενοι πολλὰ κάμπτονται καὶ συγκλῶνται, ὥσθ᾽ ὑγιὲς οὐδὲν ἔχοντες τῆς διανοίας εἰς ἄνδρας ἐκ μειρακίων τελευτῶσι, δεινοί τε καὶ σοφοὶ γεγονότες, ὡς οἴονται.

Καὶ οὗτοι μὲν δὴ τοιοῦτοι, ὦ Θεόδωρε · τοὺς δὲ τοῦ ἡμετέρου χοροῦ πότερον βούλει διελθόντες ἢ ἐάσαντες πάλιν ἐπὶ τὸν λόγον τραπώμεθα, ἵνα μὴ καί, ὃ νῦν δὴ ἐλέγομεν, λίαν πολὺ τῇ ἐλευθερίᾳ καὶ μεταλήψει τῶν λόγων καταχρώμεθα; ΘΕΟ. Μηδαμῶς, ὦ Σώκρατες, ἀλλὰ διελθόντες. πάνυ γὰρ εὖ τοῦτο εἴρηκας, ὅτι οὐχ ἡμεῖς οἱ ἐν τῷ τοιῷδε χορεύοντες τῶν λόγων ὑπηρέται. ἀλλ᾽ οἱ λόγοι οἱ ἡμέτεροι ὥσπερ οἰκέται, καὶ ἕκαστος αὐτῶν περιμένει ἀποτελεσθῆναι, ὅταν ἡμῖν δοκῇ · οὔτε γὰρ δικαστὴς οὔτε θεατής, ὥσπερ ποιηταῖς, ἐπιτιμήσων τε καὶ ἄρξων ἐπιστατεῖ παρ᾽ ἡμῖν.

his belief that words express the nature of things, and his tentative analysis of ordinary words is intended to show that the meaning he postulates was in the minds of the first framers. Many modern critics have thought the whole intention was to ridicule some contemporary efforts ; but anyone who has heard ignorant people nowadays attempt derivations, and who knows Plato's attitude, will side with Grote in asserting that the attempt was serious, though only provisional, and that Plato would readily have surrendered his results had anyone shown him a more reasonable method of procedure.

§ 423. As we cannot fix any chronological sequence, we may here turn to a small group of very interesting tracts, which are more clearly satirical in tone than the rest of the dialogues. I will not say that there is anywhere in Plato a want of this quality, but the main purpose of two at least—the *Ion* and the *Euthydemus*—is to ridicule two well-known classes of literary men. In the first Socrates cross-examines, in a tone of good-humoured banter, a popular rhapsode who has just come from a contest of epic recitation at Epidaurus, and who gives us many curious details concerning his profession, and the bold claims which the unintelligent reciters of Homer made to universal knowledge, derived from that omniscient bard. For to the Greek public Homer was strictly a *Bible*, in which beyond controversy all theology and morals were contained. The majority also maintained, though here there were doubters, that all kinds of science and practical wisdom were also to be derived from him. But when Ion confesses that he knows no other poets critically, Socrates explains this peculiarity by expounding two theories which are the direct pagan counterparts of the doctrines of Verbal Inspiration, and of Apostolical Succession in the Christian Church. He holds that the Muse inspired Homer to a certain madness, distinct from, if not opposed to, reason, which made him sing divine truths which he himself did not comprehend ; that this madness is transmitted by a *magnetic* succession to the rhapsodes, and that thus they teach truths on the ground of inspiration, which are not attained by rational discussion or inference.

It may be well to add here the remark, that the whole school

of Socrates never criticise the great poets of their nation from
æsthetic, but from moral grounds ; they never commend a passage as beautiful, but approve or disapprove of it as moral or
wise. The same may be said of the criticism in the *Frogs* of
Aristophanes, and generally of criticism before the days of
Aristotle. Perhaps this is not the smallest reason why the
beauties of Greek poetry are so natural and so unconscious.
That the Greeks of this age were susceptible to these beauties
as such is certain ; it is equally certain that they were quite
foreign to that peculiar vice of modern literature, the conscious
production and conscious analysis of æsthetic effects in poetry.
I need not here turn aside to discuss the many qualifications
and exceptions, some of them only apparent, of this law, which
the reader should verify and emend for himself. The *Ion* closes
with the ridiculous assertion of the rhapsode, that he must
at least be a good general, because he knows his Homer, in
which that art is taught ; Socrates banteringly presses him to
admit the converse, that all good generals must be good rhapsodes.

The *Euthydemus* is similarly a ridiculous picture of the arts
and devices of a pair of professional sophists—Euthydemus and
Dionysodorus. This again is an indirect dialogue, or reported
conversation by Socrates of his discussion with these two men,
who profess to teach arms, and judicial rhetoric, and virtue, but
have lately, in their toothless old age, mastered the art of Eristic,
by which they profess to silence anyone, or in which to instruct
anyone who pays the necessary fee. The dialogue wanders
into coarse and vulgar buffoonery, showing Plato in the light of
a comic artist, though I think he is deficient in wit, even where
he abounds in humour. It is, however, remarkable that the
sophists carry on the very same sort of elenchus or cross-examination as Socrates, but with a totally different object : they wish
to humble the adversary, and display their own force ; Socrates
is always intent on stimulating and suggesting, and never seeks
to confute for the mere sake of victory. There is a curious
epilogue which, as Grote says, seems like an after-thought,
which defends the pure philosopher, even such an one as
Euthydemus, against a popular half-and-half teacher, who is

neither professional orator, nor real philosopher, but a mongrel worse than either, who gives himself great airs, and knows nothing thoroughly. There seems great probability that this points at Isocrates, of whom Plato expressed high hopes in the *Phædrus*, but who had become the head of a rival school, and was now viewed with a critical eye, and not without jealousy, by the head of the Academy.

§ 424. We pass to the *Menexenus*, or funeral panegyric, which Socrates professes to have learnt from hints of Aspasia, who had, he says, taught Pericles his great harangue. This points apparently to the speech in 'Thucydides' second book, in rivalry with which Plato would seem to have composed this dialogue. He represents the art of making funeral harangues as an easy one, and desired, according to Grote, to resist the rhetors on their own ground, by showing he was equal to them in sustained eloquence. If this were indeed his object, we cannot hold that he was very successful. The eulogy of the dead is very inferior to the weighty and splendid performance of Thucydides, though it is smoother in form, and more easy to understand. Yet we hear that it was afterwards very popular at Athens, owing no doubt to the author's general reputation. The review of Athenian affairs comes down to 387 B.C., though put into the mouth of Socrates — an anachronism which causes some to reject the speech. But Aristotle's *Rhetoric* speaks of it, as of other Platonic dialogues, as 'Socrates in the Funeral Speech.' The rhetorical critics from Dionysius to Blass have paid much attention to it, and Dionysius criticises it severely in comparison with the *De Corona* of Demosthenes. Plato was no really finished rhetorician in the Greek sense. Though he laid the foundations for a far deeper and more philosophical theory of rhetoric than any of his contemporaries, he was not in form so strict and irreproachable as they were. He mixes poetical and prose words, he abounds in metaphors, he does not round his periods with accuracy. It is even remarked as regards this speech that he does not adopt the formal improvements of the Isocratic school. The hiatus is not avoided, as it is in later Platonic writings, and the emulation is evidently not with the new, but with the old rhetors, professedly with Archinus and Dion, leading citizens who were probably of the old school, and would not suit themselves to the new refinements which we shall discuss when we come to Isocrates. The *Epitaphios* ascribed to Lysias is very like Plato's speech in plan and structure, and might be regarded as its model, were we sure of its priority. As a performance in rhetorical prose, it is not equal to the speech of Agathon in the Symposium, in which the peculiarly florid and balanced style of that fashionable author seems imitated with wonderful skill.

§ 425. Great as are the merits of the dialogues already mentioned, they are far beneath the writings of the two classes which have yet to be named. The first I will term the perfect dialogues—meaning those of Plato's mature genius, in which both the negative vein and positive philosophical teaching are combined, without any loss in dramatic form or brilliancy. We may call the remaining the constructive dialogues, and discuss in relation with them Plato's political and social theories. But it seems justifiable to apply the term perfect to three pairs of dialogues, which I put in this order, because each pair expounds either the same subject or opposite sides of the same subject. They have no other connection. Thus the *Protagoras* and *Gorgias* set forth opposite views on the nature of virtue, Socrates arguing in the former that it is identical with private utility, while in the *Gorgias* he repudiates this view, and holds that virtue is totally distinct from pleasure. Again the *Phædrus* and *Symposium*, though the former touches on other subjects, are mainly dialogues in which the famous Platonic theory of Eros is expounded and defended against objections. Lastly the *Menon*, which is professedly on the teachableness of virtue, maintains this thesis by adopting the theory of the pre-existence of the soul, and may therefore be brought together with *Phædon*, which preaches its permanence after death. Of all these the *Menon* is perhaps the least striking as a literary piece, though it is philosophically very suggestive, and has inspired poets down to our own day with its magnificent conception of the antenatal life, which accounts for so many great riddles—*à priori* knowledge, noble instincts, sudden discoveries—by moving a step backward, and drawing them from the treasure-house of a former existence.[1] This hypothesis has made the dialogue more famous than its professed subject, the teachableness of virtue, upon which Socrates actually comes to a definite conclusion. Identifying virtue as a kind of *knowledge*, as Socrates consistently did, he holds that the highest kind of virtue, being such, must be communicable ; but that the ordinary virtues of men being only right opinions, are not so conveyed, but come by special inspiration of the gods. Hence it is that there are bad sons of good fathers, and that in general virtue is regarded as a moral, and not an intellectual condition.

§ 426. The *Phædon*, or last conversation and death of Socrates, is certainly the most famous of all Plato's writings, and owes this renown not only to the infinite importance of the subject—the immortality of the soul—but to the touching scenery and pathetic situation in which the dialogue is laid. Socrates and his friends in the prison, the calm cheerfulness of the victim, the distress of the friends, the emotion even of the jailor—these pictures are only paralleled in literature by the one sacrifice which was greater and more enduring than that of the noblest and purest pagan teacher. But there is one moment in the Greek prison, which stands in strange contrast to the deep sympathy and gentleness which relieve the gloom on Calvary. The wife and infant of the philosopher are removed that he may enjoy his last moments undisturbed in the comfort of philosophic converse, and there is no hint that the heart-broken woman had any claim to the most precious moments of her husband's life. Her lamentations were to him in discord with his dying song, but we feel as if the human string had snapt when the Attic martyr dared to silence it. How much nearer were the mother and the Son at the cross of Golgotha ! Yet this scene, one of the greatest in any literature, is not the main interest of the dialogue. It is the clear and cheerful promise of future happiness which has fascinated the thoughtful men of all ages, and especially those who had not obtained a hope of immortality through the adoption of the Christian faith. Before all men the dark grave stands gaping, and ever the question

---

[1] Cf. Grote, *op. cit.* ii. p. 7, and the passage quoted there from the dialogue in a note (p. 81 B).

repeats itself, What is the hereafter? This is the world-grief, the world-fear which Plato seeks to remove, and his answer has comforted patriots and martyrs in many ages and divers lands.

But the reader who imagines that here at least he will find a pure and simple strain, that, like the song of the dying swan, the notes must be clear and the melody simple and pathetic, will be greatly disappointed. The dialogue is full of hard meta-physic concerning the self-motion of the soul, its participation in the eternal ideas of a former existence, its likeness or unlike-ness to a harmony, and, moreover, concerning the nature of effi-cient and final causes. The discussion ends with an elaborate and difficult myth concerning the future state, which tries the intellect, but does not excite the emotions, of the reader. In all these features the *Phædon* bears a singular analogy to its great musical parallel in modern times, the famous *Requiem* in which Mozart declared his hopes and fears through the last hours of his failing life. Here too, at first hearing, the ear misses the simple and sweet melodies which he composed in earlier life, but is surprised with all the intricacies, all the display of wonderful learning, which heap harmony upon harmony, in-version upon inversion, subject upon subject in complicated counterpoint. It requires long familiarity both with Plato and Mozart to feel the great leading ideas, and follow the thread of the divine argument. But even to honest men who are not satisfied with the reasoning, the practical evidence that Socrates showed his own perfect conviction of its truth is perhaps the clearest and the most effective corroboration.

No doubt Plato has here introduced some metaphysic of his own. Indeed the doctrine of Ideas is so developed and prominent in the *Phædon*, that the critics place its composition long after Socrates' death, and late in Plato's mature life. But the main picture must be true, and if Plato had left us no other monument of his genius, it would have sufficed to place him in the highest rank.

§ 427. The most striking contrast to the *Phædon* is the *Symposium*, which is no doubt really greater and more bril-liant, but is so intensely Greek, that it sounds strange and even offensive to modern ears. It is an account given by

Aristodemus of a banquet at the house of the tragic poet Agathon after one of his victories, at which, together with other less famous persons, Socrates, the physician Eryximachus, Aristophanes, and by and by Alcibiades, discuss the nature and praise of Eros. The introduction is very graphic, and brings before us vividly the manners of refined society at Athens. Instead of drinking hard, which most of them had been doing the night before, or listening to a flute girl, they 'send her to play to the women within, if they like it,' and propose to speak in turn in praise of Love. The speeches are somewhat strained and mythological, especially that of Aristophanes, which is more grotesque and far-fetched than witty, and again shows that Plato had no real wit at command, in spite of his delicate humour. The speech of Agathon is, on the contrary, a very remarkable rhetorical display, and well deserves the applause which it receives from the company. It is in the old style of Gorgias, full of alliterations and conceits, and is evidently carefully copied from the poet's style. The speech of Socrates, whose passion for cross-examination breaks out several times during the dialogue, is an exposition in which he repeats the lessons he professes to have heard from the prophetic Diotima, and forms (with the *Phædrus*) the *locus classicus* for the proper understanding of the Platonic Theory of Love. But presently Alcibiades breaks in with a riotous party, and the banquet degenerates into a scene of drunkenness and almost of ribaldry. For Alcibiades, instead of praising Eros, undertakes to praise Socrates, and gives such an account of his resistance to erotic temptation, as even in Greek society is only excused by the drunkenness of the narrator. Nevertheless, the most wonderful of all our pictures of Socrates, in all his ugliness, his fascination, his deep sympathy, his iron courage, his unassailable chastity, is this panegyric of the licentious Alcibiades. The end of the banquet shows him in yet another light, as a man of so strong a head, that he can drink most men under the tables, and sit discoursing though his audience is unfit to follow him upon the analogies of the pathetic and the humorous, and how a tragic ought also to be a comic poet. This quality of resisting intoxication was prized by Plato even more than it is nowadays, as giving proof of a strong and clear intellect, not easily disturbed by outward causes.

§ 428. The *Phædrus* is a discourse in a far simpler setting— there are only two speakers, Socrates and Phædrus—but yet there are few Platonic works more full of poetry, as Socrates, by the shady banks of the Ilissus, and within view of the theatre of Dionysus, soars into a mighty dithyramb on the nature and effects of that divine impulse which leads us to long for immortality, and to seek after perfection. The position of this piece in the development of the author's system has been much disputed, but there seems now to be a sort of general agreement, even among the Germans, that it was an early work. This is most in accordance with the high expectations expressed of Isocrates, who afterwards became a rival, and is probably (above, p. 185) censured in the *Euthydemus*. It accounts also for the favourable judgment here pronounced on Pericles, in contrast to the severe remarks in the *Gorgias*.[1] As to what the critics say about the youthful exuberance of the style, and what in the translation of Zeller is called 'the want of intuitive faculty in the myth,' it seems to me discovered to suit the theory of its early composition. On the other hand, the great doctrines which Plato is supposed to have attained gradually, and long after the death of Socrates, are here almost all distinctly preached. The Reminiscence of previous existence, the Platonic Forms or Ideas, the Eros, and other points, show that if this is indeed an early work, the favourite theory of a gradual evolution in Plato must be abandoned. And this is the sensible view of Grote.

The dialogue opens with the recitation of the erotic speech alleged to be Lysias', which has been discussed above (p. 143), and to which Socrates at first replies with a sarcastic parallel speech, formally inferior to the Lysian harangue. But then craving pardon of the god, he breaks out into that wonderful rhapsody on the nature of philosophic love, which has made its everlasting mark upon human thought, and still survives in the mouth of the modern public which has no

[1] But cf. Thompson, Pref. to his Ed., and Usener, *Rh. Mus.* xxxv. p. 131.

inkling of its real sense. The identifying of all kinds of Eros as mere degrees of the same eternal instinct—the Love of the Ideal Beauty, which is coincident with the Good and the True—is no doubt a very noble theory. Above all it marks in old Attic days a very different kind of pursuit of knowledge from that of modern life, when competition for material rewards is stifling all the poetry and charm of learning. The passion for truth, which Plato held to be a love 'passing the love of women,' is now a rare thing to meet, and is regarded as an unpractical anachronism. But while we admit the poetical and æsthetic beauty of the doctrine, it must be confessed a very unfortunate specimen of the perpetual efforts of Socrates to find a common thread or connecting link between all the senses in which the same term was used in ordinary speech. It might puzzle an ignorant person of intelligence to know how Plato identified the sexual instinct with the longing to solve a mathematical problem. The desire of happiness is the desire after *the Good*, which is identical with the True—this leads us to the love of Mathematics or to any other new truth. Again the desire to possess the good must be a desire to possess it *for ever;* hence a desire for immortality, hence, when this is unattainable, the desire to procreate an *alter ego* who may represent us. And the selection of beauty for this purpose is of course the desire of possessing the Beautiful in its phenomenal manifestation, for this alone of the eternal Ideas has its illustration in sense. Such is the logic of the theory of Eros.

The latter part of the dialogue, after the famous myth comparing the soul to a chariot with ill-matched horses, is a criticism on existing Rhetoric, and suggestions of a newer and wider theory. He complains that the existing professional speakers have neither the logical nor the psychological knowledge necessary for the true art. In the first place the subject must be carefully divided, and the heads subordinated—an advice still valuable, and which, if taken to heart by the many persons who deliver *invertebrate* harangues, might raise their performances into a higher order. Secondly, the special peculiarities of the minds to be addressed must be studied, and the argument specially suited to these circumstances. As Grote observes, these conditions are too exacting, and it is not fair to attack the practical men who were training the Attic public in habits of debate, because they could not satisfy the requirements of the philosopher. But nevertheless Plato, though himself a rhetorician inferior in form to his ablest contemporaries, laid the basis of a better and more permanent philosophy of Rhetoric—developed by Aristotle to some extent, but requiring and admitting of application at all ages and among all kinds of culture. It has indeed been well shown by Spengel that the hints thrown out by Plato in this dialogue on the defects of the popular rhetoric of the day, on the importance of ψυχαγωγία, or psychological study of human character, and on the essentials of proper proofs and method, contain all the really valuable matter of Aristotle's rhetoric, and that they are silently adopted and developed by Plato's great pupil. Aristotle refers indeed to the polemic against rhetoric in the *Gorgias* for the purpose of refuting and qualifying Plato's views as there expressed. But no doubt Spengel is right, that it was not the fashion of the day to quote authorities, and that Aristotle's silence as to the *Phædrus* arises from no vulgar jealousy, but rather from cordial approval of this striking flash of Plato's far-seeing genius.

Another topic in the *Phædrus* is the comparative value of written and oral teaching, on which again we have from Plato a profoundly true, if exaggerated, theory. He despises mere written discourses. He does not believe that a man can be taught to know anything by such means. Until a man has discussed a subject with kindred minds, until he has undergone a careful cross-examining and sifting of his views, he cannot be said to know thoroughly, or have made his own, any subject. Here Plato argues with the mediæval schools, or rather against the modern universities, where the increase of examinations has compelled students to spend their time in reading many books, and remembering what they say. When the test is a *colloquium*, or discussion with the examiner, some of the resulting evils may be obviated; but even this safeguard has been for the most part abolished by the English universities, and many candidates for honours, who can write down apparent knowledge on paper, would be speechless if set down to stand the *vivâ voce* elenchus of the examiner. However, the tirade against the value of written discourses (which is repeated from the *Phædrus* in the seventh epistle) sounds strange from one of the most prolific authors of written treatises in his day, many of them expository and didactic in style.

§ 429. The criticism of Rhetoric in the *Phædrus* leads us naturally to the *Gorgias*, in which the same subject is handled at greater length, and with greater detail. Rhetoric is treated as the art of practical politics, of persuading the multitude, just like Sophistic, which aims at laying down laws both of morals and politics. Socrates, on the contrary, insists that true politics are the art of making men happier by making them better, and are therefore a consequence or deduction from ethics and from a thorough philosophy of human nature. The sophist Gorgias, like Protagoras in the dialogue which bears his name, is represented as an estimable man and a successful teacher, but not rising above the popular level, and only teaching by knack, not from any scientific principle. In the mouth of Polus and of Kallikles, two inferior followers, are put certain repulsive theories of selfish morality, of the right of the stronger, and of the happiness of power, to which Socrates replies by showing that vice is indeed misery, and that the happiest thing for the evil-doer is to suffer condign punishment, as the sick man must endure painful remedies. He all through compares vice to disease of body—an analogy least of all tenable on his theory that vice is ignorance, and that the wicked man is ignorant of his condition, and requires to be restrained and corrected by wise interference from without. Though Plato does not say it, the only disease which really suits his argument is that form of lunacy in which the patient is happy and contented under his hallucinations ; for then indeed the man who does wicked acts, without knowing they are such, is in a worse condition than he who does them with a consciousness that they are wrong.

The *Gorgias* is the greatest of all pagan protests in favour of absolute morality against the utilitarian theory, that good is pleasure, and evil pain. In this dialogue there is no account whatever taken of present pleasure, and he alone is thought a true philosopher and a good man who can despise such inducements, and follow his conscience in spite of bodily pain and torture.   The first declaration of Stoicism, and of the self-denial of our Gospel, is to be found in the splendid and ennobling argument of Socrates, who knows that he will not be followed by the mob, who feels himself isolated and disliked, but who claims the inalienable right of the honest man to think for himself, and follow those eternal laws of justice which alone can render any human soul, or any human society, permanently happy. Grote complains that in arguing against utility, and even in supporting it (*Protagoras*), Plato only supposes that coarse form which regards the purely private interest of the individual, without considering the utility of those around him. And no doubt by bringing in this latter consideration, late writers in ethics have contrived, as Grote does, to put a fair face on the doctrine of Interest.   But is not this the colouring of an ugly theory with the colours borrowed from a foreign source ? Can the regard for others be called utility or interest with any common decency of expression ? The very assertion *this is my interest* excludes in many cases those of the rest of mankind, and if these interests clash with it, to choose them is to violate the doctrine of utility in its only proper and reasonable sense. Thus the noble protest of the *Gorgias* stands, with the *Phædo*, among those writings of Plato which have not (like the *Symposium* and *Phædrus*) lost their point by a change of social conditions, and there are few of the dialogues more profoundly instructive and interesting to the ethical student of the present day.

§ 430. A remarkable contrast to it, in ethical theory, is the *Protagoras* (on the possibility of teaching virtue). This dialogue is in style and scenery not a whit inferior to the *Gorgias ;* nay, it is even a more elaborate and brilliant composition, and not even the theorists who wish to prove it an early and mistaken piece can find in it the supposed crudities of the *Phædrus.*   It has all the marks of Plato's ripe scholarship and literary perfection. Yet in it Protagoras is made the honest and persuasive advocate of the best traditional morality, whereas Socrates attacks these views, and holds that virtue is the art of computing our pleasures and pains, and making the most of the balance. To utilitarians like Grote, this theory, which is very foreign to Plato's general tone, is peculiarly attractive. Nay they even strain points to bring out this side of the Socratic ethics in other dialogues. No doubt there was a certain vulgar homeliness about Socrates, which sometimes taught the pleasant consequences of virtue as if they were its chief recommendation. It was, moreover, an excellent engine in disputation, as it opposes an intellectual computation of results to an often vague æsthetic feeling. But the real value of the *Protagoras*, as compared with the *Gorgias*, is to demonstrate Grote's theory of the mutual independence and frequent conflicts of the dialogues, which were written separately, and which each put their own point of view, often in intentional variance from the rest. Plato evidently was too genuine a pupil of Socrates not to feel the difficulties in all ethical speculations, and though he was quite ready to dogmatise, and set up a system, he was quite ready to discuss and debate its foundations. In fact, as Grote has shown beyond all question, the constructive and the sceptical sides of Plato are separate streams of thought, and he did not seek to bring them into one channel.

On another point these two dialogues are interesting. They prove the general respectability and high character of the leading sophists. Though Plato was the determined enemy of their system, though he ridiculed and censured the pretence of teaching excellence, moral or intellectual, for money, he always makes inferior followers of the great sophists—Polus, Thrasymachus, Euthydemus—the butts of his satire, and treats both Gorgias and Protagoras with respect. They are not debaters, they cannot stand a cross-examination from Socrates, but they teach vulgar morals with elegance and sincerity, and there are few finer passages than the exposition put into Protagoras' mouth of the general diffusion and teaching of virtue by all society in a civilised Greek city.[1]

§ 431. We pass to the last class—the purely or mainly constructive dialogues, in which Plato has set forth his views on the construction of the world (*Timæus*) and on the reconstruction of society (*Republic* and *Laws*), with the fragment called *Critias*.

[1] *Protagoras*, pp. 322-3.

These latter are so important from a social and political view, as well as from their great length and explicitness, that they deserve special consideration. The *Republic* is, moreover, the best composed and most perfect composition of Plato, so much so that those German critics, who assume that a man must decay in old age, will not allow it to be placed late in the catalogue. All agree that the *Laws*, if genuine, were a late work, and were intended to give a more practicable scheme than the *Republic*, both of them being, however, harmonious in principle.

But the style and tone of thinking are very different. There is no kind of Platonic excellence which is not represented in the *Republic*. There is the gentle, pertinacious, ironical Socrates in the first two books ; there is the didactic, imaginary Socrates to suit Plato's convenience in the later books. There is the finest character-painting—the resigned and mellow old age of Kephalos, the brutal frankness and impetuosity of Thrasymachus, the delicately shaded differences between Glaucon and Adeimantus, both earnest seekers after truth. There is hard-and-dry metaphysic in the fifth and sixth books ; there is a splendid myth, that of Er the Armenian, at the close of the tenth. Few of the important theories of other dialogues can be cited which are not alluded to or implied in the argument. But when there are oppositions, such as between the *Gorgias* and *Protagoras*, it is the nobler and more ideal side which is adopted. In fact, there are peculiar points of contact with the *Gorgias* and *Phædon*, and perhaps less of the erotic element than we should expect from the author of the *Phædrus* and *Symposium*.

§ 432. The formal subject of the dialogue is the enquiry, *what is justice?* It is the subject approached with such boldness, and with so direct a challenge to Socrates in the *Kleitophon*, that those who accept that fragment as genuine think it was originally intended as the opening of the *Republic*. Others again, from the negative and lively tone of the first two books, imagine that this portion was an early composition, added to and enlarged by Plato in his later and more constructive years. All these are but conjectures. What is more important to note is that the work has taken both its name and importance, not from the official, but from the indirect or accidental investigation which Socrates introduces in a huge parenthesis. The problem to be solved is the nature of justice. It is only by the assumption of a civilised polity being a system analogous to the mental constitution of an individual, and of larger and easier survey, that the conversation passes into the description of the ideal *State,* falsely called by us the *Republic,* as the absence of monarchy is by no means essential to Plato's scheme. We know in fact from the *Politicus* that he was inclined to the rule of a single head, and an absolute head too, provided the ideal character, the king-philosopher, could be found to conduct it. In the *State* or *Republic* before us, he places the control under a small number of guardians, with similar qualifications to his *Politicus,* but the number is immaterial, their relations to one another are not considered, and their authority is regarded rather as an abstract unity than as the wisdom resulting from discussion, and the decision of the majority in a consulting board. The real point, which he considers vital in the constitution, is to exclude the public from consulting on state affairs, and to confine the government to one, or to a few, select experts, who are not to be required to impart their reasons to the subject classes, or to submit to criticism.[1] This is the attitude of all those aristocratic theorists who speculated on the best form of polity in Plato's age. They were all profoundly convinced of the evils of a democracy, and still more of the inexpediency of amateur politics. The hand-to-mouth legislation of mobs, or of the casual advisers of mobs, was to them absurd on so vastly important an issue, and they considered that here if anywhere professional skill was absolutely required. The common sense or collective wisdom of a number of intelligent private men—the best form of government, according to modern notions—was by them

---

[1] Cf. his argument in the *Politicus* (pp. 292 3) beginning : μῶν οὖν δοκεῖ πλῆθός γε ἐν πόλει ταύτην τὴν ἐπιστήμην δύνατον εἶναι κτήσασθαι; his conclusion is (p. 297 B) : ὡς οὐκ ἄν ποτε πλῆθος οὐδ' ὡντινωνοῦν, τὴν τοιαύτην λαβὸν ἐπιστήμην, οἷον τ' ἂν γένοιτο μετὰ νοῦ διοικεῖν πόλιν, and therefore (p 292) : τὴν μὲν ὀρθὴν ἀρχὴν περὶ ἕνα τινά, καὶ δύο, καὶ παντάπασιν ὀλίγους, δεῖν ζητεῖν, ὅταν ὀρθὴ γίγνηται. He goes on to compare the art to that of medical men, who treat patients of all ranks and dignities, without allowing them to interfere or meddle with the treatment, often painful and distressing, which medicine and surgery prescribe.

thoroughly despised.   If any of the practical politicians, like Pericles, had really done anything great, it was to be accounted for by their partial acquaintance with deeper philosophy, and their even occasional converse with the philosophers who raised their thoughts to the general laws of the world.   Yet even Pericles had fallen vastly short of the Platonic requirements, as we may see in the *Gorgias.*

Assuming then that the public was unfit to govern itself, Plato, and with him the Greek theorists, were furthermore quite averse to allowing it even that liberty of life, which was the mark of the Athenian democracy, and which all actual states allowed their citizens in their own homes.   The general notion which governed Greek life was that the state could demand any sacrifice from the citizen, that his personal rights were as nothing in regard of any state claim, but that, provided he submitted to this demand, his private life was to be without control.   When the citizen entered the strong door of his house, he was absolute master, and it required some extraordinary violence or scandal to persuade the state to interfere.   Thus ordinary Greek politics, while holding the absolute power and claims of the state, were less particular than we are in maintaining private morality.

There was one peculiar exception—the Spartan society under the paternal despotism of the ephors.   Here the young men at least were kept under control all through their life. They lived in common, slept in common, hunted in common, and were all the time under organised supervision.   Plato applies this idea to the higher classes of his state, and, strangely enough, makes this higher caste or class the military class. The men of his day were beginning to find out that a citizen militia, torn from home and from peaceful duties, was no match for professional warriors, like the Spartans, whose discipline and experience were now being imitated by mercenary troops and paid generals.   Hence the theorist set apart a special caste as a military guard for the rest of the state, and he devotes much of his treatise to their education and maintenance.   Moreover, like that Homer whom he, though himself so saturated with his genius, ejects from his state, he will not conde-

scend to describe the life and training of the artisan or husband-
man class, but spends all his attention upon the noble warriors
in the battle of life.

§ 433. But Plato went far beyond this. He saw clearly that
while the production of other animals was carefully controlled by
men, and hence varieties and improvements in breed were
easily obtained, the production of man, the highest and most
precious of animals, was left to chance, to random fancy, to
stray passion, to pecuniary considerations ; so that congenital
defects, moral obliquities, and all other defects are propagated,
and deform the human race. This question was then, and has
ever since been, so surrounded with a cloud of sentiment, and
entwined with the sacred ties of family affection, that the very
discussion of it is almost intolerable, and only a few advanced
thinkers are even yet to be found who will venture to urge
this necessary condition for the physical and therefore intellectual improvement of mankind. Mr. Jowett, no old-fashioned
conservative, can see how the abolition of private property, and
a community of goods, may yet become the condition of a more
advanced culture, and how the assertion of private rights and
interests may be a hindrance to the public good. But he recoils
even from imagining a society without permanent marriages,
without apparently a home or family ties, and where the propa-
gation of the race was directed and controlled by the state.

It is usual to speak of Plato's theory as the *Community* of
wives—a gross libel on the philosopher, who guarded the relations of the sexes in the strictest way, as long as they lived
together for the state, who made marriage, so to speak, a
'sacrament,' and punished every sin against its sanctity as
impious.[1] But though he does not give details on this point, it
appears that his marriages were to last only for a season, and
when the necessity for a new union of citizens arose, the persons

---

[1] The only point in this part of the *Republic* which is in any sense *immoral* is the license given to the guards who are past the stated age for
marriage. They are not restricted, except in this, that they are not to
produce any children, or, if they do, to make away with them. This is
the point on which modern ethics may well censure the highest Greek
morals.

who had formerly cohabited had no claim to remain together, nor were the parents to know their own children, whom the state took and educated.

It should be observed, that though Plato had no actual model for these temporary marriages, there was at Sparta a greater regard paid to the breeding of the human race, and with good results, than in any other civilised society of either ancient or modern times. This care had certainly advanced to the point of disregarding all the usual sentiment as to the sanctity of married life, for Plutarch tells us facts (in the *life* of Lycurgus) which show how easy the adoption of Plato's scheme might have been at Sparta.[1] The really remarkable point about the matter is this : that in the state where temporary husbands were allowed, and where the production of a healthy and beautiful race was made the paramount consideration, no decay in female honour, no collapse of family ties, or of the influence of home, ever took place. Spartan wives and mothers were, on the contrary, the noblest and purest in Greece. Accordingly, Plato could have pointed to Sparta as the only state which approximated to his ideal polity in freeing the relation of the sexes from the shackles of mischievous sentiment, and nevertheless as the only state in which the physical improvement of the race was undoubted, while the chastity and refinement of both sexes were not impaired. In other respects the Spartans had fallen short (not in degree, but) in principle. They had apparently thought about the equality of the sexes, according to certain legends about Lycurgus, but the weaker sex had proved itself the stronger in resisting the lawgiver, and the education and training of women had accordingly suffered. Plato proposes that in his caste of guards both sexes shall receive the same treatment. Again, as to education, the ignorant and vulgar ephors would of course fall far short of Plato's philosophic elders, who seem rather framed on the model of the Pythagorean brotherhood. Hence music, as well as gymnastic, was to be taught on philosophical principles, and with a view to educate

---

[1] Schömann (*Gk. Antiq.* i. pp. 214, 267, Eng. tr.) thinks that even *polyandry* was sanctioned, but only on late evidence. He cites Polybius, *Excerpt. Vatican.* xii. 6, p. 819 (Ed. Hultsch); but cf. Part II   p. 68.

the faculties and feelings of the mind rather than the muscles of the body. On Plato's theory of the tripartite division of the soul, the intellect must be developed by philosophy, the affections by music, while the union of both is to keep in check the lower appetites.

§ 434. But no real reform can take place in education without a complete reform in religion, and hence Plato goes to his extremest length when he proposes to abolish Homer, the Bible of the Greeks, and all other poetry based on the ordinary theology. He thinks a totally new religion is requisite for pure and sound morals. The deity must be one and the author of all good. He must be passionless, without variableness or shadow of turning, without love or jealousy, without pride or interest. All defects in the world are to be attributed, not to his want of benevolence, but to his want of omnipotence in controlling the original necessities of things. New myths must be invented and circulated in place of the amours and wars of the gods, such myths no doubt as those of which he has himself given specimens in many of the dialogues, and not least in the end of this dialogue. The control of the whole polity is placed in the hands of a small number of elders, chosen from the caste of guards, who have been so trained in speculative philosophy, and so steeped in the contemplation of the Ideal Good, and True, and Beautiful, that they will be persuaded with difficulty, and only as a matter of duty, to undertake the regulation of human affairs.

But the great work is so full and suggestive that no adequate analysis can find a place here. I must omit the determination of justice as the proper relation of the various divisions of the soul, like that of the various orders in the state, as well as the curious history of the various aberrations from right polity in the state, and right morals in the individual, with which the later books are occupied. To one feature, however, I will call attention. It is fashionable among Christian theologians to say that the pagan world, and especially the Greeks, had no consciousness of sin, no real feeling for the pollution of moral guilt. If such persons would take the trouble to read the picture of the tyrant (ix. 1), they would find the portrait of a stricken conscience never equalled, so far as I know, from Plato's day till the days of Macbeth and Richard III. in Shakspeare's drama.

§ 435. Plato's Deuteronomy, the *Laws*, may best find its place as an appendix to the far greater *Republic.* It professes to be the second best constitution, and one surrendering many points to the strong national prejudices which were openly violated or disregarded in his earlier and more complete system. It may also be regarded as a third alternative, if we consider that the absolute control given to the 'kingly artist' in the *Politicus*, and to the select few elders in the *Republic*, is here vested in an established code of laws, which are administered by a sort of timocratic democracy. It abandons expressly the theory of the *Politicus*,[1] that a code of fixed laws is only a make-shift to meet average cases, and the want of special knowledge in the ruler, so that the ideal king will not hesitate to punish the wicked according to his own judgment, and in violation of existing legislation, as he is the highest and best judge of the necessary changes in laws, and the varying requirements of a complex human society—τὴν τῆς τέχνης ῥώμην τῶν νόμων παρεχόμενον κρείττω. But if the philosopher-king, or the council of perfectly educated elders, who know the Forms or Ideas of Things, and act accordingly, cannot be found, we must only establish the best possible code, and invest it with the dignity and sanctity of a Divine Revelation. This had already been foreshadowed in the *Politicus*.[2]

Upon the fiction of a new foundation in Crete, a nameless Athenian stranger undertakes to describe its proper constitution, and does so in a detail, and with a minuteness exceeding that of Plato's other works. But though Aristotle cites the nameless Athenian as Socrates, nothing can be more contrasted with the real Socrates than the tone and method of this lawgiver. He is with great propriety called an Athenian, for as the *Republic* might fairly have been excogitated by a philosophic Spartan, if such could exist in the fourth century, the *Laws* are distinctly modelled upon the older Attic

[1] pp. 294-7. [2] pp. 297, sq.

constitution.[1] As the board of elders represent the ephors,
so the Code of Laws represents the venerable work of Solon,
protected by an invisible, or nocturnal council, which has
no logical place in the scheme. This contrast of ideals—
Spartan in the *Republic*, Athenian in the *Laws*—runs all
through the works, and it has long been recognised by critics
that the chief value of the latter is in pointing out to us details
of Attic law, which we only know through the adaptation of
Plato. It is interesting to find the philosopher in his old age
conceding even so much to the democracy which his soul ab-
horred, and deigning to make Attic models serve him for even
a partially ideal state. But truly the *Laws* are a work of his
old age, and if the testimony of Aristotle assures us of their
authenticity in the literal sense, we may agree in a higher and
spiritual sense with the Germans who will not accept it. For in
the *Laws* the real Plato is dead, just as the real Edmund Burke
is dead in the *Letters on the French Revolution*. The spirit of
Socrates is gone from him, as his figure pales out in the later
dialogues, and an evil spirit is troubling him. All his fame, all his
piety, all his earnestness, have not been able to stay the spirit of
scepticism which his dialectic had worked. The rejection of
popular theology was bringing with it the decay of morals. The
philosophers were found to be bad citizens, for the questioning
of principles had induced laxity of practice. The world is
so bad, and evil is so predominant, that he even advances
in one isolated passage to the theory of a second world-soul,
the author of mischief in creation, and the opponent of the
good Demiurge in the *Republic*. So then the dying theorist
composes a great palinode, in which he protests that his principles are perfectly consistent with even Athenian principles.
He shows that, with some practical modifications, these will suit
a Platonic state, and that on one capital point he will even abandon the task of his life. When the laws are once established on
philosophical foundations, he will make peace with the orthodox
crowd, and forbid all discussion and dialectical practice. Let

---

[1] The commentators note that many social points are taken from Sparta.
This is true; but the main body of the work is on the details of legislation,
which are almost all Attic in principle.

us but agree upon our religion, and I will defend it with all the
vigour of the narrowest religionist. I will make mere heresy
in opinions, though accompanied by a blameless life, punish-
able with five years' imprisonment ; I will visit the graver (and
more usual) cases with the penalty of death. Verily, if this be
so, the sentence on Socrates was just, and may be defended
from the *Laws* of his favoured disciple. Accordingly he
banishes a strictly philosophical education in the Theory of
Ideas even from his magistrates, and substitutes mathematical
training, together with the sanctions of religion—in fact, a
Pythagorean rather than a Platonic ideal.

We have in Greek literature many instances of intellectual
power unimpaired in advanced age, and not a few of our
greatest remaining monuments are the latest work of their
authors. The *Laws*, if genuine, are then a remarkable and
exceptional case of senility, curious and valuable in its way,
but no fair evidence of the real greatness of its author. There
is no doubt great dignity, and even oracular splendour about it ;
like the Deuteronomy ascribed to his Hebrew rival, the *Laws*
of the Attic Moses combine solemn homily with precept,
burning exhortation with command ; the old man's former
grace and subtlety flash out here and there. But there is
something pitiable, as well as pathetic, in the rage of this royal
thinker, who, like Lear, has brought up ungrateful children,
and they have turned against him.

§ 436. The *Epinomis*, an appendix of very doubtful authenticity, goes in detail into the education of the Nocturnal Council,
to whom is entrusted in the *Laws* the general care of the constitution. It consists chiefly in a theological study of Astronomy,
to which Plato seems really to have inclined in his later or
Pythagorean epoch. So likewise the fragmentary *Critias*, and
the projected *Hermocrates*, were to give illustrations of the
carrying out of the ideal principles of the *Republic* in history.
For this purpose the *Critias*, and also the opening chapters of
the *Timæus*, give a curious and imaginary account of the condition of Attica thousands of years before, when she entered
into conflict with the power of the great continent Atlantis,
which lay beyond the Pillars of Heracles—a strange and much

discussed anticipation of the discovery of America, which the Abbé Brasseur de Bourbourg[1] has actually received as a genuine historical tradition. To him the civilisation even of Egypt is originally brought from the older, and once more advanced, western continent. But these splendid dreams, as well as the abstruse physical theories of the *Timæus*, cannot detain us here. I will only call attention to the freedom with which Plato (and other philosophers of his day) treated the facts of history as a vehicle for moral improvement. The genuine historic sense, and thorough conscientiousness as to facts, which we all admire in Thucydides, seem to have made no impression upon Attic society. Plato especially, who preaches the use and morality of fiction for didactic purposes, does not hesitate to invent (in the *Critias*) and distort[2] previous history— his account of the Dorian migration and its results being contrary to what we can deduce from the evidence. Thus, while the rhetors handled history as a branch of oratory, Plato handled it as an adjunct to ethics, and dressed up the older annals of the Greeks to suit his purposes as a sort of moral fairy tale.

§ 437. The above very inadequate review of Plato's works will afford the reader a better means of judging their author than a mere literary description of his genius. Nevertheless, a few points may be suggested in addition to what appears from the foregoing pages. Few readers of a single dialogue, even of the *Republic*, would imagine or anticipate the extraordinary fascination exercised over European thought by Plato from his own day to the present. It is the fashion to deduce all the later schools of philosophy from the real Socrates ; but perhaps the Platonic Socrates may have replaced him more completely than we imagine. The Stoic ideal of the wise man, standing apart from and above the crowd, more precious in himself and to himself than to others, or to the members of a Greek city—this ideal is clearly drawn in the perfect philosopher of the *Gorgias*, the *Politicus*, the *Crito*. The deeper and sounder aspects of Epi-

---

[1] *Commission Scientifique de Mexique,* vol. iii.—the splendid work promoted by the Emperor Napoleon III.

[2] *Laws,* pp. 691, sq.

curus' Search for Pleasure appear in the *Protagoras*. The Peripatetic goods of 'mind, body, and estate,' indeed the whole of their system, comes directly from Platonic teaching. Need I add that the sceptical Academics found their forerunner in the Agnostic Socrates of the earlier dialogues, and that the Alexandrian fusion of Judaism, Egypticism, and Christianism could find no fitter book to form their philosophical Bible than the works of Plato. This exaltation of Plato by the school called the neo-Platonic is perhaps the most curious and the greatest tribute to his genius. No argument can so convince us of the veneration, of the sanctity, of the absolute authority of any book in the minds of men, as the desire of ages which have drifted away from its principles still to claim and to obey its authority, by dint of allegorising, and sublimating, and mysticising its doctrines. The scholars of the Renaissance, the Cambridge Platonists, Berkeley, Malebranche, and a host of later intellectualists, have sustained to the present day the spirit, and to some extent the doctrines of Plato.

But apart from the history of philosophy, apart from those metaphysical theories which only attract the few choice and subtle spirits of an age, what do we not owe to him in literature? The form of the philosophical dialogue, constantly copied by later Greek philosophers, but by all of them without dramatic genius, has fascinated even in English literature some of our greatest masters of style, such as Bishop Berkeley and Walter Savage Landor, nor have *Symposia* been wanting even in the ephemeral literature of the present day. Both the sceptical and the constructive sides have been imitated. The vulgarest atheist will still put his arguments in the form of a Socratic elenchus, and the deepest thinker will strive to use it in laying the foundations of his system. Above all, the construction of an ideal state has been a model imitated, as Mr. Jowett says, 'by a goodly band of followers.' Cicero's *Republic*, Augustine's *City of God*, More's *Utopia*, are among the greatest, and perhaps even Hobbes' *Leviathan*, and Mandeville's *Fable of the Bees*, owe some of their celebrity to a far-off and distorted reflex of Platonic genius. Great practical books of statesmanship, such as Aristotle's *Politics*, and Machiavelli's *Principe*, would not disown at least the suggestions of contrast. Still more fruitful has Plato been in throwing out scattered guesses at truth, and bold inferences from unrealised principles, which ever attract and stimulate those who will think more thoroughly and fearlessly than the vulgar masses. Thus in the *Republic* he has anticipated the Mediæval Church, in which the spiritual control by a few, and a strict subordination of the rest to those specially selected and educated, were realised beyond his most ardent hopes. So too he anticipated a great reform of religion, and from the summit of his Mount looked upon a promised land which his people should inherit. And while he went a long way beyond even the present age in his theories of the improvement of the race by rational and careful selection of parents, and proper attention to the physical antecedents of humanity, he was so far from degrading the female sex in social importance, that he distinctly asserted the equality of the sexes and the rights of women in the strongest nineteenth-century spirit. Again, on the laws of war, he distinctly asserts (though here in agreement with the higher minds of his day) the laws of what we should call Christian warfare, of humanity to Hellenic prisoners, of regarding Hellenic troubles as family quarrels, to be celebrated by no trophies or triumphs. His guesses in physical science are not less curious and interesting.

§ 438. But with all this strange modernness, Plato is a Hellene of the Hellenes. His prospect does not include any non-Hellenic races. Though he acknowledges the culture and the learning of the Egyptians. and borrows, or affects to borrow, splendid myths from other barbarians, the fusion of Jew and Greek, of bond and free—the Hellenism of a later age—is far beyond his vision. He shares with Isocrates the old, I had well-nigh said the vulgar, Greek admiration for the most retrograde and narrow of the Hellenes, the Spartans ; nay, he is so exclusive and aristocratic in spirit, that he will hardly condescend to consider the lower classes, and conceives, like every other Greek of that day, even his ideal society to be a select body of equals amid a crowd of unprivileged inferiors and of slaves. This it is which gives to Plato's Communism a character so radically distinct from all the modern dreams known by the same name, or from the early Christian society described in the *Acts of the Apostles.* It was essentially an aristocratic Communism, and was based not on the equality of men, but upon their inherent and radical disparity. It was really the Republic of the select few, exercising a strict and even intolerable despotism over the masses. Here again, in spite of the modernness of the Socratic conception of the philosopher as a privileged dissentient, of the rights and the dignity of the individual and his conscience—here again Plato falls into the purest fourth-century Hellenedom, when he constructs an ideal state, or a code of Laws, in which this dissentient can be allowed no place. To protect such an individual, with all his nobility, and his inestimable good effects on those around him, the actual Athens of Plato's day, as Mr. Grote says, was a far safer, happier, and better abode. There democratic habits and common sense had modified and softened those theories of state interference, which no individual thinker of that age seems able to shake off.

All these profound contradictions were doubtless the cause of that increasing gloom and morbidness which seem to have clouded Plato's later years. He did not believe in the perfectibility of the human race. Even his ideal Polity, if carried into practice, is declared by him to contain the seeds of a necessary decay. The human race was not advancing, but decaying. Dialectic and free thought led to scepticism ; acquiescence in received ideas to ignorance and mental apathy. We may almost infer from the silence of contemporary history concerning his later years that, beyond his immediate disciples, he was neglected, and regarded as an idle dreamer. Yet if this was so he but verified his own prophecies on the social position of the true philosopher.

§ 439. In his style he is as modern as in his thinking. He employed that mixture of sober prose argument and of poetical metaphor, which is usual in the ornate prose of modern Europe, but foreign to the character and stricter art of the Greeks. This style, which is freely censured by Greek critics as a hybrid or bastard prose, was admirably suited to a lively conversation, where a sustained and equable tone would have been a mistake.[1] But when Plato attempts formal rhetoric, as in the reply to Lysias in the *Phædrus,* or in the *Menexenus,* we find how true was the artistic feeling of the Greek schools, and how this greater genius, with its irregularities, falls below the more chastened and strictly formal essays of professional orators. He is said in his youth to have inclined to dramatic poetry, but his aversion to dramatising passion was so ingrained, and his love of analyzing the play of intellect so intense, that we may imagine him producing very dry and unpopular tragedies. Yet his appreciation of the great poets, though his criticisms of them are always moral, and never æsthetic, was certainly thorough, and told upon his style. Above all, he shows a stronger Homeric flavour than all those who professed to worship the epics which he censured. His language everywhere bears the influence of Homer, just as some of our greatest and purest writers and speakers use unconsciously Biblical phrases and metaphors. It is also very remarkable that he is not only the first Greek author who confines the name of Homer to the Iliad and Odyssey, but that the text he used was apparently that established afterwards by Aristarchus against the inferior and faulty copies used by Aristotle and later critics.[2] The effects of the rhetoric of his rival Isocrates are also to be remarked in him, though he seems never to have adopted with any strictness that avoidance of hiatus which is a distinctive mark of Isocratic prose.[3] Hence we see in Plato the child of his age and yet its leader, the most Attic of Athenians, and yet a disaffected citizen, a profound sceptic, and yet a lofty preacher, an enemy of the poets, and yet a rhapsodist himself, a thinker that despaired of his own people, and yet, aloft on his Pisgah of speculation, looking out with prophetic eye upon a far future of better laws, purer religion, and nobler life.

[1] Albinus (*Isagoge,* c. 2) well sums up its characteristics : τὸ Ἀττικόν, τὸ εὔχαρι, τὸ ἀπέριττον, τὸ ἀνενδεές. It is remarkable that Aristotle, in his *Politics,* calls the dialogues specially by one of the epithets here denied — τὸ περιττον ; but he is evidently speaking of the matter, not of the technical prose style.

[2] Cf. Sengebusch, *Diss. Hom.* ii. p. 118.

[3] Cf. above, p. 186, on the *Menexenus.*

§ 440. *Bibliographical.* As regards the external history of the text, there is no doubt that the dialogues were early conveyed, in very good copies, from the Platonic school at Athens to the Alexandrian library, where they were commented on with care, especially by Aristophanes and Eratosthenes. There were even editions brought out with the critical marks devised for the Homeric texts,[1] a fact which shows the great esteem in which they were held ; and the very term χωρίζοντες was applied in this controversy. Unfortunately we have little remains of Aristophanes' work except the grouping in trilogies of some dialogues, mentioned by Diogenes, and two references (I think) in the extant scholia. The neo-Platonists and the Roman schools of philosophy studied and criticised the text diligently. The rhetor Libanius composed good arguments, and our scholia quote both Didymus and Aristarchus. But some of them are distinctly composed by Christian writers, as, for example, the note on the Sibyls to the *Phædrus.* These scholia, which are on the whole good, are scanty on many of the dialogues, though very full on others. Thus the first *Alcibiades*, the *Gorgias*, and above all the *Timæus*, have very ample notes, while the *Protagoras*, *Parmenides*, and *Ion* have hardly any whatever. They have been separately published by Bekker (1824) in a convenient form.

Passing to the MSS., which are good and numerous, it is agreed that far the highest authority belongs to the splendid Bodleian codex, dated in the year 896 A.D., and therefore one of our oldest classical MSS. There is an equally ancient Paris MS. for the *Republic, Laws,* and *Timæus.* The rest have been described and classified by Bekker in his edition, which other editors follow. I have now to add that among the papyri sent home by Mr. Flinders Petrie, Mr. Sayce and I have found (June 1890) fragments of a copy of the *Phædo*, in a careful hand not apparently later than the first century. These fragments, which we have deciphered, form two separate groups, and are from pp. 69-73 and pp. 80-85 (marginal figures) of the text respectively. The recension differs from our *textus receptus* frequently in the order of the words ; and admits hiatus where it has been avoided

---

[1] Cf. Vol. I. § 32, note.

in our texts. We hope to print these precious fragments for
Mr. Petrie shortly. The printed editions, commentaries, and
translations are so numerous, that it would be a great task
to enumerate even the principal ones.[1]   Long after the Latin
version of Ficinus (1483) came the Aldine folio of 1513, dedicated to Leo X., not even now a rare book.   Every great
press, or editor of Greek texts, since that time has produced
a *Plato.*   I particularly avoid the philosophical side of Plato
in this literary history, and therefore pass by his ancient rivals
and pupils, who belong strictly to the history of philosophy, but
I cannot avoid making an exception to my silence on the great
library of Platonic philosophy in favour of Mr. Grote's admirable and not sufficiently esteemed work.   In our time the best
texts are Bekker's, Stallbaum's (with full commentary, 1835–61),
and the Zurich edition (1839).   An interesting and rare book is
the seven dialogues printed by the Dublin University Press, as
its first book, in 1738.   The special editions of separate dialogues
up to date are given in the prefaces to each dialogue in Stallbaum's edition.   But some good English commentaries have
since appeared, such as W. H. Thompson's *Gorgias* and *Phædrus*
(1868), Badham's *Philebus* (1855), Geddes', and A. Hind's
Phædo (1884) and *Timæus* (1889), L. Campbell's *Theætetus,*
Sophistes, and *Politicus,* Wayte's *Protagoras,* Warren's *Republic*
(five books, Macmillan, 1889).   Mitchell's *Index Græcitatis*
was printed at Oxford 1832, and there are many able papers by
Mr. H. Jackson in the *Journal of Philology.*   In addition to
Manuel Chrysoloras' translation of the *Republic,* about 1397
(printed by Cassarini, Venice, 1624), and Ficinus' early Latin
translation, we have an English version of the *Apology* and
Phædo in 1675 ; Dacier's French in 1699, reproduced in England 1701 ; Sydenham's in 1760 (several dialogues) ; abridg-
ments of the *Phædo* and *Theætetus* by Leibnitz ; Davies and
Vaughan's *Republic* -- an excellent book ;   F. J. Church's
Euthyphro, Apology, Crito and *Phædo* ;   Dr. Wright's *Phædrus,*

---

[1] Nicolai, *LG.* i. pp. 508–27, gives a catalogue of the myriad works on
Plato, to which I refer the special student.   Yet he omits to mention Mr.
Jowett's translation.

Lysis and Protagoras (both in the Golden Treasury Series) ; V. Cousin's French version in 1822 ; Schleiermacher's, and the Stuttgart translation by various scholars (1869) ; and now, finally, Mr. Jowett's five volumes, with excellent introductions which give us the literary side of Plato perfectly. Neverthe-less, this great book by no means supersedes the admirable work of Grote on Plato, in which we have the curious pheno-menon of a Positivist expounding the great Idealist with sym-pathy and generally (I think) with fidelity. The recent German literature on Plato is reviewed in Bursian's *Jahresbericht* for 1887 (vol. 50, pp. 134 sqq. ending with vol. 53, pp. 186 sq.).

INDEX TO PART I.

www.ingramcontent.com/pod-product-compliance
Lightning Source LLC
Chambersburg PA
CBHW030113030726
47498CB00007B/2369